ESSAYS IN APPLIED PSYCHO-ANALYSIS

BY
ERNEST JONES, M.D., F.R.C.P.

VOL. I

International Universities Press, Inc.
NEW YORK   NEW YORK
1964

Third Impression

PRINTED IN THE UNITED STATES OF AMERICA

PREFACE

SINCE the first edition of *Essays in Applied Psycho-Analysis* was published, in 1923, so much new material has accumulated that it has been decided to issue the present edition in two volumes. The number of essays has increased threefold. A quarter of the former edition is reproduced, with some additions, in the present volume; the first essay in it has been separately published in book form by Messrs. Gollancz under the title of *Hamlet and Oedipus*.

The essays in the present volume appear in chronological order. My thanks are due to the publishers for permission to reproduce them, and notes are added to indicate where and when they were first printed. The following paragraph is taken from the original preface.

'The light which psycho-analysis is capable of throwing on the deeper problems of human thought and conduct is only beginning to be appreciated. The field over which it can be applied is almost indefinitely large. The parts touched on in the present volume(s) constitute of course only a selection, yet they are sufficiently diverse: political psychology, artistic and literary creation, national and individual characterology, and the study of superstition, history, religion, and folk-lore.'

E. J.

CONTENTS

		PAGE
I.	On 'Dying Together', with Special Reference to Heinrich von Kleist's Suicide	9
II.	An Unusual Case of 'Dying Together'	16
III.	The Influence of Andrea del Sarto's Wife on his Art	22
IV.	The Case of Louis Bonaparte, King of Holland	39
V.	War and Individual Psychology	55
VI.	War and Sublimation	77
VII.	A Linguistic Factor in English Characterology	88
VIII.	The Island of Ireland: A Psycho-Analytical Contribution to Political Psychology	95
IX.	The Relation of Abnormal Psychology to Social Psychology	113
X.	The Inferiority Complex of the Welsh	128
XI.	Mental Heredity	133
XII.	Psycho-Analysis and Biology	135
XIII.	The Problem of Paul Morphy: a Contribution to the Psychology of Chess	165
XIV.	Psycho-Analysis and Mental Hygiene	197
XV.	The Individual and Society	206
XVI.	The Psychology of Constitutional Monarchy	227
XVII.	How Can Civilization be Saved?	234
XVIII.	Evolution and Revolution	254
XIX.	The Psychology of Quislingism	276
XX.	The Psychology of the Jewish Question	284
XXI.	Psychopathology and International Tension	301
XXII.	The Death of Hamlet's Father	323

I

ON 'DYING TOGETHER'

WITH SPECIAL REFERENCE TO HEINRICH VON KLEIST'S SUICIDE[1]

In a recent interesting monograph on Heinrich von Kleist, Sadger[2] has called attention to a number of considerations bearing on the psychology of the impulse to die together with a loved one, to share death in common. As it is possible in a special journal to pursue an analysis more freely than in writings intended for a lay audience, I wish to comment here on two points in this connection which Sadger —I assume, with intention—left untouched.

Of the general psycho-sexual significance of the idea of death nothing need be added here. Freud, Stekel, and others have fully described the masochistic phantasies in which the idea may become involved, and this is also clearly illustrated in Sadger's monograph. The common mythological and folk-loristic conception of death as a spirit that violently attacks one mainly originates in this source.

The question of 'dying together' is, however, more complicated, the tendency being determined by several motives. The most obvious of these is that underlying a belief in a world beyond, a region where all hopes that are denied in this life will come true. The wish-fulfilment comprised in this belief subserves, of course, a similar function

---

[1] Published in the *Zentralblatt für Psychoanalyse* (September 1911), Jahrgang I, p. 563.
[2] Sadger, *Heinrich von Kleist. Eine pathographisch-psychologische Studie*, 1910.

to that operative in the neuroses and psychoses; the consolation it yields, as is well-recognized by theologians, is naturally greater at times when life is filled with disappointment and sorrow. The same is true of the desire to die together with one's beloved, as is well illustrated by the accessory factors that helped to drive von Kleist to suicide.[1] With him, however, as Sadger clearly shows,[2] there was a specific and irresistible attraction toward the act, one which is not at all accounted for by the attendant circumstances. Most psycho-analysts will probably agree with Sadger's conclusions[3] that 'the wish to die together is the same as the wish to sleep and lie together (originally, of course, with the mother)', and that 'the grave so longed for by Kleist is simply an equivalent of the mother's bed'. Von Kleist's own words plainly confirm this: he writes, 'I must confess to you that her grave is dearer to me than the beds of all the empresses[4] of the world'. The idea that death consists in a return to the heaven whence we were born, *i.e.* to the mother's womb, is familiar to us in religious and other spheres of thought.

Deeper motives connect the subject with that of necrophilia. First of these may be mentioned the sadistic impulse, which can be inflamed at the thought of communion with a dead person—partly through the helpless resistlessness of the latter, and partly through the idea that a dead mistress can never be wearied by excessive caresses, can endure without limit, is for ever loyal. The latter thought of the insatiability of the dead often recurs in the literature on vampirism; it is indicated in the verses where Heine, in his dedication to 'Der Doktor Faust', makes the returned Helena say:

[1] Sadger, *op. cit.* pp. 60, 61.　　[2] Sadger, *op. cit.* pp. 56-8.
[3] Sadger, *op. cit.* p. 60.
[4] Empress, like Queen, is a well-known unconscious symbol of the mother.

ON 'DYING TOGETHER'

Du hast mich beschworen aus dem Grab
Durch deinen Zauberwillen,
Belebtest mich mit Wollustglut—
Jetzt kannst du die Glut nicht stillen.

Press deinen Mund an meinen Mund;
Der Menschen Odem ist göttlich!
Ich trinke deine Seele aus,
Die Toten sind unersättlich.

(Thou hast called me from my grave
By thy bewitching will;
Made me alive, feel passionate love,
A passion thou canst never still.

Press thy mouth close to my cold mouth;
Man's breath is god-like created.
I drink thy essence, I drink thy soul,
The dead can never be sated.)

In my psycho-analytical experience of neurotics, necrophilic tendencies have further[1] invariably been associated with both coprophilic and birth phantasies. Freud[2] first pointed out the connection between the two phantasies just named, and this has since been amply confirmed by most observers. On the one hand, faecal material is dead matter that was once part of a living body, but is now decomposing, facts that make it easy for an association to be formed between it and a corpse; and on the other hand it is, according to a common 'infantile theory', the material out of which children are made, and, in the form of manure, is a general fertilizing principle. Love for, or undue horror at, a dead body may thus betoken a reversion

---

[1] The connection here implied between sadism and coprophilia is discussed at length in a later paper republished as chapter xxxi of the author's *Papers on Psycho-Analysis*, 2nd edition.

[2] Freud, *Sammlung kleiner Schriften*, Zweite Folge, p. 168.

to the infantile interest and fondness for faecal excrement. This explains the frequency with which the twin motives of (1) a dead woman giving birth to a child, and (2) a living woman being impregnated by a dead husband, occur in folk-lore, literature, mythology, and popular belief.[1] Interteresting indications of both, which need not be detailed here, are to be found in von Kleist's short story, 'Die Marquise von O.'. The same combination of coprophilic and birth phantasy probably underlay his remarkable proposal to Wilhelmine von Zenge that they should leave everything else and adopt a peasant's life; as is well known, when she refused to fulfil this 'love condition' he heartlessly broke off their engagement. Sadger quotes the following passage of his in this connection: 'With the Persian magi there was a religious law to the effect that a man could do nothing more pleasing to the gods than *to till a field, to plant a tree, and to beget a child.*[2] I call that wisdom, and no truth has penetrated yet so deeply into my soul as this has. That is what I *ought* to do, I am *absolutely sure.* Oh, Wilhelmine, what unspeakable joy there must be in the knowledge that one is fulfilling one's destiny *entirely* in accord with the will of Nature.' I thus fully agree with Sadger[3] when he maintains that this has a hidden sexual meaning. I have further observed, though I do not know if it is a general rule, that patients having this complex often display an attitude of wonderful tenderness towards the object of their love, just like that of a fond mother for her babe; this was very pronounced in von Kleist's final

[1] Numerous examples of this are quoted by Hanusch, *Zeitschrift für deutsche Mythologie*, Jahrgang IV, p. 200; Hock, *Die Vampyrsagen und ihre Verwertung in der deutschen Literatur* (1900), pp. 24, 37, 43 ; Horst, *Zauber-Bibliothek* (1821), Erster Teil, p. 277; Krauss, *Slavische Volksforschungen* (1908), p. 130; Sepp, *Occident und Orient* (1903), p. 268.

[2] The italics are mine (in this instance only).

[3] Sadger, *op. cit.* p. 62.

ON 'DYING TOGETHER'

outburst of 'dithyrambic rapture' towards Henriette, with its 'exchange of pet names that bordered on lunacy'.[1]

Sadger further comments on the 'travelling' significance of dying together. The connection between the ideas of death and travel is primaeval; one thinks at once of the Grecian and Teutonic myths of the procession of dead souls, and of Hamlet's 'undiscovered country, from whose bourn no traveller returns'. The fact, now becoming generally recognized since Freud first called attention to its importance (*Die Traumdeutung*, 1900), that children essentially conceive of death as a 'going away', as a journey, evidently renders this association a natural and stable one. With von Kleist it can be brought into line with his curious mania for travelling, which seemed so objectless and inexplicable to his friends. Two motives in this connection lie fairly near the surface. In the first place, death is conceived of as a voyage of discovery, as a journey to a land where hidden things will be revealed; I have had several religious patients whose curiosity, sexual and otherwise, had been largely transferred on to this idea.[2] Sadger points out how passionate was von Kleist's desire to reach *absolute, certain truth*,[3] and quotes his statement: '*Education* seemed to me the only goal worthy of endeavour, *truth*[4] the only wealth worthy of possession'. When he studied Kant's destructive criticism of the concept of the Absolute, and of a life hereafter, he was shaken to the depths of his being. He wrote: 'And my only thought, which my soul in this utmost tumult laboured on with burning dread, was always this: thy *sole* aim, thy loftiest goal, has declined'. In the

[1] Sadger, *op. cit.* p. 59.
[2] One of my patients eagerly looked forward to discovering in the next world the authorship of the Letters of Junius!
[3] Sadger, *op. cit.* p. 62.
[4] On the intimate association between the ideas of truth and nudity see Furtmüller, *Zeitschrift für Psychoanalyse* (1913), Bd. I, p. 273.

second place, a journey can be undertaken in company, and it is significant that in von Kleist's fugue-like escapes this was practically always so. Sadger traces this tendency ultimately to the infantile desire to defy the father and escape with the mother to some distant place where he cannot disturb their mutual relations; therefore dying together can signify in the unconscious to fly with the mother and thus gratify secret desires.[1] The travelling mania is one of many tendencies that may come to expression in flying dreams,[2] and in this connection I should like to throw out a few suggestions. Freud traces the ultimate source of these dreams to the pleasurably exciting chasing of childhood,[3] and has also laid special stress on the relation between bodily movements in general and sexuality.[4] In several psycho-analyses I have found associated with this various anal-erotic motives, which may therefore furnish something towards the later desires. The fact itself that the common expression for defaecation is 'movement', and for faeces 'motion', points to an inner connection between two subjects that at first sight appear to be quite unrelated.[5] I need not here go into the different grounds for the association, but will only remark that when the act of defaecation is especially pleasurable it is apt to acquire the significance of a sexual 'projecting',[6] just as of urine

[1] Sadger, *op. cit.* p. 60.
[2] It is perhaps not without interest that the name of the woman with whom von Kleist departed on his endless journey was Vogel (*i.e.* 'Bird').
[3] Freud, *Die Traumdeutung*, 2e Aufl., p. 195.
[4] Freud, *op. cit.*, 2e Aufl., pp. 53, 54. See also Sadger, 'Haut-, Schleimhaut- und Muskelerotik', *Jahrbuch der Psychoanalyse*, Bd. III, p. 525.
[5] This association plays a prominent part in the common symptom known as *Reisefieber*, and in the allied 'packing' dreams.
[6] It is noteworthy that the common vulgarism for the act is etymologically cognate with the word 'to shoot'.

and semen. I have collected much evidence, from both actual psycho-analyses and from folklore, which I hope to detail elsewhere,[1] indicating that (*a*) this connotation of sexual projecting, and of movement in general, is especially closely associated in the unconscious with the act of passing flatus,[2] and (*b*) that this latter act, on account of the idea of penetration to a distance, is sometimes conceived of by children as constituting the essential part of coitus, which thus consists of expelling flatus into the female cloaca. The latter phantasy would, through its association with movement (and therefore flying through a gaseous medium—the air), be particularly well adapted to find expression, together with the other coprophilic, sadistic, and incestuous tendencies referred to above, in the love-condition of dying together, and I would suggest that it might be worth while to investigate future cases of the kind from this point of view.

[1] Since the present paper was written this has been done in two monographs published in the *Jahrbuch der Psychoanalyse*.

[2] It is noteworthy that the common vulgarism for this both in English and in German singularly resembles the German for travel, 'Fahrt'.

II

AN UNUSUAL CASE OF 'DYING TOGETHER'[1]

The following dramatic event, which took place here[2] this week, seems to lend itself to some considerations of psycho-analytical interest.

A man and wife, aged thirty-two and twenty-eight respectively, went from Toronto to spend a week-end at Niagara Falls. In company with several other people they ventured on to the great bridge of ice that forms every winter just at the foot of the Falls, and which then joins the American and Canadian shores of the river. The ice-bridge began to crack and drift from its moorings, and a river-man, who knew the locality well and who was on the ice at the time, shouted to the others to make for the Canadian side where there was more chance of getting ashore. The couple in question ignored this advice and rushed towards the American shore, but were soon stopped by open water. They then ran in the other direction (about 150 yards), but when about 50 yards from safety the woman fell down exhausted, crying 'I can't go on! let us die here!' The husband, aided by another man, dragged her onward until they reached the edge. This was 3 yards from the shore, and the intervening water was covered with soft ice. The river-man begged them to cross this, pointing out that the ice would prevent their sinking, and guaranteed to bring them to safety; he demonstrated the possibility of the feat by crossing himself, and later by

[1] Published in the *Zentralblatt für Psychoanalyse* (May 1912), Jahrgang II, p. 455.
[2] *I.e.* Toronto.

AN UNUSUAL CASE OF 'DYING TOGETHER'

returning to save another man. The woman, however, declined to take the risk, and her husband refused to go without her. The mass of ice now began to drift down the river, breaking into smaller pieces as it went, and slowly but surely approaching the terrible Rapids that lead to the Niagara Whirlpool. In an hour's time they had drifted to where a railway bridge crosses the ravine, over 60 yards above their heads, and were on the point of being caught up by the swift rapids. A rope, with an iron harpoon at the end, had been lowered from the bridge and this was obviously their last hope of safety. As the ice-floe, now moving rapidly, swept under the bridge, the man successfully seized the rope, but apparently the woman refused to trust to it unless it was fastened around her. At all events the man was seen to be vainly fumbling, with fingers numbed by cold, to tie the rope around his wife's waist. Failing in this in the short time at his disposal before the floe passed onwards, he flung the rope aside, knelt down beside the woman and clasped her in his arms; they went thus to their death, which was now only a matter of seconds.

These are the main facts as published in all the newspapers. The only additional ones I could discover, from a friend of mine who happened to know the couple well, were: that they were devotedly fond of each other, that they had been married for seven years, and that they, the woman in particular, were sad at never having had any children.

The husband's conduct does not call for any special comment, being dictated by sufficiently obvious motives. To these I will only add that he was in the presence of a large audience, the banks of the ravine being lined by thousands of people who had accumulated during the fateful hour, and that it would be difficult or impossible for a man to hold up his head again if he deserted any woman in such a situation, let alone his own wife.

There is, however, more to be said about the woman's conduct, or rather lack of conduct. It is evident that she was throughout overcome by panic and fright, or else convinced of the inevitableness of the fate awaiting her. Her efforts at escape were either paralysed or else *actively hindering*, and she did not respond even to the powerful motive of saving her husband. Now it is known to psycho-analysts, as Freud first pointed out in reference to certain dreams,[1] that emotional paralysis is not so much a traumatic effect of fright as a manifestation of inhibition resulting from a conflict between a conscious and unconscious impulse. A familiar example is that of a woman who cannot protect herself with her whole strength against being raped, part of her energy being inhibited by the opposing unconscious impulse which is on the side of the assailant. The question thus arises whether any such process can be detected in the present case. If so, then the woman's conduct would have to be viewed as expressing an unconscious desire for death, an automatic suicide. The available evidence, as just narrated, is so meagre that any hypothesis of this kind must necessarily be very tentative, but when correlated with psycho-analytical experience in general the probability of its being true is, in my opinion, very considerable.

There is no reason to believe that any desire for death that might have existed could have been other than symbolic; indeed the description I obtained of the woman's state of mind on the day before the calamity makes the idea of any direct suicidal intent highly improbable. We have therefore to ask what other ideas could have been symbolized by that suicide. It is known, through analysis, not

[1] Freud, *Die Traumdeutung* (1900), p. 228.

only that the ideas of sex, birth, and death are extensively associated with one another, but also that the idea of dying in the arms of the loved one—*'gemeinsames Sterben'*—symbolizes certain quite specific desires of the unconscious. Of these, which have been pointed out especially by Sadger[1] and myself,[2] one in particular may be recalled —namely, the desire to beget a child with the loved one. The unconscious associative connections between this desire and the notion of common suicide are too rich and manifold to discuss here; besides which they are now well enough known to justify one in assuming an understanding of them in informed circles. I will therefore content myself with indicating some of the respects in which the present situation was adapted for supporting this associative connection.

The association between Niagara and death, especially suicide, is one that has been enforced by countlessly repeated experiences. It is not so generally known, however, that the association between it and birth is also very intimate. Niagara is a favourite honeymoon resort—possibly more so for Toronto people than for those of other places in the neighbourhood, on account of the romantic journey thither across the Lake of Ontario. So much is this so that Niagara town is commonly known—in Toronto at all events—as 'the Baby City', from the high percentage of conceptions that date from a visit there. The couple in question were very fond of spending their holidays there, the unconscious attraction being possibly the same as that which drew women of old to the Temple of Aesculapius and which still draws women to various healing waters. They had never been there before in winter-time, a rather strange circumstance, for it is almost as popular with

[1] Sadger, *Heinrich von Kleist* (1910), pp. 59-62.
[2] Chapter I of these Essays.

Toronto people in the winter as in the summer because of the beautiful ice effects to be seen at that time. It is conceivable that they were this time drawn by the idea of winter (death, cold, etc.) which was beginning to correspond with their attitude of hopelessness about ever getting a child.

Coming next to the calamity itself we see how similar was the conscious affect investing the two ideas which we suppose became associated; the hope of giving birth to a child was almost as small as that of escaping from the threatened doom. That this doom was one of drowning—in the horrible form of being swept under in an ice-cold whirlpool—is a circumstance of considerable significance in the light of all we know about the symbolic meaning of water in general and of drowning in particular (cf. Freud, Rank, Abraham, Stekel, etc.). If the whole story were told to one as constituting a dream one would have no hesitation in interpreting it as a childbirth fantasy of a sterile woman, the floating *on a block of ice* in a dangerous current of water, in company with the lover, in sight of all the world and yet isolated from it, the threatening catastrophe of drowning, and the rapid movement of being passively swept to and fro (in the paper referred to above I have insisted on the significance of movement in this connection)—all this forms a perfect picture.

Though the actual situation was not a dream but a grim reality, nevertheless the circumstances detailed above are just such as would, especially in a moment of acute emotion, strongly appeal to the latent complex in question and stimulate it to activity. It should be remembered that, in times of despair (defeat, severe illness, danger, enfeeblement, approaching death, and so on), there is a universal tendency to fly from reality by having recourse to the primitive system of thought (Freud's primary *Lustprinzip*,

Jung's *phantastisches Denken*), mostly in the form of infantile wishes relating to the mother; indeed I have elsewhere[1] expressed the opinion that the idea of personal death does not exist for the unconscious, being always replaced by that of sexual communion or of birth. We may thus imagine the woman in question as reacting to her frightful situation by rapidly transforming it in the unconscious and replacing reality by the fantasy of the gratification of her deepest desire. The external outcome of this act of transformation illustrates very well the contrast between the practical value of the pleasure principle and that of the reality principle.[2]

One might speculate whether the outcome would have been different if the woman's thoughts concerning childbirth had been more accustomed to assume the common form of the fantasy of saving, or of being saved.[3] It is even possible that this fantasy was operative, and that her objection to being saved by the river-man and by the men who were holding the rope from the bridge was due fundamentally to her excessive marital fidelity, to her determination that no one should save her except her husband. But at this point our speculations become so filmy as to float away into the region of the completely unknown.

[1] *Journal of Abnormal Psychology*, April 1912.
[2] See Freud, 'Die zwei Prinzipien des psychischen Geschehens', *Jahrbuch der Psychoanalyse*, Bd. III, p. 1.
[3] See chapter x of my *Papers on Psycho-Analysis*, 1918.

III

THE INFLUENCE OF ANDREA DEL SARTO'S WIFE ON HIS ART[1]

It has been a problem to many generations of art students to explain why Andrea del Sarto, in spite of his stupendous gifts in every branch of painting, should have failed to reach the front rank as an artist. The more carefully his work is analysed in detail the more wonder does it wring from the spectator, and especially from the connoisseur. His drawing was unrivalled in its flawlessness, and defies all criticism; he was the finest colourist of his day, and in this respect has never been excelled except by a few of the Venetian school; of chiaroscuro he was an absolute master; his composition was well-nigh perfect in its harmony; his frescoes remain to-day to show us the highest that could be reached in this domain; and his technical skill was applied with a sensitiveness of tact, a sureness of judgement, and an excellence of good taste that are beyond reproach. It is little wonder, therefore, that, even by a critical generation, he was given the title of 'il pittore senza errori'. Added to these accomplishments must be reckoned that he lived in Florence, a contemporary of Raphael and Michelangelo, at the time when the Renaissance art reached its very acme, before there was yet any serious sign of the decadence that was soon to set in, and when the very air was thrilling with inspiration. Yet, in spite of all this, we are confronted by the startling fact that Andrea never attained true greatness in his art, that there is something

[1] Published in *Imago* (1913), Bd. II, p. 468.

essentially lacking in his work which robs it of any claim to rank with that of the greatest masters.

A few quotations from expert judgements will describe both Andrea's excellences and his defects far better than I can pretend to do. Sir Henry Layard considers his earliest remaining work (in the Annunziata), done at the age of twenty-two, to be 'an instance of the highest level, in point of execution, attained by fresco',[1] and Leader Scott also says of it, 'this might well be classed as on the highest level ever reached in fresco'.[2] Guinness writes of him: 'He interprets the secrets of nature with a force so completely victorious over every difficulty of technique that the effort appears to be to him but as child's-play, and his utterances are but a further manifestation of her intimate mysteries. . . . The works of men like Buonarotti and Leonardo betray a hundred subtleties of invention, and astonish with a sense of difficulties aimed at and overcome. But Andrea knew none of these complexities; difficulties of technique did not exist for him. . . . The supreme gift which had early gained for him the title *senza errori*, and the native simplicity of his character, left him without desire to startle; he aimed at nothing beyond the reach of his facile brush, and the longer the spectator beholds his works the deeper grows his admiration before their absorbing unity and *ensemble*. . . . It is this quality of natural simplicity and lack of exaggeration which makes del Sarto to so large a degree the artist who appeals to artists rather than to the ordinary public, who do not understand the noble simplicity of his work, and his stupendous powers of technique.'[3] Of Andrea's masterpiece, the Madonna di San Francesco, he says, 'the beauty of this picture is

---

[1] Layard in the 5th edition of Kugler's *Handbook of Painting* (1887), Part II, p. 457. [2] Leader Scott, *Andrea del Sarto* (1881), p. 92.
[3] Guinness, *Andrea del Sarto* (1899), pp. v, 57, 58.

beyond praise', and of the Scalzi frescoes that 'their technique reveals the almost superhuman force of the artist, who—within the limitations of chiaroscuro—has here proved himself a complete master of colour. . . . They have been equalled by no other artist in Italy.'[1] Of the famous Last Supper picture he writes, 'No other word but brilliant will express the jewel-like sense of colour and noble drawing which strike the eye on entering the refectory of the Salvi convent. It was the beauty of this marvellous creation which saved it from destruction during the siege of Florence, when the soldiers who would have razed the convent to the ground stopped spell-bound as they burst into the refectory and were confronted by the noble drama which the artist's brush had so vividly portrayed.'[2] Bottari speaks of Andrea's Tabernacolo as 'a divine picture, one of the most beautiful works which ever issued from the hand of man',[3] and similar panegyrics are common enough. A sufficiently high one is contained in Michelangelo's remark to Raphael:

> Friend, there's a certain sorry little scrub
> Goes up and down our Florence, none cares how,
> Who, were he set to plan and execute
> As you are, pricked on by your popes and kings,
> Would bring the sweat into that brow of yours![4]

[1] Guinness, *op. cit.* pp. 21, 44, 45.
[2] Guinness, *op. cit.* p. 42. Vasari's account of this episode (vol. iii, p. 224) is that the picture was saved by the officer in command. The more florid version seems to have originated with Varchi (*Storie florentine*, vol. iii, p. 186).
[3] Quoted by Guinness, *op. cit.* p. 32.
[4] This is the rendering given by Browning in his poem on Andrea. The original, of which it is a free translation, may be found in Bocchi's *Bellezze di Firenze*. It may be of interest in this connection to recall that Andrea once copied a picture of Raphael's (Leo X) for Ottaviano de' Medici so skilfully as completely to deceive Giulio Romano, who had helped Raphael to paint the picture.

ANDREA DEL SARTO

Andrea's defects are most pithily summed up in Reumont's phrase, 'Greatness is lacking in his works'.[1] They were the equivalent of masterly prose, not of poetry. He seems to have had no inner vision, no inspiration, no ideal, and his pictures fail to move the observer to anything more than a sense of admiration at their abstract beauty and perfection; he leaves one cold at heart, and never conveys any feeling of a something beyond that has been mysteriously revealed. Reumont writes, for instance, 'Del Sarto's Madonnas are expressive of a fresh, blooming, often robust nature, but they do not wear the halo of the spiritual, of the inexpressible, of the yearning towards heaven, with which we love to see the head of the Virgin encircled, and without which she loses her finest charm'.[2] Guinness puts it more apologetically thus: 'But if the soul of Andrea lay in things of sense, and he missed the vision of ideal beauty, the secret of visible beauty was truly his, and was rendered by him with consummate skill. . . . He courted no rivalry, he employed no tricks, he feared no imputations of want of originality, but went directly to his goal, attaining, as was, alas, inevitable with his want of poetic idealism, the fault of faultlessness. In the Birth of St. John the skilled hand of the artist has grown almost mechanical in its ease; the grand attitude, the noble drapery, the perfect equipoise of composition well-nigh oppress by their very perfection; and this last great fresco of the Scalzo series betrays the weakness as well as the strength of Del Sarto.'[3] Vasari sums him up as follows: 'In him art and nature combined to show all that may be done in painting, when design, colouring, and invention unite in one and the same person. Had this master possessed a somewhat bolder and more elevated mind, had he

---

[1] Reumont, *Andrea del Sarto* (1835), p. xv.
[2] Reumont, *op. cit.* p. 75.   [3] Guinness, *op. cit.* pp. 44, 57.

been as much distinguished for higher qualifications as he was for genius and depth of judgement in the art he practised, he would beyond all doubt have been without an equal. But there was a certain timidity of mind, a sort of diffidence and want of force in his nature, which rendered it impossible that those evidences of ardour and animation, which are proper to the more exalted character, should ever appear in him; nor did he at any time display one particle of that elevation which, could it but have been added to the advantages wherewith he was endowed, would have rendered him a truly divine painter: wherefore the works of Andrea are wanting in those ornaments of grandeur, richness, and force, which appear so conspicuously in those of many other masters.'[1] Browning, in his 'Andrea del Sarto'—a poem that contains a brilliant descriptive analysis of the painter and which betrays a wealth of psychological insight[2]—makes him realize both his capacity and his deficiency:

> I can do with my pencil what I know,
> What I see, what at bottom of my heart
> I wish for, if I ever wish so deep—
> Do easily, too—when I say, perfectly,
> I do not boast, perhaps: . . .
>
> . . . . .
>
> There burns a truer light of God in them,[3]
> In their vexed, beating, stuffed and stopped-up brain,
> Heart, or whate'er else, than goes on to prompt
> This low-pulsed, forthright craftsman's hand of mine.
> Their works drop groundward, but themselves, I know,

[1] Vasari, *Lives of the Most Eminent Painters* (English Translation, 1851), vol. iii, pp. 180, 181.
[2] The reason why this is so good is perhaps because it contains a considerable piece of unconscious self-analysis on the poet's part.
[3] *I.e.* his rivals.

Reach many a time a heaven that's shut to me,
Enter and take their place there sure enough,
Though they come back and cannot tell the world.
My works are nearer heaven, but I sit here.

.   .   .   .

Ah, but a man's reach should exceed his grasp,
Or what's a heaven for? All is silver-grey
Placid and perfect with my art: the worse!

The prominent characteristics, therefore, of Andrea's work are his perfection of technique, his astounding facility,[1] his unforced sincerity and natural simplicity; with these go a lack of inspiration, an absence of 'soul' or of deep emotion, an incapacity to express either a great poetical or religious idea, or an ideal thought of any kind. There have been two explanations given of this striking antinomy, and they are usually held, no doubt with right, to be mutually complementary rather than contradictory. The one invokes an inborn lack of that indefinable quality called genius, the other the unfortunate influence of the painter's wife. The first of these will not be entered upon here, but it is our intention to consider the second from the point of view of psycho-analysis, and to see whether more light can in this way be thrown upon it.

The essential facts of Andrea's life that bear on our problem are as follows. The exact date of his birth is disputed, but was certainly in the July of either 1486 or 1488, more probably the latter. He was the third of six children, having two older brothers. He became acquainted with Lucrezia del Fede, when she was the wife of another man, about 1511 or 1512,[2] and married her, after her husband's

[1] He never painted shades one above the other, like other painters; all was finished from the first laying on, and with an unerring accuracy and sureness of touch.
[2] His first known portrait of her is to be found in the Nativity fresco of the Annunziata, painted at some time between 1511 and 1514.

death, in 1513. He was thoroughly infatuated with her, sacrificed both his artistic prospects and the esteem of his friends in order to marry her, and, at her bidding, deserted his parents, whom he had previously supported; this infatuation lasted, apparently without the slightest intermission or change, until the end of his life. His wife was unquestionably a beautiful and attractive woman, but the character generally given her is decidedly the reverse of favourable. She is said to have been haughty, exacting, vain, entirely selfish, extravagant, and domineering. It is thus intelligible that the whole situation brought about an estrangement between Andrea and his friends, who regarded his conduct as that of a blind fool. Vasari writes on this point: 'When the news became known in Florence the affection and respect with which his friends had always regarded Andrea changed into disapproval and contempt.... But he destroyed his own peace as well as estranged his friends by this act, seeing that he soon became jealous, and found that he had besides fallen into the hands of an artful woman, who made him do as she pleased in all things. He abandoned his own poor father and mother, for example, and adopted the father and sisters of his wife in their stead; insomuch that all who knew the facts mourned over him, and he soon began to be as much avoided as he had previously been sought after. His disciples still remained with him, it is true, in the hope of learning something useful, yet there was not one of them, great or small, who was not maltreated by his wife, both by evil words and despiteful actions: none could escape her blows, but although Andrea lived in the midst of all that torment, he yet accounted it a high pleasure.'[1]

[1] Vasari, *op. cit.* p. 194. Vasari should speak with some authority on this matter, for he was one of the pupils in question. He is unfortunately an unsafe author to rely on, being given both to distortion and confabula-

Andrea was badly paid for his work, probably because he had no rich patron; for the Annunziata frescoes, for example, he got only 70 lire each. Some five years after his marriage he was asked by King Francis to come to the French court, an invitation which he accepted with alacrity; he was absent from Florence altogether from May the 25th, 1518 to October the 17th, 1519. In Fontainebleau he was received with every mark of esteem, was highly honoured by the King and his court, and was richly paid for his work; he is said to have painted over fifty pictures while in France—though doubtless some of these were by his pupil Squazzella whom he took with him—and for one alone he received 2100 lire. The contrast between his previous sordid existence and this life of opulence and admiration must have seemed to him nothing less than magical. Pressure on the part of his wife, however, who was probably envious of his lot and also desirous of resuming her sway over him, led him to return to Florence. According to Vasari: 'She wrote with bitter complaints to Andrea, declaring that she never ceased to weep, and was in perpetual affliction at his absence; dressing all this up with sweet words, well calculated to move the heart of the luckless man, who loved her but too well, she drove the poor soul half out of his wits; above all, when he read her assurance that if he did not return speedily, he would certainly find her dead. Moved by all this, he resolved to resume his chain, and preferred a life of wretchedness with her to the ease around him, and to all the glory which his art must have secured to him.'[1] He

tion, but the main points of the present story are to be confirmed from other sources, *e.g.* from Andrea's own portraits of himself and his wife.

[1] Vasari, *op. cit.* p. 206. King Francis is said to have entrusted him with large sums of money to buy pictures for him in Florence, but which Andrea squandered on his wife. This widely accepted story, however,

promised the King faithfully that he would soon return to France, hoping to induce his wife to come back with him, but once home he was kept prisoner by his wife, who refused to go to France; her principal motive in this refusal is said to have been her reluctance to leave her father, a part which throws some light on her general hysterical disposition. Andrea thus flung away his brilliant prospects, resumed his old life of misery and poverty, and became more despised than ever for his conduct; it is related that for some time he was afraid to show himself in the streets of Florence on account of the sneering remarks he overheard.[1] He made attempts a little later to regain King Francis's favour, and sent him several pictures, but the King never forgave him or took any further notice of him.

Of the rest of Andrea's life there is not much to be told. He spent it in relative obscurity and poverty; for instance, for the two finest of the Scalzi frescoes, the Carità and Verità, he was paid 20 lire (in 1520), and for his Entombment picture he received merely a bunch of candles, the price also of his Madonna of Zanobi Bracci. His wife was his principal model, and so obsessed was he with her appearance that her features recur again and again in all his female types. He lived with his wife, her daughter, and her sister, thus in an altogether feminine atmosphere, and died in January 1531 (at the age of forty-two) of the plague, deserted by his wife who feared to expose herself to the infection. The quality of his work, with certain exceptions, steadily deteriorated during these twelve years,

---

seems to have been one of Vasari's inventions, for recent investigation of the King's accounts, which were kept with scrupulous exactitude, shows that he gave Andrea no money except for the work he had done. (See Guinness, *op. cit.* pp. 28, 29.)

[1] Reumont, *op. cit.* p. 113.

although they naturally betray a greater ripeness and self-confidence; according to Guinness, 'for the most part his best works were painted before he was thirty-two'.[1] (*i.e.* before the year he decided not to return to France). Layard says that 'his facility led later to increasing mannerisms and emptiness',[2] and it is certain that his lack of inspiration became more and more evident during these last years.

Our problem, therefore, is to ascertain, if possible, how much of his failure is to be ascribed to Lucrezia's influence, and in what precise way did it produce its effect. History has furnished us with many examples showing that passionate and enduring devotion to a beautiful woman is not always fraught with the happiest consequences to a man's career, but at least it has been given the credit of inspiring his art if he was a painter or poet. Must we be robbed also of this illusion? Yet the judgement of the critics is that the petty annoyances caused by Lucrezia's behaviour, the way in which she drove her husband to devote himself to making money instead of to enriching his artistic capabilities, and the general squalidness of feeling resulting from her lack of appreciation and imagination, conspired to kill in Andrea whatever soul he might have had, and stifled his genius for ever. To quote again from Browning's poem:

Had you, with these [beauties] the same, but brought a
    mind!
Some women do so. Had the mouth there urged
'God and the glory! Never care for gain.
The present by the future, what is that?
Live for fame, side by side with Agnolo!
Rafael is waiting: up to God, all three!'
I might have done it for you. So it seems.

[1] Guinness, *op. cit.* p. 56.   [2] Layard, *op. cit.* p. 460.

Perhaps if we examine more closely the precise mental relationship between the two mates, calling to our aid psycho-analytical knowledge in so doing, we may reach a clearer understanding of the way in which it affected Andrea. As soon as we do this it becomes clear that love could not have been the sole feature comprising his attitude towards Lucrezia, and that our understanding of the situation must be imperfect unless we also take into consideration the influence of other emotions, especially that of hate.

There are several good reasons for coming to this conclusion. In the first place, there is in all people a certain amount of ambivalence of affect, so that it is hardly possible for an intense and lasting emotion to be aroused without its opposite at the same time being stimulated and an increase being caused of the natural counter-tendency. Especially is this so when, as in the present case, the emotion is unusually strong, for then it is almost inevitably accompanied by a counter-emotion (of variable intensity) in the unconscious.

In the second place, no man could have suffered what Andrea did from his wife without its provoking a natural resentment. To be foiled in his aspirations and ambitions, to be henpecked and hampered in his daily work, to be cut off from his friends and relatives, to have his life spoilt in every respect except one (that of possessing the woman he loved): these are things that would provoke even the mildest man. Whether the one compensation counterbalances all the rest, that is, to be sure, another matter. We may grant that with Andrea it did, so that he definitely preferred his present life to existence without Lucrezia, but he would not have been human if, side by side with this constant devotion, there was not produced in him as well a counter-reaction of (repressed) hate. Further, the fact that he was able to enjoy such a life of torment indicates a pleasure in suffering, a masochism, that is always accompanied by its opposite in the unconscious, namely sadism, with the tendency to hate that is apt to go with this; we shall recur to this in a moment.[1]

Thirdly, and perhaps most important, there is a deeper ground for supposing that Andrea's love for his wife was connected with unconscious emotions of a very different kind. For there is reason to believe that the normal homosexual component of the love-impulse, particularly the feminine variety of this, was unusually developed with him. It is at all events certain that before his marriage he entered into the enjoyment of male society with an unusually keen zest.

When he was twenty-one years old he was persuaded by an older friend, Franciabigio, to leave his master and to set up in a studio and lodgings which the two were to share in common; for a time they even signed their work in common. After living a year or so thus, Andrea changed his lodgings so as to be in the same street as two other friends, Sansovino and Rustici. His relations with Francia are described as having been 'of the closest possible friendship' while of his friendship with Jacopo Sansovino, Vasari writes, 'nay, so close an intimacy and so great an affection was subsequently contracted by Jacopo and Andrea for each other that they were never separate night or day'.[2] During this time Andrea is said to have been a great favourite in his circle, to have delighted exceedingly in lively society, and to have taken a leading part in various jokes,[3]

---

[1] The account of Strindberg's marriage, given in his *Confessions of a Fool*, is an ample illustration of this paragraph.
[2] Vasari, *op. cit.* vol. iii, p. 184.
[3] Vasari, *op. cit.* vol. v, pp. 72-6; Scott, *op. cit.* pp. 86, 87.

not always too refined,[1] that were played in the clubs of which he was a member. It is not to be supposed that the surrendering of these pleasures through his marriage cost him nothing.

It is not without significance that the friends to whom he was most especially attached were all older than himself; Francia by five years, Sansovino by two, Rustici by fourteen, and so on. One cannot avoid connecting this with the fact that he had two older brothers; in many of his pictures one sees this mirrored by the portrayal of a playful rivalry between the infant Jesus, sheltering in his mother's arms, and one or more older boys (St. John the Baptist, etc.).[2] Pointing in the same direction as these facts is the description of Andrea's disposition as that of 'a gentle, diffident, mild-mannered and modest man.' Finally, if Vasari's statement is true, that Andrea was 'tormented by jealousy',[3] we have the plainest evidence of homosexuality, for an obsessional jealousy[4] is an almost certain indication of this.

In these circumstances Andrea's attachment to his wife may be regarded, at least in part, as denoting a flight from

[1] Most of these were connected with food. To those familiar with Ferenczi's work on homosexuality it may be of interest to know that Andrea took an especial interest in the matter of eating; he did his own marketing every morning in order to secure the choicest tit-bits of his favourite articles of diet, covered the walls of his house with frescoes representing scenes of cooking, table-laying, etc. (these are still to be seen), and was so fond of good living that, according to Vasari, it shortened his life by lowering his resistance to the plague.

[2] Dr. Havelock Ellis has called my attention to an indication of homosexuality shown in Andrea's art. According to Brücke (*Schönheit und Fehler der menschlichen Gestalt*, p. 39), he gave his angels boys' arms, instead of the more customary girls' arms.

[3] Vasari, *op. cit.* vol. iii, p. 194.

[4] There is no reason to believe that Lucrezia was in reality unfaithful to him.

his repressed homosexual tendencies. She became at once his anchor of salvation, to which he must cling at all costs, as well as the barrier against the satisfying of his repressed desires. As his refuge from himself she increased his love; as the person who deprived him of the pleasure of male society she increased his hate. This hate could not be allowed to become conscious because the reason for it was repressed, and could therefore manifest itself only by evoking an exaggerated amount of love to counterbalance it.

In his attitude towards his wife there was thus a constant conflict. The matter is still further complicated by the probability that much of his homosexual masochistic desire must have found satisfaction in her peculiar temperament; in other words, he loved her as a woman loves a man,[1] a common enough occurence in marriage. We can

---

[1] He sometimes actually depicted her as a man, particularly (and appropriately enough) as Michael, the Christian god of war.

Of other complex-indicators in his paintings I will mention three. (1) On the pedestal of the Madonna in his masterpiece, mentioned above, are several harpies, which are, of course, entirely out of place in a subject of this character; so far as I know it is the only instance of a Pagan motive occurring in any of Andrea's works, and it is so striking here as to have given the picture the name of the 'Madonna dell' Arpie'. Critics have been completely mystified by this, but, if my suggestion concerning Andrea's *unconscious* attitude towards his wife is correct, it should not be difficult of explanation. (2) A favourite topic of Andrea, which he painted no less than five times, is Abraham's sacrifice of his son Isaac. Critics comment on the wonderful benignity of the father in these pictures, and the implicit trust and self-surrender displayed by the son as he sees the father's knife approach. In view of our remarks above on Andrea's homosexual masochism, this also becomes more comprehensible. (3) Andrea shows a special preference for painting figures seated cross-legged on the floor, in the graceful composition of which he developed a remarkable skill. It is hard not to connect this with the fact that his father was a tailor and that later in life Andrea changed his surname from Agnolo to del Sarto (Sarto = tailor).

hardly think otherwise when we contrast his own meek disposition with her domineering haughtiness; it is also significant that she was some four years older than himself. Reumont's description of him as 'a good-natured, modest, unpretentious but weak man entirely at the mercy of his own impulses as well as of his dominant wife'[1] is in full accord with this conclusion.

We now begin to understand better the enormous hold that Lucrezia possessed over Andrea. His love was maintained in a constant state of high tension because it had to serve, in addition to its own functions, that of damming back both repressed hate and homosexuality. She could demand anything of him, and treat him however she liked, for without her he was lost; he could not afford not to love her.

Returning now to our main problem, of the influence of the situation on Andrea's art, we may wonder why the current conflict did not throw him back towards older, infantile ones (regression), from which he might derive deeper sources of stimulation, or at least why he did not seek an escape from them in his work. One answer to the former question probably is that the infantile complexes were either not strong enough to attract the driven back libido or else were incapable of being sublimated in the desired direction; this is, it is true, an unsatisfactory sketch of an answer, but to fill it in would mean the opening up of many topics other than those we are here concerned with. Another answer, applicable to both questions, is that the current conflicts were of such a kind as to allow no escape from them, even in phantasy. How could Andrea sink himself into his art (flight into work) when there was Lucrezia in the body, with him at every moment? She was practically his sole model, she ordered the

[1] Reumont, *op. cit.* p. 214.

workshop, directed what her husband was to do and what not (according to what she thought would best pay), and left him no moment of peace in which to develop his own individuality. With right could Browning make him say,

> So—still they[1] overcome
> Because there's still Lucrezia,—as I choose.

The last three words express the core of the situation. The love for Lucrezia, with its superadded sources that we have indicated above, was stronger than all else, including even the desire for artistic expression, so that in this sense it may perhaps be said that she was responsible for the ruin of his genius. It would be a more accurate way of putting it to say that she forced the internal battle, which is necessary for all artistic creation, to be fought out in the current details of everyday life, and so allowed him no opportunity to gather strength and inspiration that could be applied to higher aims. Her domineering masterfulness enabled her to choose the scene of battle, and her egocentricity demanded that she should be the centre of it.

But after all, the reason for the situation lay at least as much in Andrea as in Lucrezia. If she had never existed he would probably, with his special temperament, have found another Lucrezia. And here one cannot help feeling the difference between a masculine, creative temperament and a feminine, receptive one, whether they occur in the body of a man or a woman being irrelevant. Scott says very justly in this connection: 'In looking at Andrea's pictures one sighs even in the midst of admiration, thinking that if the hand which produced them had been guided by a spark of divine genius instead of the finest talent, what glorious works they would have been! The truth is that Andrea's was a receptive, rather than an original and

[1] *I.e.* Raphael and others.

productive mind. His art was more imitative than spontaneous, and this forms perhaps the difference between talent and genuis.'[1] As regards the development of Andrea's art, therefore, Lucrezia may practically be said to have played little more than the part of a lay figure; it was his temperament that made her mean to him all that she did. The problem is thus reduced, like so many psychological ones, to one of temperamental constitution. If Andrea had not been what he was, Lucrezia could not have played the part in his life that she did; but it is probable that if *she* had not been what she was he still would have tried to make her play that part, *i.e.* she still would have been to him the man, and not the helpmate woman. One side of his nature was developed, but not the other. I must once more quote from Browning's poem.

I know both what I want and what might gain,
And yet how profitless to know, to sigh
'Had I been two, another and myself,
Our head would have o'erlooked the world!' No doubt.

. . . . . .

In this world, who can do a thing, will not;
And who would do it, cannot, I perceive;
Yet the will's somewhat—somewhat, too, the power—
And thus we half-men struggle.

In short, if Andrea had been able to react differently towards his everyday difficulty, he might have displayed the genius of a creator instead of merely the talent of an skilful craftsman. He might have been an artist, and was —only a painter.

[1] Scott, *op. cit.* pp. 72, 73.

IV

THE CASE OF LOUIS BONAPARTE, KING OF HOLLAND[1]

THE life-history of Louis Bonaparte, the brother of the great Napoleon and the father of Napoleon III, is of no special interest in itself, but it acquires some extrinsic importance through the part he played in contributing to his brother's downfall, an event the interest and significance of which is such as to make worth while any attempt to throw further light on the problems surrounding it. For it was Louis' attitude towards his brother's views that precipitated the incorporation of Holland in the Empire, and so added one more to the nations that presently rose and overthrew Napoleon. An attempt will here be made to increase our understanding of this attitude by adducing some psychological considerations regarding Louis' personality.

The problem can be shortly described as follows:[2] Louis was made King of Holland by Napoleon's will on June the 5th 1806, with the very grudging consent of the Dutch. He had hesitated considerably before accepting the proposal, and, once having done so, he proceeded to take up an independent position in opposition to his

[1] Read before the American Psychopathological Association, May 8, 1913; published in the *Journal of Abnormal Psychology* (December 1913), vol. viii, p. 289.
[2] The original authorities from which the following details are taken are for the most part dealt with in Atteridge's *Napoleon's Brothers*, Rocquain's *Napoléon et le roi Louis*, and in Masson's works, so that it is not necessary to give individual bibliographical references here.

brother. Napoleon's object was, of course, to bring Holland more directly under his own control than before, to merge her interests in those of France, and to make her join in his great contest with England. It was just a few months before he issued his famous Berlin decree, after which he went on to league the whole of the Continent against England in the blockade that was intended to starve her into submission by paralysing her export trade. Holland was at that time the chief point at which this trade entered the Continent, so that she could not remain neutral, and had to take one side or the other. To join with Napoleon would involve the practical destruction of her own trade, with extreme economic distress until the end of the war, but it was essential to his project that she should make this sacrifice, for which she might be recompensed by the restoration of her colonies if England were conquered. Her narrower national interests were therefore of necessity opposed to the general Continental scheme that Napoleon was aiming at, and Louis, although he had been sent to Holland purely for the purpose of supporting and enforcing this scheme, chose to adopt the Dutch point of view and hinder his brother's plans. He would not admit that he was merely a French prince governing what was practically a part of the Empire, in the interests of the latter as a whole, but regarded himself as an independent sovereign whose duty it was to rule in the interests of his subjects, a laudable enough aim if his view of his situation had only happened to be in conformity with the actual facts. This attitude, which was indicated on the day of his State entry into the Hague by his allowing hardly any French to take part in the procession, in which Dutch cavalry formed the escort, became more and more pronounced as time went on, in spite of the most vigorous protests from Napoleon, and it extended to the whole sphere of government. In a book written many years later he stated that he entertained throughout different views from his brother on every question that concerned Holland, on the problems of conscription, religion, trade, war, and so on, as well, of course, as on the all-important matter of the Continental blockade. The efforts of the French officials were vain in their endeavour to suppress the wholesale smuggling that was rendering the blockade inefficacious, and Napoleon became more and more exasperated. Finally, he was driven to undertake the gradual absorption of Holland into the Greater France he was then building up. Louis, seeing clearly whither his brother was trending, first consented to surrender all his territory up to the banks of the Meuse, but three months later, when the French army was ordered to march into Amsterdam, he abdicated in favour of his son and fled surreptitiously into Bohemia (July 3, 1810). His whereabouts were discovered two weeks later, but he resisted all Napoleon's entreaties and commands to return to France, and proceeded to Graz, in Styria, where he lived until just before the fall of the Empire. The incorporation of the whole of Holland into France immediately followed, and this led to chronic discontent and insurrection which lasted until the final overthrow of the French yoke in 1814.

The thesis here maintained is that Louis' conduct was not altogether due to his political blindness in refusing to recognize the inexorable facts of his situation, but was in part determined by his personal attitude towards Napoleon, a matter that becomes more intelligible in the light of modern psychopathology. His lack of co-operation with his brother was not confined to the period of his short Dutch reign, but extended over some seventeen years, until the end of the Empire. Both before these years and after them he was an enthusiastic supporter and defender of his brother, so that we see two opposite tendencies manifesting themselves in his life. More than this, the beginning of the period of hostility synchronized with a complete change in his general character and disposition; we may therefore suspect that we have to do here with something that lay near to the core of his personality.

I proceed now to give an account, as brief as possible, of Louis' life, particularly in regard to his relations with his brother. As is well known, he was Napoleon's favourite brother, was educated personally by him, and was for many years hardly separated from him. Napoleon attached him to his staff when he was barely sixteen, and he remained in this position, passing through various stages of promotion, for the greater part of the next three years, from shortly after the fall of Toulon until nearly the end of the first Italian campaign. He seemed at this time to be a very active and promising officer; at the battle of Arcola he distinguished himself by acts of especial courage and daring, and at Lodi he is said—though this has been denied—to have saved Napoleon's life. Just after this, when he was in his twentieth year, came about the striking character change, which was to reduce him for the rest of his life to being little more than a useless encumbrance to all about him. It followed on a serious illness, of which we shall say more presently, and was marked by moodiness, depression, irresolution, seclusiveness, and self-withdrawal, and above all by a most pronounced valetudinarianism. His main and permanent interest now became the care of his health; he tried one after another every cure, spa, and health resort within reach, and he used this as a pretext to refuse, or to hesitate about accepting, all the duties that were successively imposed on him. In other words, he became a confirmed hypochondriac. He protested against going to Egypt with Napoleon, and was with him there only three months when he got permission to return to France. Three years later he refused to accompany his brother in the second Italian campaign that was to end in Marengo, going instead to Aix. In 1806 he hesitated about accepting the crown of Holland on account of the dampness of the Dutch climate, and when his brother overruled his objections he stayed in his new kingdom only a month before leaving for Wiesbaden, leaving the government in the hands of his ministers; within a week of reaching Holland he had written to Napoleon saying that he was suffering from the change of climate and must have a holiday. In the following year, in the contest with Prussia that culminated in Jena, he hesitated to join the army, was filled with concern lest the English should descend on Holland, and behaved throughout the campaign in such a pusillanimous and timorous manner as to convince even his brother that he was totally unfitted for military command. The year after, Napoleon, seeing that he did not serve his purpose in Holland, offered him the crown of Spain, but Louis refused it, on the ground that he was pledged to Holland. Two years later came his abdication and retirement to Graz. When the Russian campaign was embarked on he remained in Graz, prophesying disaster to his brother. At the beginning of 1813 he wrote to Napoleon offering his services on condition that his kingdom was restored, a demand that he repeated several times throughout the year, and in November he came to France, staying at his mother's château at Pont-sur-Seine. Napoleon pointed out that he was being hampered in his efforts to come to terms with the Allies by his brother's absurd pretensions to the throne of Holland at such a moment, and gave orders to Cambacérès, the Arch-Chancellor of the Empire, that if Louis did not make his submission within two days he was to be arrested. Louis fled to Switzerland, but late in January of 1814 he came to Paris and made his peace with Napoleon, whom he now saw for the last time. He was asked to assist his brother Joseph in the defence of Paris, but he deserted it on the eve of the Allies' attack. On Napoleon's return from Elba he refused to join him, stayed in Italy making sinister prophesies, and was the only one of the brothers—not even excluding the recalcitrant Lucien, who returned from England after a seven years' exile—to take no part in the Hundred Days.

During, therefore, the whole of Napoleon's period of power Louis had either refused to co-operate with him or else did so only very grudgingly and half-heartedly. Yet there were occasional moments even in this time when his old devotion to his brother reasserted itself, particularly when the latter seemed in danger; an example of this was when Napoleon was given up for lost in Egypt after the destruction of his fleet, Louis being unceasing in his insistence that the Directory should spare no efforts to send reinforcements to Egypt and relieve his brother. As was mentioned above, Louis' attitude towards his brother once more underwent a change after the downfall of the latter, and still more markedly after his death. He busied himself in his later life with making replies to Napoleon's detractors, and wrote a book, for instance, in answer to Sir Walter Scott's *Life of Napoleon*, in which he made the savagest attacks on the integrity of this author. The following passages may be quoted from this volume, as indicative of his present attitude towards his brother: ' Napoleon is the greatest man that has ever lived'; 'Since the world has existed there has never appeared a general, a conqueror, or a King, who can be compared to him'. His own delusion of persecution he parallels, through the process of identification, by developing a similar one in regard to his brother:

'I am absolutely convinced that this gigantic undertaking [the expedition to Russia], as well as the affairs in Spain, and the taking over of Holland and the Papal States, were simply snares into which the people about him managed to seduce him, by means of his extraordinary love of fame and his equally unlimited striving to make France ever greater and mightier'; 'He would have achieved the most brilliant and decisive of all his successes had Paris only been able to hold out for a few days' (and not been surrendered through treachery).

In attempting to understand better this ambivalent attitude that has just been outlined we have first to ask ourselves whether it cannot be explained as a natural reaction to Napoleon's own rather similar attitude towards his brother. This can best be described as one of striking over-estimation of value, followed later by a gradual disappointment and increasing annoyance. To call it an alternation of love and hate, which we plainly see in the case of Louis, would be to give a very imperfect and incorrect description of it, although—and this is an important point—the external manifestations of it might be so interpreted by someone who experienced this alternation himself, just as the normal conduct of a parent is often in this way interpreted by an over-sensitive child. For Napoleon's treatment of Louis did actually resemble that of an over-fond parent on the one hand and that of an over-stern one on the other, and no doubt Louis interpreted it as such. A few illustrations will make this clearer, and it will help our understanding of the situation if we try to imagine the effect that the attitude described would have on a boy who doted on his clever and masterful brother, eight years older than himself.

Louis' first memory of his brother was that of a young officer of seventeen, on his first leave of absence to visit his Corsican home. Nearly five years later, in January 1791, Napoleon took him back with him to Auxonne, where he educated him personally and supported him at his own expense by dint of making serious sacrifices. At this time Napoleon was enchanted with his young pupil-brother, wrote home that 'he will turn out a better fellow than any of us others', and prophesied a great future for him. For a few years Louis developed promisingly and seemed to be fulfilling all the hopes his brother had built on him. It took a long time to destroy this illusion, and Napoleon clung to it for years after it had been dissipated for everyone else who knew Louis. In 1801, for instance, after Louis' disappointing behaviour in the Egyptian and second Italian campaigns, and four years after the change in his disposition noted above, we find Napoleon saying, 'There is no longer any need of bothering our minds about looking for my successor. I have found one. It is Louis. He has none of the defects of my other brothers, and he has all their good qualities.' It was only gradually that he renounced this project of making Louis his successor, and then he replaced it by adopting Louis' eldest son, much against the father's will. Not until the Prussian campaign of 1806 did Napoleon realize his brother's total incapacity. From this time on his treatment of Louis became even more arbitrary than before, though he had always had a way of disposing of him that savoured of the spirit of ownership. His attitude in the later years showed still more clearly his characteristic alternation between the kindness for a favourite brother and the annoyance of a despot at one who constantly disappointed and failed him. Thus in March of 1810, on hearing that his brother had left his Kingdom for a health resort, he writes to de Champagny, the Minister for Foreign Affairs, 'Prince Louis is to retire from the States of Baden instantly, else

THE CASE OF LOUIS BONAPARTE

he is to be arrested and shut up in a French fortress to expiate all his crimes',[1] while two months later, in a letter to Louis himself, he refers to him as 'a prince who was almost a son to me'. Three days after this friendly letter he writes to his brother, 'Write me no more of your customary twaddle; three years, now, it has been going on, and every instant proves its falsehood', adding in a postscript of his own handwriting, 'This is the last letter I shall ever write to you in my life'. In another two months he is writing to Lebrun, his Lieutenant-General in Holland, expressing the strongest solicitude and love for Louis. In the November of 1813 he writes to Cambacérès, 'I am sending you a letter from King Louis, which appears to me that of a madman', and the day after sends him instructions to have Louis arrested unless he gives in his submission; but two months later he is receiving Louis in the Tuileries with the greatest kindness.

If we now compare the attitudes of Napoleon and Louis towards each other, we see that there are marked differences in the two cases. Napoleon's attitude is perfectly consistent throughout, and is in accord with his whole character. It is that of a masterful man who becomes disappointed at not being able to make the use he had hoped of someone he had over-estimated to begin with, and it is practically identical with his attitude towards many of his followers, such as Junot, Masséna, Murat, and others. Any change in his treatment of Louis is quite intelligible in the light of this, and needs no further explanation. In any case it cannot be regarded as the *cause* of Louis' change in attitude, for this had preceded it by several years and must therefore have been the prior one. Louis'

[1] This letter, and other similar ones, was omitted from the Correspondence of Napoleon, published in the reign of Louis' son, Napoleon III, and they have only recently been made public.

attitude, which was obviously much more personal, gives, on the other hand, the impression of proceeding from some inner conflict, and this inference is greatly strengthened both by the fact that the change in it was accompanied by a severe neurotic disturbance and by a number of other considerations which will presently be mentioned.

It is already not difficult to surmise what the nature of this conflict must have been, namely his homosexual attraction to Napoleon, and having this key we can unlock most of the problems here under discussion. That the homosexual component, of the feminine variety, was unusually pronounced in Louis there is little room to doubt. To judge from the stories of his dissipations in the intervals of the Italian campaign, he was making a manful attempt to overcome this tendency and to develop the heterosexual side of his nature, when the event happened that was to change his whole life and ruin his happiness. This was an attack of venereal disease, which caused in his twentieth year a long and serious illness, and which left him a hypochondriacal invalid, permanently crippled by what in all probability was gonorrhoeal rheumatism. From this moment he became a changed man. The influence that such an event may exercise in the case of a man of a certain disposition is well known to us from experience in daily practice, and has often been illustrated in history, notably in the case of Nietzsche. A pronounced misogyny is apt to develop, aided by the primary weakness of the heterosexual instinct, and the only avenue of escape from the homosexual tendency is thus violently closed. In Louis' case the event threw him back for a time on his old love for Napoleon, and we find Josephine in 1800 making to Roederer the strong statement: 'He loves Bonaparte as a lover does his mistress. The letters he wrote to him when he left Egypt are so tender as to make tears come to one's eyes.' This remark is made by a woman who disliked her husband's brothers, and who had a rich experience in what love letters should be like; the significance of the remark is not therefore to be underestimated.

Louis' misogyny, however, was far from being absolute, and he made several further attempts to find consolation in the arms of woman. Early in 1798 he had fallen in love with a school-friend of his sister, a niece of Josephine, but Napoleon interfered and put an end to the affair by taking the girl from school and promptly marrying her to one of his adjutants, Lavalette. In his disappointment Louis plunged into reckless dissipation in Paris, but his soldier brother again stepped in, carried him off to Toulon on the way to Egypt, told him to stop playing the fool, and made him march reluctantly along the path of military glory. Four years later Napoleon again undertook to direct his love-instinct, this time in a more positive way by getting him to marry Josephine's daughter, Hortense. Louis at first sulked, and fled to his country estate at Baillon in order to avoid the young lady, but he ultimately gave his consent to the wedding, which took place on March 3, 1802, when he was twenty-four years old. From the point of view of happiness the marriage was, as might have been expected, a complete failure. Within a few weeks his old dreamy restless mood again took possession of him, his wife became anxious and unhappy, and after two months of married life he abandoned her in Paris, so that she had to return to her mother. Seven months later a son was born, Napoleon Charles (the names of his brother and father), and the rumour became current that Napoleon was the father. It is practically certain that the rumour was false, but it was so persistent and so widespread throughout Europe that Napoleon, after making an effort to discredit it, reconciled himself to it and concluded that, since he meant to make the boy his heir and successor, it would not be altogether a bad thing if it was believed that he was his own son.

From this time Louis' old affection for his brother disappeared more completely, and was more obviously replaced by a mixture of suspicion and smothered hatred. It is not definitely known to what extent he shared the popular belief about his son, but his subsequent conduct makes it highly probable that he was unable altogether to dismiss it from his mind. He was jealous of Napoleon's intense fondness for the boy, and refused to allow him to be chosen as the successor to the Imperial throne for fear that Napoleon might adopt him and take him away; later on he refused to let his son be given the crown of Italy, and for the same reason. At the same time he gave his affection, not to his eldest son, but to the second one, about whose paternity there was never any question. His married life lasted six or seven years, and was a series of jealous quarrels with occasional reconciliations, such as during his wife's passionate grief over the death of their eldest son. She was prostrated by the occurrence, and was sent to recuperate at Cauterets, in the Pyrenees; from here rumours reached Louis of her being too friendly with Decazes and Verhuell, two of his officials, and he now came definitely to believe in her infidelity. A third son, who later became Napoleon III, was born the next year, and Louis took the view, probably an incorrect one, that he was not the father, although he publicly recognized the boy as his own. He was permanently estranged from his wife after the Pyrenees visit, and in December 1809 he formally petitioned for a separation. This was the very month in which Napoleon was arranging his divorce from Josephine, a circumstance which cannot be a coincidence, for it was a most inopportune moment; it clearly shows how Louis was still identifying himself with his brother. A family council was called together, according to the French law, and to avoid scandal an informal separation was arranged, which lasted until Hortense's death twenty-eight years later. Not long after this Napoleon's son was born, Marie-Louise's child, and Louis, who was now in retirement in Graz, reacted to the news as though the event had been purposely arranged as a personal blow against himself. He became more embittered than ever against the Emperor, who, according to him, had robbed him of his throne, taken his children from him, and had now produced a son himself who was to steal the heritage of Louis. The last relation he had with his wife was to bring a law-suit against her on the fall of the Empire to get possession of his elder surviving son, the one concerning whose paternity there was no question; he was granted this by the courts, but Hortense refused to part with the boy.

An interesting matter, and one which throws much light on Louis' conduct at the most important period of his life, is that his reactions in the sphere of international politics to a large extent duplicated those of his personal life in relation to his brother, a process known as introjection (Ferenczi). This is well brought out in a book he published some nineteen years after his abdication, from which I quote the following passage: 'Since a great State must necessarily exert a important influence on the others, I wanted this influence [in the case of France and Holland] to be the result of friendship, of good treatment, of mutual inclination and of benevolence on the part of the stronger one in regard to the weaker, so that the interest of the latter would come into accord with its inclination'. This is evidently a parallel of his idea of what Napoleon's attitude should be towards him personally. How far he carried the identification of himself with Holland is illustrated by his cherishing the delusion that his former kingdom was mourning his absence and longing for his return, and this at the end of 1813, at a time when the Dutch were rising in insurrection against the French yoke and were massacring French officials in large numbers; Louis even went so far about this time as to write to a number of prominent men in Amsterdam assuring them that he would soon be amongst them again and that their (!) desire to have him as their permanent King would be gratified.

We may now sum up the preceding discussion. Thanks to the investigations of the past few years it is known that delusions of jealousy and delusions of persecution, the two most characteristic symptoms of the paranoid syndrome, are practically pathognomonic of repressed homosexuality, in which they take their origin, and on this ground alone, quite apart from the other evidence detailed above, we are justified in concluding that here lay the root of Louis' trouble. The delusions of persecution are the expression of disappointed love, and are brought about by means of a double inversion of the underlying content. The love is replaced by hate, a process often enough pointed out by poets and writers, and the emotion is ascribed to, or projected on to, the person towards whom it was originally directed. This explains how it is that such delusions always begin in reference to persons whom the patient had loved, though they usually extend later to others who replace these in his imagination. Finding that he cannot love them he hates them instead, and fancies that they hate him. In Louis' case this delusion remained chiefly localized to Napoleon, but we noted a tendency to extension in his conviction that Napoleon, with whom he here identifies himself, was the victim of a carefully laid plot to lure him to destruction. The psychological structure of delusions of jealousy is still simpler, there being merely a projection of the emotion without any change in the nature of this. The patient accuses his wife of loving a man whom he himself would like to love. This also, like the previous one, may get generalized, and with Louis we see examples of both kinds. He suspects his wife of having sexual relations first with Napoleon, and then later with other men, members not of his actual family, but of his symbolic family, his court. It is instructive to see that the second of these suspicions, being a more disguised manifestation of the homosexual wish, is allowed to come to more open expression than the first one; the latter was a fixed idea, while the former was hardly more than a half-avowed suspicion.

It is not really correct to speak of delusions with Louis, at least not in the strict psychiatric sense of the word, for it is rather a question of preconscious beliefs which his reflective judgement was able to a great extent to hold in check. Louis never became a true paranoiac, though he certainly exhibited definite paranoid tendencies. All through his life we see him struggling against these, and against the homosexuality from which they sprang. As an instance of the devices he adopted to defend himself against his delusional tendencies may be quoted the following: Some years after Napoleon's death he published the statement that his brother had never been unfaithful to Josephine; Napoleon, whose amours were the talk of Europe, and who was known to have had at least thirty mistresses during his wedded life with Josephine! The object of this attempt at self-deception on Louis' part is quite plain; if Napoleon had never betrayed Josephine, it was a guarantee that he could never have betrayed Louis and that the latter's suspicion regarding his wife had been unfounded. By such desperate measures as this Louis kept his abnormal tendencies to some extent within check, and so managed to preserve his reason, but it was at a heavy cost, at the expense of becoming a nervous invalid for the whole of his life. He sacrificed his health rather than his reason, and he had no energy left to make him a useful member of society.

Of the bearing that Louis' conduct had on his brother's plans, of the difference it made to the course of history, and the not inconsiderable extent to which it contributed, directly and indirectly, to the downfall of the Empire, this is not the place to speak; the object of the present paper is merely to illustrate that knowledge gained from psychopathology, and unobtainable in any other way, may be of service in helping to elucidate even purely historical problems.[1]

[1] Mention may be made here of two other attempts to apply psychoanalytical knowledge to an historical problem: Abraham: 'Amenhotep IV (Echnaton). Psychoanalytische Beiträge zum Verständnis seiner Persönlichkeit und des monotheistischen Aton-Kultes.' *Imago* (1912), Bd. I, p. 334; and Flügel: 'On the Character and Married Life of Henry VIII', *International Journal of Psycho-Analysis* (1920), vol. i, p. 24.

V
WAR AND INDIVIDUAL PSYCHOLOGY[1]

THE aim of this essay is to raise the question whether the science of Psychology can ever show us how to abolish War. It is a question that must have occurred to many of those who have been able to reflect on the events of the past months, and it is one of the most far-reaching questions that mankind as a whole has to face, one on which its future may to a great extent depend. We are beginning to realize as never before—for it is to be supposed that at the time of other cataclysms, such as during the destruction of the Roman Empire, mankind was less conscious of itself than now—how powerful is the check that War may impose on the advance of civilization, and the sight, together with the accompanying horrors, has naturally stimulated the desire, always widespread even in times of peace, to devise, if possible, a means of surmounting this formidable obstacle.

This desire has already manifested itself in the devising of many schemes, mainly legal and political—from systems of international policing to conventions for compulsory arbitration—and the evidently unworkable nature of these may be taken as a measure of the emotional pressure that has brought them into being. It is characteristic of emotional states that they lead to attempts at immediate action instead of to thought, the preliminary investigation necessary to secure suitable action being dispensed with. The general attitude of pacifists is that, both on the moral

[1] Published in the *Sociological Review* (1915), vol. viii, p. 167.

and the material side, the evils of War are evidently greater than its benefits, even if the latter are admitted, and that consequently steps must be taken at all costs to prevent its occurrence. The sense of urgency is felt so acutely that any calm study of the factors involved is regarded as an intolerable delay, while any expression of doubt as to the desirability of the goal is repudiated with impatience. Ill-considered and, in all probability, unsuccessful action is the natural result of such an attitude. Certain cooler-headed and more thoughtful people, on the other hand, who take a longer view of the question, realize better its complexity, and see that the matter demands an intimate knowledge of human motives, desires, and emotions. They therefore turn to Psychology for assistance in a problem which obviously belongs to its domain, and ask psychologists how it is to be solved. It is the purpose of the present essay to consider what kind of answer can be given to such an inquiry.

Now this answer must always be the same whenever any science is approached with a similar question, one with a purely utilitarian aim. Suppose for example, that an engineer is asked to devise a plan for carrying out a given practical purpose, *e.g.* building a bridge. He can answer the questions about the possibility of the undertaking, the means that would have to be adopted, and the probable cost, in lives and money, that would be incurred. What would not be in his sphere is the question of whether or no the undertaking *should* be entered upon. All he can do is to supply the data relating to the points just mentioned, leaving to the promoters of the undertaking the decision of whether they considered it worth while to carry it out. Science is thus the handmaid of the human will: it is not within her province to dictate what ought to be done in a given situation, but only to point out what will have to be done if a desired end is to be attained.

Psychology, however, holds a peculiar rank among the sciences in that it is concerned also with the instrument of valuation, the mind. When approached with a utilitarian problem, therefore, it has two additional functions to fulfil which do not appertain to any other science. In supplying the data to enable a decision to be made it has first to answer the three questions mentioned above, viz., as regards possibility, means, and cost. But there are two further sets of important data that Psychology has to supply. The first of these relates to the decision that a given end must be achieved, the second to the choice of means. Fundamentally the two points come to the same, it being the place of Psychology in both cases to call attention to the mental factors that may unconsciously influence decision, so that they may be taken into consideration in making a judgement. This is a matter on which the greatest emphasis has to be laid, because the importance of such factors is commonly neglected or else grossly underestimated, and it will therefore be discussed here at some little length. Coming now to the question at issue, whether Psychology can teach us how to abolish War, we see that the first thing to do is to restate the problem under the following headings: Is it possible? If so, how can it be done? What would the cost involve? And, finally, what is the full significance of the desire to accomplish this end?

It may as well be said at once that Psychology can as yet give no positive answer to any one of these questions, a fact which, for the impatient, will forthwith dispose of any further interest in whatever it may have to say on the matter. With those, however, who are chary of nostrums, and brave enough to suspend their judgement until the painful process of attaining truth is achieved, the following considerations should carry weight. In the first place, Psychology is already in a position to offer a considerable body of information directly bearing on the problem, and, in the second place, it is only through a richer and deeper knowledge of Psychology that a final solution of it is possible. It is hardly likely that this conclusion will be doubted on reflection, for it should be evident that even physical factors, *e.g.* economic ones, owe their influence only to the effect they have on human motives and instincts: it is in the sphere of these latter that we have to seek in order to obtain a better understanding of the causes of War.

It will be expedient to open the discussion by considering further the important matter mentioned above—namely, the influence of emotional factors on decision and judgement. Within the last twenty years a method of investigation, known as psycho-analysis, has been devised and elaborated by Professor Freud of Vienna, which has permitted access to a hitherto veiled part of the mind, designated the Unconscious, and the explorations thus carried out have yielded information of very considerable value about the unsuspected significance of this more emotional region of the mind. It would appear from these investigations that man is endowed with a far more intense emotional nature than is generally imagined, and that powerful barriers exist, the function of which is to restrain its manifestations. All the emotions of which we become aware, either in ourselves or in others, represent only tricklings through from the volcanic reservoir that is pent up in the unconscious region of the mind, *i.e.* that region of which we are unconscious. The dams that impede a freer flow of emotion are the restrictions against uncurbed action that have been painfully acquired during the civilization of the race and the training of the individual, and the reason for their existence is the fact that the pent-up or 'repressed' emotional life is of a rude and savage character incompatible with the demands of civilized standards. In this buried mental life, which is prevented from readily translating itself into action, phantasies play a very extensive part, and these are fundamentally of a pleasurable kind. Any disagreeable piece of reality that may succeed in penetrating to this region of the mind is at once treated as material to be used for the building up of some pleasurable fancy; it is remoulded in terms of some wish, and thus robbed of all its unpleasant features. The Unconscious cannot endure any contradiction of its desires and imaginings, any more than an infant can; intelligibly so, because it mainly comprises the infantile and inherited portion of our mind. Perception and, in an even higher degree, judgement are thus grossly distorted by these powerful emotional agents.

We are, it is true, to some extent familiar with this process of distortion in conscious mental life also. The expression 'the wish is father to the thought' is proverbial, and everyone will admit, in the abstract, that prejudices can influence opinions and judgements, at least those of other people. The science of History, and in a very imperfect way that of Law, makes some attempt at estimating and allowing for errors due to this factor, and in scientific research it is generally recognized that evidence of an emotional influence (jealousy, ambition, etc.) casts suspicion on the validity of the conclusions and even on that of the observations. But what is not generally recognized is that influences of this nature are far more extensively exerted than might be imagined, and that the most potent ones are those proceeding from sources of which we know nothing, namely from the unconscious region of the mind. In an emotional situation, such as is evoked by a horror of war, any judgement arrived at will infallibly be dependent only in part on the external evidence; in a greater part on unconscious emotional influences. If, therefore, we desire to form a judgement purely on the relevant evidence, *i.e.* a judgement that is in accord with reality and so is likely to be permanent, it is essential to neutralize the influence of those other factors, and this, of course, cannot be done until it is known precisely what they are. As will presently be explained, this knowledge can be adequately based only on a study of Individual Psychology.[1]

Similar considerations apply to the causes of War. The causes of any given war are exceedingly numerous, and these are usually so interrelated as to make the unravelling of them one of the most difficult of tasks; it is further notorious that success in this undertaking is rarely more than approximate. The most important part of the task is, of course, not the mere enumeration of a list of causes, but the ordering of them according to their scale of values. They constitute a hierarchy in this respect, and may be divided into the exciting causes, which merely precipitate the war, and the deeper or more underlying ones, which bear the main responsibility for it. Whereas popular opinion concentrates its attention almost exclusively on the former, the philosophic historian seeks to uncover and comprehend the latter. How difficult this is may be judged from the circumstance alone that it takes about a century before all the material is published on which alone valid conclusions can be founded. In the present war, for example, it would seem impossible as yet to answer even the apparently elementary and simple question of which was the more important causative factor leading up to it—

[1] This term seems to have been appropriated of late to denote only Adlerian psychology, but in 1915 this was not so.

the so-called inevitable conflict between Teuton and Slav or the need for German expansion overseas; in other words, whether the War is primarily one between Germany and Russia or between Germany and England.

Supposing, however, that all the political factors bringing about a certain war have been elucidated, we are still left with the problem of the causation of war in general. That is to say, the question arises whether there is not in the human mind some deep need, or some set of recurrently acting agents, which tends to bring about wars more or less regularly, and to find or create pretexts for wars whatever the external situation may be. This would involve the conclusion that man cannot live for more than a certain period without indulging his warlike impulses, and that history comprises an alternation of wars and recuperations. Another possibility, not identical with the preceding, though allied to it, is that man tends to prefer the solution of various socio-political problems by means of War to their solution in any other way: this might be because of the instinct just referred to or else because the other solutions are more difficult and irksome, or it might be due to both reasons combined. There is undoubtedly much that could be adduced in favour of this view, unpalatable as it may seem, and we should be prepared, in any unbiased investigation, for the possibility that it is true. We have, for instance, the unvarnished fact that wars do invariably recur in spite of the best intentions to the contrary, and it might very plausibly be argued that what happens historically is a periodic outburst of warlike impulses followed by a revulsion against War—usually lasting for one or two generations—which is again succeeded by a forgetting of the horrors involved and a gradually accumulating tension that once more leads to an explosion. This feature of periodicity would be well worthy of a special study,[1] but we must leave aside here historical questions of a kind which are not directly germane to the psychological considerations of the present paper.

Returning to the problem of the Psychology of War, we may at this point consider an objection that is likely to be brought against the mode of approach here adopted, namely, that of Individual Psychology. Many will take the view that, since War is obviously a social problem, it should be either to Sociology or Social Psychology that we should have recourse in order to obtain a better understanding of the nature of it. This might even more strongly be urged in the case of modern war, which is essentially the affair of whole societies, and in which the social phenomena of imitation, contagion, crowd psychology, and mass suggestion play an important part. Fully to meet this objection would necessitate a detailed discussion, impossible here, of the relation of Social to Individual Psychology in general. There are two schools of thought in the matter, the main point at issue being as follows: On the one hand it is contended that it is possible to pursue the subject of Social Psychology independently of the data afforded by Individual Psychology, on the ground that there are peculiar data pertaining to the interaction of social mass units which are provided by the former subject and which are accessible only to those who make a study of it. The second school maintain the contrary of this, namely, that Social Psychology must throughout be based on Individual Psychology, for three reasons.

[1] Several writers, for example, have commented on the interesting circumstance that, on the four last occasions, the turn of the century has roughly coincided with a general European war of the same nature, consisting, namely, in a coalition against the predominance of the most powerful nation.

In the first place, the unconscious emotional influences and prejudices spoken of above affect judgement to a much greater extent in the domain of the mental than in that of the non-mental sciences, so that a student of Social Psychology is at a grave disadvantage unless he has, on the basis of Individual Psychology, submitted his own mind to a thorough analysis and in this way acquired a knowledge and control of the distorting influences in question. In the second place, the study of motives, emotions, instincts, etc., can for technical reasons be properly carried out only by the methods of Individual Psychology, where the material is susceptible of objective experimental control. Finally, there is good reason to believe that in what may be called the 'social situations' that are the subject of socio-psychological study no new factor is added that may not be observed apart from such situations. 'Social' mental activities are nothing more nor less than the sum of individual mental activities. The reason for this has been pointed out by Wilfred Trotter,[1] who in his essay on the most exquisite of socio-psychological forces—the herd instinct—adduced considerations to show that man is literally never anything but a social animal, and that all the agents specially insisted on by social psychologists, mob infection, press suggestion, etc., are constantly operative under all circumstances. The reason why some social psychologists have been misled into adopting the opposite conclusion is largely that the manifestations of certain instincts acted on by 'social situations' may differ somewhat in their external form from those occurring apart from these situations, the underlying unity of the two sets being overlooked.

Something may profitably be said at this point on the

[1] *Sociological Review*, 1908. Reprinted in his *Instincts of the Herd in Peace and War*, 1916.

mode of operation of these 'social situations', for the matter has a direct bearing on the problem of the essential nature of War. It is necessary to recur to a topic mentioned earlier, that of the 'repressed' unconscious impulses that are incompatible with civilized standards of thought and behaviour. The normal fate of these impulses is not annihilation, as might be supposed from the fact of their total disappearance from view in the course of education and development. On the contrary, they remain active throughout life, and furnish probably the greatest part of all our interest, energies, and strivings. They cannot manifest themselves, however, unless they first go through a process of transformation, to which the name 'sublimation' has been attached, whereby the energy investing them becomes diverted along other, associated channels that accord better with the demands of social standards. The deflection of an ungratified maternal instinct into philanthropic channels is a familiar instance of this. Mental disorder, including the various forms of 'nervousness', results from an inability of this process to work smoothly, and the very great prevalence of this in one shape or another, from slight eccentricities and character anomalies to the gravest kinds of insanity, affords some measure of how imperfect is the sublimating mechanism. Further, there is present in the mind a constant tendency to relapse in the direction of cruder and more primitive manifestations of the repressed impulses, and advantage is taken of every excuse to do so: examples are the relaxation of standards of modesty in clothing at the seaside and on the stage, the conduct responsible for the recent agitation about 'war babies', and the temporary paralysis of ethical restraints by alcohol. Now the influence of social situations is very apt to be in just this direction of undoing the effects of sublimation, thus leading to the adoption of a lower or more primitive standard of behaviour.[1] A mild example of this may be seen in the circumstance that most committees will display types of behaviour, involving perhaps injustice, meanness, inconsiderateness, and lack of responsibility of a kind that would be disavowed by any single member acting independently. The bloodthirsty and often indiscriminate cruelty of mobs is notorious, and in general it may be said that any large body of men can be got to commit acts that would be impossible to the component individuals. But it is important to realize that this massive social contact creates none of these impulses; it only releases them by affording a certain sanction to them. The impulses themselves are deeply rooted in human nature, and lead to endless other manifestations besides those just indicated. These fall into three main groups: (1) social, those of social value, produced by sublimation; (2) asocial, those of no social value, neurotic and other mental disturbances, due to a partial failure of the sublimating process, *i.e.* to mental conflict; (3) anti-social, due to paralysis of sublimation, whether this be brought about by massive social contact or in any other of the numerous ways in which this is possible. The manifestations of social situations so largely studied by social psychologists must, therefore, in no sense be regarded as isolated phenomena.

It is from this point of view that we obtain what is perhaps the most profitable perspective of the nature of War. The essence of War surely consists in an abrogation

[1] The reason why the influence of social situations is most often in the direction of lowering the standards of thought and behaviour can only be briefly indicated here. It is because sublimations are mainly individual creations, whereas the unconscious repressed impulses are more uniformly and generally distributed; a relapse, therefore, takes place in the direction of the greatest common measure of the whole, *i.e.* in the direction of these impulses.

of standards of conduct approved of by the ethical sense of civilized communities. By this is meant that in War an attempt is made to achieve a given purpose by means which are otherwise regarded as reprehensible. The best proof of this statement is to be found in the simple fact that no nation or government dares to assume the responsibility for initiating any war. At the present time, for instance, they are one and all engaged in an eager search for sanctions to justify their action in proceeding to war, and a cynical observer might almost say that the chief conflict in the war is over the question of who began it. On every side it is agreed that to have caused the war is a disgrace, the blame for which must at all costs be imputed to the enemy. To admit responsibility for it is universally regarded as tantamount to a confession of guilty wrong-doing, the thought of which is too painful to tolerate. Every nation whole-heartedly maintains the view that it was forced to go to war, regretfully and entirely against its will, by the wicked machinations of some other nation. Now this is just the attitude which in private life we see adopted towards any anti-social act or any act of which the ethical sense of the community does not approve. The person concerned makes every endeavour to shift his guilt or responsibility on to others or on to circumstances, and seeks to defend his conduct under cover of all imaginable excuses, pretexts, and rationalizations. This need for defence is in itself a proof that the act runs counter to the prevailing ethical sense. Seen from this angle, peace may be compared with the institution of monogamy, which society accepts in theory, but never in practice.

It is plain that the actual deeds of which War consists are so counter to the conscience of mankind that they can never be deliberately performed without some preliminary vindication; otherwise it would be mere murder and destruction of the savagest kind. The general theory of War is, of course, that the deeds comprising it are in themselves wholly repellent and abhorrent, but that they are justified by the necessity or desirability of the purpose to be achieved. As was indicated above, however, an alternative and equally possible view is that the repressed impulses leading to warlike acts accumulate such force from time to time as to incline the scales in favour of a bellicose solution whenever the opportunity offers itself in the form of problems otherwise difficult of settlement. Nietzsche, in *Thus Spake Zarathustra*, contrasts the two attitudes thus: 'Ye say it is the good cause which halloweth even war? I say unto you: it is the good war which halloweth every cause.' The fact that the second view appears repugnant and almost unthinkable is in itself no evidence against its possible truth, for *ex hypothesi* it relates to the unconscious and repressed part of the mind, the part that is repudiated by our waking consciousness, but which none the less exerts the greatest influence on the latter. It is not without significance that every belligerent tends to impute to his enemy this motive for War; the Germans have a proverb *Der Hass sieht scharf*; which means that hate enables one to uncover the motives of an enemy to which the latter is blind.

Even if we accept the more flattering view of War, to the effect that 'the end justifies the means', it is necessary to remember that historically the attitude of mind implied in this has frequently been allowed to serve as a cover for acts in which the means supplied the principal motive—a familiar instance being the passion for cruelty indulged in under the cloak of the Inquisition. It is an empirical rule of wide validity in psychology that the consequences of an act, so far as they could have been predicted, have to be taken into account as a probable motive, and usually the chief one, in performing the act, even when the author of it repudiates this conclusion. Applying this rule to the present question, we are led to ask whether the terrible events of War, the cruelties and so forth, are not connected with the underlying causes of War itself. Therefore, for more reasons than one, it remains a problem for psychological investigation whether the end or the means of War must be regarded as the ultimate cause of it. There is reason to suppose that both are operative, and also that the second set of factors is seriously underestimated, but it would be valuable to know which of the two is the more important. It will thus be necessary to institute studies into two broad groups of motives, on the one hand, those alleged by the conscience, and, on the other, the darker ones to be discovered only by a more indirect mode of approach. A few words may be added concerning each of these groups, so as to indicate some of the directions in which further research would seem to be desirable.

Most of the motives belonging to the first group can be summed up under the word Patriotism, for it is much to be doubted whether the operations of cosmopolitan financiers have ever directly dictated the outbreak of any war and they have rarely been a factor of any importance at all. Patriotism, or devotion, love and loyalty towards one's country (or smaller unit), involves the willingness to fight for its interests, this taking the various forms of defending its material interests, avenging a slight on its honour, extending its prestige and importance, or resisting encroachments. The ultimate psychological origin of this complex sentiment is to be found mainly in the individual's relation to his parents, as Bacon hinted in his remark that 'Love of his country begins in a man's own house'.[1] It has three sources—in feelings about the self,

[1] *De Aug. Scient.* Bk. VI, ch. iii.

the mother, and the father respectively. The last-mentioned is probably the least important of the three, but is more prominent in some cases than in others, leading then to patriarchal conceptions in which the head of the state is felt to be the father, and the state itself the father's land. More significant is the relation towards the mother, as is indicated by the fact that a country is, as a rule, conceived to have the feminine gender (in the expression *la patrie* we see a fusion of both conceptions). Most important of all is the source in self-love and self-interest, where the self becomes more or less identified with one's fellow-citizens and the state is a magnified self. Psycho-analysis has shown that these three feelings are far more complex and deeply rooted than is generally supposed, and that they exert a correspondingly weighty influence in the most manifold relations of life, often in quite unsuspected ways. On the precise fate of these feelings during the stage of early mental development depends the greater part of a man's character, dispositions, including the form of his Patriotism, whether aggressive, assertive, vainglorious, or the contrary; it would be tempting to compare the type of Patriotism usual in different countries with the various types of family relationship characteristic of each, for instance in Germany, England, and America. Even the finer shades of conduct in diplomatic relations, and the decisions on intricate questions, are to a large extent determined by the precise manner in which the three feeling complexes just mentioned have been developed and interconnected; it should not be forgotten that the greater part of them is unconscious, an example being the concealed hostility towards the father and passion for the mother that makes up what has been called the Oedipus complex.

The second group of motives concerns a darker side of human nature. It is necessary to penetrate behind a veil which is well adapted to obscure it. This is the veil of restraint and discipline, the inculcation of obedience, loyalty, and devotion to the military unit and its commander, attitudes of mind which are akin to the first group of motives just discussed; they can hardly be regarded as important causes of War, for the emotions concerned are just as easily indulged in times of peace. Behind the façade, however, are to be discerned evidences of far less respectable motives. War is, of course, the replacement of peaceful methods of dealing with certain other people, through discussion, consideration, and so on, by the method of brute force, and that this reversion to a more primitive level of civilization is of its very essence is shown by the nature of the deeds that throughout compose it. Civilized warfare is a contradiction in terms, for under no circumstances is it a civilized act to blow another person's head off or to jab a bayonet into him, nor can we, after recent events, be any longer subject to the illusion that it is possible to exclude savagery from the warfare of civilized nations. Four repressed instincts play a cardinal part in all war: the passions for cruelty, destruction, lust, and loot. It is popularly held that the manifestations of these are incidental to War, and not inherent in it; that they are regrettable, though perhaps unavoidable, complications which should be reduced to a minimum. But it is found in practice that where one of these passions is suppressed another flames out the more to take its place; one army may rape where the other loots. The most puritanical army of which we have record, Cromwell's Ironsides, indulged in orgies of sacrilege, pillage, and massacre— under, of course, the usual cover of military necessity, etc. One of these passions, the lust to kill, is so indispensable that, without it, an army would be paralysed. The full analysis of these various passions, the sadistic blood-lust, the impulse to pillage and destroy, and so on, is of obvious importance for a proper understanding of their significance in regard to both the causation and conduct of War.

Where, therefore, the romantic idealist sees only the pure flame of patriotism feeding noble impulses to heroism and self-sacrifice, the psychologist detects the operation also of deeper forces dating from a past that is only too imperfectly overcome. Behind the guise of altruism work impulses of a more egoistic order, and who shall say which of the two is the more important, the visible or the invisible? What can definitely be asserted is that there is no hope of attaining to a real understanding of the meaning of War unless both are taken into full account and appraised at their true value. Whoever undertakes a psycho-analysis of men deciding to enlist in war-time will be astonished at the complexity and strength of the unavowed motives darkly impelling him and reinforcing his altruism, from the fascinating attraction of horrors to the homosexual desire to be in close relation with masses of men, and one can only urge scepticism and caution in accepting conclusions on these and allied matters until our knowledge of every layer of the human mind is more complete than it is at present.

It may also be not out of place to sound a warning for those who accept the view that War is a reversion to a more savage state of conduct, but who draw the inference that the way to avoid it is through a still greater repression of the more primitive instincts that we inherit from the past. Doubt is cast on the validity of this apparently plausible conclusion by the following considerations. The investigations of psycho-analysis[1] have shown that the influence on conscious life of these impulses that are in a

[1] Those wishing to inform themselves further on this subject may be referred to the writer's *Papers on Psycho-Analysis*, 2nd edition, 1918.

repressed state in the unconscious mind is of an altogether unsuspected importance, and, what is more, that they are indestructible. Through the process of sublimation, however, they become of the highest value in furnishing much of the energy for our social activities, so that the only hope of diminishing their anti-social effects is to further this process. Now, sublimation takes place automatically when repression is carried up to a certain point, the repressed impulses finding another outlet. In this there is necessarily an element of renunciation (of the original aim of the impulse), a circumstance which imposes an inevitable limit on what is possible in this direction. There are not wanting indications suggesting that we are nearly reaching the limit of natural sublimation, and when this happens there comes about a very unsatisfactory state of affairs. For if repression is carried too far, the energies in question revert to their unconscious sources, and lead either to neurotic disorders or to an accumulated tension which may be followed by an outbreaking of the impulses in more or less their original form. A lessening of the repression in such a case will allow better sublimation to take place than before.

If the present situation of civilization is accurately described in these terms, it follows that there are only two possible ways of dealing further with these unruly impulses, and it is likely that both will be adopted when such matters are better understood. One is to relax the repression at points where it has lost its value and become harmful; certain aspects of the sex problem (more intelligent organization of the marriage institution) occur to one in this connection. This is like the plan which we, alone among the nations, have adopted in the governing of subject races, and still more so in our relations with the Colonies. What the opposite attitude leads to is well shown historically by the French Revolution and the American War of Independence. This principle has also been adopted socially in many spheres, notably in that of penology, and always ultimately with beneficial results. The other plan, which is not only compatible with, but also related to the first, consists in preventing excessive repression by allowing children to be more aware of certain sides of their nature, and so substituting conscious control for blind repression. A corollary of this is the provision of suitable outlets for the impulses in question; the value of various sports in this connection is undoubtedly great. One of the appeals made by War is that it offers a permissible outlet for a variety of impulses that are insufficiently gratified in times of peace; this is often described as the spirit of adventure seeking to escape from humdrum conventionality. The credit of first clearly perceiving that War could never be abolished unless suitable outlets were provided for the impulses leading to it belongs to William James. In his famous essay on 'The Moral Equivalents of War' he suggested that such impulses should be deliberately guided into suitable paths, an example he gave being Alpine climbing to gratify the desire for danger. What was completely lacking in his day, however, was any knowledge of the springs of conduct and of the unconscious sources of warlike impulses. Thanks to Freud's penetrating researches, we are now at least in a position to undertake further investigations in this direction which hold out every promise of that success.

The argument of this paper may now be recapitulated. It is the place of Psychology to point out the almost irresistible tendency of the mind to believe that a given aim is possible of achievement when there is present a burningly intense desire to achieve it. Under these circumstances the mind tends greatly to underestimate the difficulties in the way, and also the cost involved. Psychology has further to ascertain what this judgement of values depends on and ultimately signifies. When all the data involved are put before those who have to pass such judgements, it is quite possible that reflection may lead to reconsideration of the criteria on which there had been a tendency to make a hurried decision.

Although these considerations are evident enough, psychological knowledge has realized that it is far harder to apply them than is commonly imagined, and proffers the explanation of this: namely, that the main influences distorting judgement are unconscious ones, the persons concerned being therefore unaware of their effect. This matter has a direct bearing on judgements relating to the causation and preventibility of War. It is at present quite an open question whether it is possible for mankind to abstain from War, whether the desire to abstain at all costs does not fundamentally signify something more deleterious to human development than the contrary attitude, and whether the psychological benefits that regularly recurring warfare brings to a nation are not greater than the total amount of harm done, terrific as this may be.

Some clues were then indicated for the direction in which psychological research may profitably be further developed with a view to determining the ultimate meaning of War in general. This has to reach beyond the ostensible motives given by the belligerent, and to inquire also into the nature and origin of the various warlike impulses, the presence of which is indispensable for a bellicose solution of a problem ever to be regarded as tolerable. It is even possible that the strength of these impulses, for the most part concealed from view, is greater than that of the conscious motives; in any case, they are certainly of importance in rendering the latter more acceptable and plausible. Something has been said also about the source of the warlike impulses and about the possibility of finding other than warlike outlets for their activity.

It is only when we have a fuller understanding of the motives and impulses concerned in War based on a detailed and exact knowledge of Individual Psychology that we can begin to form a just appreciation of the merits and demerits of War and of its general biological and social significance. War furnishes perhaps the most potent stimulus to human activity in all its aspects, good and bad, that has yet been discovered. It is a miniature of life in general at its sharpest pitch of intensity. It reveals all the latent potentialities of man, and carries humanity to the uttermost confines of the attainable, to the loftiest heights as well as to the lowest depths. It brings man a little closer to the realities of existence, destroying shams and remoulding values. It forces him to discover what are the things that really matter in the end, what are the things for which he is willing to risk life itself. It can make life as a whole greater, richer, fuller, stronger, and sometimes nobler. It braces a nation, as an individual, to put forth its utmost effort, to the strange experience of bringing into action the whole energy of which it is capable.

The results of this tremendous effort are what might have been expected. On the one side are feats of dauntless courage, of fearless heroism, of noble devotion and self-sacrifice, of incredible endurance, of instantaneous and penetrating apprehension, and of astounding intellectual achievement; feats which teach a man that he is greater than he knew. The other side need not be described in these days of horror. To appraise at their just value these two sides of war, to sound the depths as well as explore the heights, what is this other than to know the human mind?

Postscript.—After reading this essay the late Lord Davies, who was passionately desirous of preventing future wars, approached me with the inquiry of how much psycho-analytic research would be needed to aid him in achieving his goal. When I said 'a couple of centuries', he withdrew his interest, saying he must find a shorter cut—which proved to be the League of Nations Society. How completely ineffective that short cut was we now know to our cost. My answer has been subsequently expanded in Edward Glover's *War, Sadism and Pacifism* (1933), 2nd edition.

VI
WAR AND SUBLIMATION[1]

It is proposed to discuss in this paper the relationship of the uncivilized impulses of man to the civilized ones, with special reference to the problems in this connection suggested by the spectacle of war. The term 'sublimation' in the title does not, therefore, cover the whole ground of the paper, for, although the process denoted by this is perhaps the most characteristic of those whereby the one set of impulses becomes subordinated to the other, it is by no means the only process of the kind.

In the conduct of war, and implicit in the very conception of war, sundry impulses come to expression of a kind that are apparently non-existent, or at all events latent, in the same people during peace, and with which we are hardly familiar outside the criminal classes; they may include such disapproved-of tendencies as cruelty, deceit, and ruthless egotism, with such acts as killing, looting, and savagery of various kinds. This statement, it is true, does not accord with the popular and romantic view of war, which holds that it is valid only of the enemy, and that the conduct of the soldiers on its own side differs from that in peace in merely one particular, namely, in the fact that they kill their opponents. That it should have to differ even in this particular is regarded as an unfortunate necessity, and in no way related to any innate desire to kill. But it does not need very much knowledge of the unvarnished facts to realize the outstanding truth that, in

[1] Read before the British Association for the Advancement of Science; Section of Psychology, September 10, 1915. Published in the Reports of the Association, vol. 85, p. 699.

war, things are done by large numbers of men on both sides of a kind that is totally foreign to their accustomed standard of ethical conduct during peace, and the question arises, what is the source of the impulses thus vented and the relationship of these impulses to the controlling forces of civilized life?

An important clue to the problem is afforded by the circumstance that similar impulses are readily to be detected in the conduct and mental attitude of most children in the first few years of life, although their significance here has, for certain reasons, been greatly underestimated. It should be evident that if an adult were to display the same disregard for the rights and feelings of others, the same indecency, cruelty, and egotism as that characteristic of the infant, he would very definitely rank as an asocial animal, and it is partly this remarkable contrast between the two, separating them into two worlds, that accounts for the extent to which the continuity of individual life from the infant to the adult is generally overlooked. There can be no doubt that the asocial impulses we are discussing are part of the inherited characteristics of mankind, and it is throughout intelligible that both the infant and the savage stand in this respect nearer to the animals from which we are descended. In the course of individual development these impulses are replaced by tendencies of an opposite nature, such as consideration for others, honesty, altruism, and horror of cruelty. It is generally believed that they disappear owing to the implantation or development of the more civilized tendencies, but psycho-analytic investigations show that the process is more subtle and complex than is indicated in such a statement. There is an intricate inter-relationship between the two sets of tendencies, the precise details of which should form an important subject of study. A foundation for such study is the conclusion arrived at by all psycho-analysts, and perhaps one of the most startling of their conclusions, that the primitive, asocial tendencies never really disappear at all, but continue their existence throughout life in the buried, unconscious region of the mind. This part of the mind, indeed, essentially consists of the impulses that we are considering, that is, of all the wishes, longings, and instinctive tendencies that are incompatible in their nature with the ethical and civilized standards prevailing in consciousness, and which, consequently, have been split off from consciousness, prevented from entering it, and kept 'repressed' into the unconscious. From here the asocial impulses exert a far more considerable influence on conscious activity than might be imagined, and they may even be called the ultimate source of such activity. It is with the interaction between the unconscious and consciousness that the science of psychoanalysis is primarily concerned.

A description of the normal unconscious mind would astonish and assuredly shock its owner. It is absolutely non-moral in nature, or, as judged by conscious standards, immoral. Through it course all manner of unrestrained fancies and desires, characterized by a complete disregard for the ethical and aesthetic canons of social life. A wish for the death of another person, even that of a loved relative, may arise on the slightest provocation, the crudest forms of indecency are gratified in the imagination, and the most extravagant flights of self-glorification are indulged in to the heart's content. In short, the picture may bear no resemblance to the person's conscious character.

The interest that the knowledge of the unconscious has for the psychological understanding of the phenomenon of war is twofold. In the first place, as I have suggested elsewhere,[1] it is probable that the constant pressure of these savage, unconscious impulses plays a part, the extent of which is quite unknown, but which may be very great indeed, in raising the threshold of acceptability for pacific solutions of international difficulties, and thus operates, probably in periodic waves, in favouring a bellicose one. In the second place, we find in war an instructive example of the type of influence which has the power of releasing repressed impulses, and thus allowing external manifestation of them in a fairly direct form; it is with this latter question that the present paper is chiefly concerned.

In order to understand what happens in the release of a repressed impulse we have next to consider the fate of such an impulse under various circumstances. This fate is manifold, but there are two broad groups of processes that may come about, the distinction between which I wish to emphasize at the outset. The repressing forces may, on the one hand, profoundly affect the impulse itself, or, to be more accurate, its mode of functioning; or, on the other hand, it may merely hold the impulse in check. The external result is very similar in both cases, the conduct of the person falling into line with what is demanded by social convention, but the psychological difference between the two is profound, though its full social significance is only evident under the stress of influences, such as war, which inhibit the action of the repressing forces.

The repressed impulses, as of course all impulses, are of a dynamic character, and they exert a constant activity in the direction of external expression, which is called in psycho-analysis the 'wish-fulfilment'. In this, however, they meet with the opposition of certain forces of a contrary kind, which emanate partly from without, and partly from within. The main source of them is the pressure of edu-

[1] See Chapter V.

cation in the widest sense, exerted first by the parents and later on by the whole cultural environment as well, though no doubt the child is born with a susceptibility to this influence in the form of various predispositions. A simple illustration of the effect of repression is the case where the impulse is, as it were, weakened and made milder on its path towards expression, the resulting manifestation agreeing in kind, but not in intensity, with the original impulse. In this way, for instance, a definitely sexual attraction may reveal itself consciously as merely a slight liking, manifesting itself externally in the form of polite intentions, and a murderous desire may come to expression merely as a chuckle whenever the object of the feeling meets with a slight reverse of fortune, or as a cordial opposition to whatever views he may hold. In such cases as these the repressing force presents itself in the form of an obstacle, a filter through which the affect accompanying the repressed impulse can only percolate.

It will readily be seen that the social consequences of a process such as that just indicated may be entirely satisfactory, the energy investing the repressed impulse being neither lost nor dammed up, but being applied in a quite permissible and even advantageous social direction. But only too often the process does not go on so smoothly as this. The repressed affects may, for instance, become heaped up in the form of an unconscious complex, from which they can then be discharged in an excessive manner on to an associated conscious idea, leading to a violent distortion of judgement, a common example of which is a strong political bias unconsciously dictated by self-interest. More serious consequences still will be noted presently.

We have next to speak of the transformations that may be brought about in the actual impulses themselves. Perhaps the most typical of these, and the most extensively studied, is that known as 'sublimation'. This has been defined by Freud[1] as 'the capacity to exchange an originally sexual aim for another one which is no longer sexual, though it is psychically related to the first'. By it is meant not a vague displacement of normal sexual desire by another, unrelated interest, but an unconscious and automatic deflection of energy from the individual biological components of the sexual instinct on to other fields which are symbolically associated with the first. It is a process that concerns the life of the young child far more than that of the adult, and it must clearly be recognized that it refers much more to the peculiar and less differentiated form of sexuality known as infantile sexuality than to the familiar adult type.[2] It will be remembered that, for reasons that cannot be gone into here, Freud includes under the term 'sexual' many processes, especially in childhood life, to which it is not usually applied. Be that as it may, the fact that energy and interest can be in this way deflected from the sexual sphere is well recognized by psychologists and educationalists, although its importance and the extent to which the process normally goes on without being remarked are certainly as a rule underestimated.

The primary impulses that have to be modified before attaining adjustment to the standards of social life may for practical purposes be divided into two groups, according as they serve the interests of the individual or those of the species. The latter, the sexual impulses, are transformed by sublimation in the manner just indicated. The other set, which may be called the impulses belonging to the ego, including the aggressive ones, are equally in need of modification for social purposes, for in their original

---

[1] *Sammlung kleiner Schriften zur Neurosenlehre*, Zweite Folge, p. 181.
[2] This subject is developed in a chapter of my *Papers on Psycho-Analysis* (1918), chap. xxxv.

shape they are quite ego-centrically orientated and tend to function in ways that ruthlessly ignore the rights and feelings of other people. A characteristic process whereby these egoistic impulses become modified is through their becoming invested with erotic feeling, the word erotic being here used to denote all possible varieties of love. They are in this way subordinated to the mutual interests of the individual and his environment, and direct pleasure is experienced in their functioning along lines that are acceptable to civilized social standards.

In both these cases we may speak of a refinement of the primary impulses, the very nature of which is profoundly affected. A curious circumstance, however—one that cannot be illustrated by any analogy from the physical world—is that the impulses continue to exist side by side in both their original and in their altered form. A possible explanation for this may be reached from consideration of the varying depth in the unconscious to which the educative influence penetrates, for it is certain that it never affects the repressed impulses down to their ultimate source in the inherited instincts. Evidence for the truth of this statement may be obtained from the analysis of dreams, in which the repressed impulses are to be discovered in their original form, and sometimes with very little disguise. The practical external result, none the less, is that the individual's conduct is in complete accord with the ethical, aesthetic, and social standards of civilized life, and that it is so without any sense of compulsion, but as a spontaneous and natural expression of the personality. One may say that adoption of these standards has become second nature, so thoroughly are they incorporated into the personality. A further important matter is that this state of affairs is a durable one, and will stand a considerable amount of strain. The individual is in no sense dependent on external approval, but will act well whatever the circumstances, even when to do so is to his manifest disadvantage; it is not in his power to do otherwise.

The refinement just described is, of course, the ideal more or less consciously aimed at by civilizing agents, though it is not often fully achieved. In contrast to it stand other effects of repression, which, though they may equally result in 'good' behaviour, do so merely through exercising an external pressure, there being no change whatever in the nature of the impulses themselves. It is as though the individual consented to behave well, against his nature, because the consequences would otherwise be disagreeable in the form of social disapproval, dislike, or actual punishment. Like Nietzsche's 'culture-Philistines', they obey and follow an ideal that is not really their own, and it is therefore intelligible that their allegiance to it can never be absolutely depended on. They are usually under a certain strain, and are always subjected to more or less inner mental conflict, though the greater part of this may be unconscious. Superficially it may not be easy to distinguish the two types just described—and of course the line between them is in no sense an absolute one—but the difference becomes pronounced when the stress of external social pressure is removed. In these circumstances the conduct and standards of the type first described remain relatively unchanged, while those of the second type rapidly deteriorate. A trite illustration of what is meant may be seen in connection with table manners and other personal habits; with some people these remain quite the same whether they are alone or in company, but with the majority of people this is certainly not so. The same is true of much more important matters, including the cardinal laws of morality. When an individual no longer feels himself to be under the eye of the social censor he becomes more true to himself, and the result of this will depend on whether his primitive instincts have undergone a real refinement by civilization—in the way indicated above—or only an apparent one. There are many circumstances under which this may happen. The sensitiveness to the social censor may be paralysed by physical agents, for example, alcohol or the toxins of bodily disease (*e.g.* syphilis of the brain), or they may be temporarily inhibited by the action of powerful emotions, such as anger. More serious socially is the situation when the change is not in the individual, but in the conscience of the social body itself. This is the secret of the so-called 'danger of mob violence', when the passions are no longer restrained because the surrounding social attitude has ceased to be inimical to their functioning. To the same category belong many of the phenomena of war, indeed the most essential ones. The lust for murder, for instance, which slumbers in every man's heart, runs counter to the strongest possible disapproval and penalties on the part of the state and of society in general; in war time, society, however, not merely averts its gaze but deliberately incites this lust and affords it full opportunity for gratification.

Psycho-analytical experience fully accords with the evidence at present being yielded by the War in the conclusion that the refinement of our primitive instincts has proceeded to a far less extent than we flatter ourselves, and that the large majority of people belong to the second type described above, where this refinement is more apparent than real.[1] And there is still more to be said in the same direction. Society, after making the discovery that a level of conduct which is natural to the few can be compelled from the many, has been encouraged to raise

[1] See a recent paper to the same effect by Freud, 'Zeitgemässes über Krieg und Tod', *Imago* (1915), Bd. IV, p. 1.

her standards still higher, to an extent that an increasingly large number of people find it difficult to comply with. The forced efforts to do so result in a variety of artificial reactions, character peculiarities, over-compensations, neurotic symptoms, and so on, all of which are necessarily unstable in nature. As Freud puts it, such people may be said, in a psychological sense, to be living beyond their means. When the real test comes, *i.e.* when they are left to their own resources without the supporting pressure of a civilized environment, their false acquisitions fall away from them just as a *parvenu* loses his veneer of good manners in similar circumstances, and they revert to a lower level of conduct. An inexplicable change seems to have come over them, but this change is only in their external behaviour; their real nature remains what it always was. All that has been lost is a false ideal, an illusion.

In this paper I have done nothing but sketch the outlines of a problem which I believe to be of great importance for psychology, and for social psychology in particular. Further investigation is needed to determine in what precise details the two types differ, and how these differences come about, why it has proved possible for one man to incorporate a given civilized standard into his inmost nature—to identify himself with it, as would be said psycho-analytically—and not for another.

Postscript I.—As a little instance of the irrationalities of war-time emotions, I may mention that I nearly got into serious trouble for 'aiding the enemy' by allowing this essay to be reprinted in the *International Review*, an impartial periodical published in Switzerland which the Germans averred was 'pro-Ally' and the Allies 'pro-German'. The view apparently held was that my essay would so increase the sales of this little periodical that

Germany, who was (wrongly) supposed to profit by it financially, would be able to continue the war for years longer! I even had the honour of being rebuked for my sins in a *Times* leader.

Postscript II.—On re-reading this more than thirty-year-old essay I perceive that insufficient distinction is drawn in it between murdering and killing. A civilized man should be able to kill when necessary, but never to murder. Murder is always connected with a sense of guilt either consciously or unconsciously, because the forbidden crime ultimately related to the primal criminal wish to murder a parent. Pure killing, on the other hand, may be a part of reality, *e.g.* in self-defence, with no such reference. Naturally in warfare both acts may be committed, being one reason why it affects differently the mental integrity of different people.

VII

A LINGUISTIC FACTOR IN ENGLISH CHARACTEROLOGY[1]

THE definition of national character traits is notoriously treacherous ground, but in all attempts to describe those most typical or general among English people, one is always mentioned with such unvarying emphasis that it is hard to resist the conclusion that it must relate, however roughly, to some group of observable phenomena. I refer to the striking insistence of the English on propriety, which is commented on not only by practically all foreign observers, but also by Americans and our fellow-subjects from overseas, not to speak of the 'Keltic fringe' in our own islands. That it degenerates into prudishness here more often than in any other country, at least in the Old World, will also, I think, be widely admitted. The trait is probably to be correlated in some degree with the proneness to reserve, the absence of social gifts, the dislike of betraying emotion of any kind, and the horror of self-display, vaunting, braggadocio, gasconade, rodomontade —one sees that we have to use foreign terms to indicate attitudes so foreign to us—which also belong to the judgements passed on the English by foreigners. Psychologically the group in question might perhaps be described in McDougall's language as a deficiency in the self-regarding instinct. Psycho-analysts would call attention to the secondary nature of the phenomena as indicating the existence of what is called a reaction-formation, and indeed

[1] Read before the British Psychological Society, March 14, 1920. Published in the *International Journal of Psycho-Analysis*, 1920, vol. 1.

that something is being actively controlled or avoided is fairly evident; they would probably ascribe the traits to a reaction against more than one complex, repressed exhibitionism being perhaps the most prominent. However this may be, it has occurred to me that there is possibly a connection between this group of character traits—which, for convenience, might be referred to as the propriety trait—and a peculiar historical feature in the development of the English language, but before submitting this idea for your consideration I shall have to make a few remarks on some general psychological aspects of speech.

There are good grounds for believing that speech originally was a far more concrete activity than it now is, and it has indeed been maintained that all speech represents pretermitted action.[1] Plain indications of this are to be observed among less cultivated human beings, especially children and savages. Freud,[2] for instance, following Groos, points out that children treat words as objects in the various games they play with them, while Frazer,[3] in his section on Tabooed Words, brings forward a mass of evidence illustrating the extraordinary significance attached by primitive races to words and especially to names. He says, following Tylor: 'Unable to discriminate clearly between words and things, the savage commonly fancies that the link between a name and the person or thing denominated by it is not a mere arbitrary and ideal association, but a real and substantial bond which unites the two in such a way that magic may be wrought on a man just as easily through his name as through his hair, his nails, or any other material part of his person. In

---

[1] Ferenczi, *Contributions to Psycho-Analysis* (1916), p. 120.
[2] Freud, *Der Witz und seine Beziehung zum Unbewussten* (1905), p. 105.
[3] Frazer, *Taboo and the Perils of the Soul* (1911), chapter vi.

fact, primitive man regards his name as a vital portion of himself and takes care of it accordingly.' He cites[1] the example of the Sulka of New Britain, who, when near their enemies, speak of them as 'rotten tree trunks', 'and they imagine that by calling them that they make the limbs of their dreaded enemies ponderous and clumsy like logs.' This example illustrates the extremely materialistic view which these savages take of the nature of words; they suppose that the mere utterance of an expression signifying clumsiness will homoeopathically affect with clumsiness the limbs of their distant foemen. Another illustration of this curious misconception is furnished by a Caffre superstition that the character of a young thief can be reformed by shouting his name over a boiling kettle of medicated water, then clapping a lid on the kettle and leaving the name to steep in the water for several days.' Of the innumerable examples from the field of taboo one may be quoted:[2] the Alfoors of Poso are not only not allowed to mention the names of their parents-in-law, a common enough prohibition, but if such a name happens to be the same as that of a thing—*e.g.* in English a Mr. Lake—then they may not mention even this thing by its own name, only by a borrowed one. Even with us the use of bad language by children is treated as a sin of no mean order, and the law of England can still condemn a man to imprisonment for making use in public of certain forbidden (obscene) words, the utterance aloud of the heinous words being in both cases regarded as equivalent to a nefarious deed.

The nature of this primitive material conception of words and speech can be described more exactly. One of the conclusions emerging from Freud's work on the psychology of wit and of dreams is that all words originally

[1] Frazer, *op. cit.* p. 331.   [2] Frazer, *op. cit.* p. 340.

possessed distinct motor and perceptual qualities, which they gradually lose more or less completely in the course of mental development. As has been interestingly expounded by Ferenczi,[1] there is a class of words, namely, obscene words, which, probably because of their being excluded from the usual course of development, still retain these qualities in a full measure. On the perceptual side Ferenczi[2] remarks that a word of this kind 'has a peculiar power of compelling the hearer to imagine the object it denotes in substantial actuality', and adds, 'one may therefore infer that these words as such possess the capacity of compelling the hearer to revive memory pictures in a regressive and hallucinatory manner'; he calls attention to the fact that delicate allusions to the same ideas, and scientific or foreign designations for them do not have this effect, or at least not to the same extent as the words taken from the original, popular, erotic vocabulary of one's mother-tongue. On the motor side the following three illustrations may be mentioned: the aggressive tendency which Freud has shown to underlie the uttering of obscene jokes—this being a substitute for a sexual aggression; the curious perversion of coprophemia in which the sexual act consists solely of uttering indecent words to women; and the obsessional neurosis, where the act itself of thinking is curiously sexualized in the preconscious in such a way that the impulsion to think certain thoughts comes as a substitute for forbidden acts. In all these cases the act or thought or speech is psychologically the full equivalent of an actual deed.

As was remarked above, in the course of mental development the motor and perceptual elements become more and more eliminated from words, and in purely abstract thought they disappear altogether. It may be recalled

[1] Ferenczi, *op. cit.* chap. iv.   [2] Ferenczi, *op. cit.* p. 116.

that Galton many years ago pointed out how much less capable of abstract thought are, as a rule, persons of a pronouncedly visual or auditory type as contrasted with those whose thought processes contain only feeble perceptual elements. One may also, in this connection, refer to Freud's latest conclusion on the unconscious,[1] namely, that the essential difference between unconscious and conscious ideas is that the former consist only of ideas (which easily regress to images) of the object or process, whereas the latter contain as well the idea of the corresponding word. Thus, unconscious mentation and abstract thought stand at the two opposite ends of the scale in this respect, the ideas of the former being near to perceptual imagery, those of the latter being almost completely divested of it.

It is evident that this process of gradual abstraction effects a great economy of thought; indeed, without it none of the higher forms of thought could occur. It is probable that this economical factor is of prime importance in bringing about the process in question, but it has to be remarked that this is accompanied by other important psychical changes as well, which probably also stand in a causal relation to it. I refer to the inhibition in feeling that goes with the progress from the motor-perceptual stage to the abstract one, and the valuable saving in expenditure of emotional energy that this signifies. There is thus a double economy, an intellectual and an affective one. The affective economy, to which I wish to draw special attention, may be illustrated from two sides. On the one hand, when there is a need to express unusually strong feeling recourse is commonly had, through regression, to the use of just those words which have retained their motor and perpetual elements, as in oaths and obscene language, a

[1] Freud, *Sammlung kleiner Schriften zur Neurosenlehre*, Vierte Folge (1918), p. 334.

procedure much more manifest in the male sex because of their having been to a less extent the subject of repression in this sex. The desire for expression combined with a sense of incapacity for it, so common in the young, similarly results in the recourse to slang. On the other hand, when there is a special need to inhibit feeling, recourse is had to the use of abstract, or at all events less familiar, words. It is well known that an otherwise forbidden idea can be readily expressed if only it is veiled in a euphemism or translated into a foreign tongue. Most books on sexology, for instance, contain whole passages written in Latin. The reason is that the vulgar, familiar words would tend to arouse embarrassing feelings, in both speaker and hearer, which can be avoided by the use of foreign, unfamiliar, or abstract words which have been acquired only in later years.

After this long digression I now return to the theme of English characterology. Without entering on a discussion of the numerous individual, social, or racial forces making for repression and inhibition, I can only think that such a process must be favoured if one of the main instruments by means of which it is carried out is peculiarly accessible. Thus, if it is unusually easy to give vocal expression to forbidden ideas in a way that inhibits the development of feeling, it seems to me to follow that, in such circumstances, feeling will be more readily and extensively inhibited. Now it is clear that this is just the situation in which the English race has been placed for nearly a thousand years. The Saxon and Norman languages, after living side by side for about two centuries, gradually coalesced to form English, but to this day there is in most cases an obvious difference in the 'feel' of the words belonging to each, and still more between words of Saxon origin and Latin words more recently introduced than their Norman-French precursors. All literary men recognize the distinction clearly, and every text-book dealing with style in writing urges the student to choose the Saxon words wherever it is possible without being precious, as being more vivid, robust, and virile, *i.e.* because of their greater capacity to arouse plastic images and feeling-tone. Our store of synonyms is unequalled by that of any other European language, and the difference in the respects I have mentioned between such pairs as house and domicile, fatherly and paternal, book and volume, is quite patent. The existence of this double stratum of words enables us to indulge in fastidiousness to a degree not open to any other nation. Most culinary terms are, for historical reasons, of Romance origin, and the difference between being invited to a dish of veal or pork and one of calves' flesh or swine flesh is very perceptible. No other nation is unable to use its native word for belly if need be, but we have to say 'abdomen', and that only with circumspection. In English a lady is gravid, pregnant, or *enceinte*, there being no single native word to describe the phenomenon. The process in question can often be followed in its stages, such as when the Saxon word 'gut' gets replaced first by the Norman-French 'bowel', and then, when this is found too coarse, by the Latin 'intestine'.

The suggestion I make, therefore, is that the development of the outstanding English character trait of propriety has been fostered by the peculiar nature of the English language, one resulting from the success of a Norman adventurer some nine hundred years ago.

Postscript.—A current example of the thesis of this essay is afforded by the repugnance, or even resentment, at the Government's adoption of the butchers' offensive terms 'carcase meat' and 'offal' to describe the viands doled out to us.

VIII

THE ISLAND OF IRELAND[1]
A PSYCHO-ANALYTICAL CONTRIBUTION TO POLITICAL PSYCHOLOGY

IT must often have struck dispassionate observers as a curious problem that Ireland should differ so profoundly from both Scotland and Wales in her reaction to the stimuli provided by England. On the extent of the difference it is not necessary to dwell; the evidence of it is to-day before our eyes. It is the object of this paper to suggest along psycho-analytical lines that one important factor effecting this difference, the geographical relationship of the countries, operates in a more subtle and complex manner than might be suspected. In so doing it is clear that we are deliberately isolating one factor only and have no intention of underestimating the numerous other well-recognized ones, historical, racial, dynastic, religious, economic, and so on.

Most people would, I think, agree that the psychological motives impelling Scotland and Wales to unite amicably with England are more evident, and call less for explanation, than those which have perpetuated strife between Ireland and England. The relations between Scotland and England, for instance, are typical of those subsisting between two strong and well-matched men, who after a period of angry fighting agree to be reconciled and to join in a partnership of mutual benefit. This issue was doubtless facilitated by the circumstance that the race and culture of both countries were predominantly Anglo-

[1] Read before the British Psycho-Analytical Society, June 21, 1922.

Saxon; indeed, with the exception of the Western Highlands, the differences between Scotland and Northern England are hardly greater than those between Northern and Southern England. The same reason cannot be evoked in the case of Wales and England, where both the racial and cultural differences are profound, and yet the two nations have found it possible to live harmoniously together in the closest contact for many centuries; nor can it be said that the dynastic union in Tudor times played more than a transitory part in producing this result. One might liken the relation of the two countries to each other as resembling that between two brothers of unequal size, with good-humoured tolerance on the one side and a combination of petulance and admiration on the other.

Between England and Ireland, on the other hand, we have a continuous record of dragooning, despoiling, and bullying on the one side and of dogged and contumacious resistance on the other, there being relatively little attempt at any period in the past seven centuries to agree to any form of tolerable union. The first question that arises is whether the state of affairs represents a perfectly natural reaction on the part of Ireland to an exceptional degree of tyranny from England or whether, on the other hand, there was not some special feature in the Irish character that provoked friction and prevented the union that one has seen in various parts of Europe between different nations and races.

Being concerned here only with the nature of the Irish reaction, I intend to pass by any analysis that might be instituted into England's attitude. That the latter cannot be held responsible for the whole situation is clear from a comparison between Wales and Ireland. The position of Wales in respect to England has been for many centuries, from a purely military point of view, identical with that of Ireland, so that the greater resistance offered by Ireland against absorption into the United Kingdom could hardly have been due to any better possibility of success. It seems safe, therefore, to search for some explanation in the national differences between the two peoples. The task here at once becomes obscure, for there is no profound racial difference between the two. Both Irish and Welsh consist essentially of a Mediterranean stock, with a primitive Neolithic substratum, which in both cases completely accepted, presumably through conquest, the Keltic culture and language. We can hardly ascribe any far-reaching national importance to the greater admixture of Danish stock in some of the coastal regions of Ireland or to the more complete Romanization of the Britons. Yet within historical times we note three outstanding divergences in the behaviour of the two peoples: (1) Wales early established a relatively harmonious relationship with England, which has always proved impossible with Ireland; (2) Ireland was uninfluenced by the Reformation, whereas Wales passed to the extreme of radical Protestantism; (3) the Welsh have, on the whole, been a more peace-loving people than the Irish, both nationally and individually.

Of the many factors accounting for this result, the only one with which we are here concerned is the circumstance that Ireland is an island. It has often been pointed out that the psychology of islanders tends to differ from that of related peoples on the mainland, and we ourselves are no exception to that rule. The insularity of the British, with all that that word connotes, is proverbial on the Continent. It is probable, however, that the relative size of the island is of considerable importance in this connection, and that the insularity of, for instance, Australia, Japan, and Great Britain is a very different thing from that of smaller islands, even though there may be features common to them all. The numerous ways in which the geographical fact of insularity may influence the mentality of the islanders, the sense of aloofness, peculiar forms assumed by the desire·for security, and so on, would make an elaborate chapter, from which it is only possible here to select one special aspect. This aspect concerns the tendency of the geographical insularity to become unconsciously associated with particular complexes, affording in this way a certain mode of expression for these.

The complexes to which the idea of an island home tends to become attached are those relating to the ideas of woman, virgin, mother, and womb, all of which fuse in the central complex of the womb of a virgin mother. This means, of course, one's own birthplace. In the secret recesses of his heart every male being cherishes the thought that his mother is a virgin, this representing the repudiation of the father which psycho-analysis has shown to be a normal constituent of the universal Oedipus complex. That important consequences in life may follow, as will presently be indicated, from the association of one's actual home and country with the profound source of feeling just mentioned is not surprising.

The evidence for the existence of this unconscious association is of two kinds. On the one hand, there is the psycho-analysis of individual phantasies about wonderful islands, which are so common as to provide a constantly recurring theme for poets and novelists. In such investigations I have repeatedly obtained unequivocal evidence of the association in question. Secondly, one finds, scattered throughout literature and mythology, innumerable references to a special mystical appeal that islands make to the imagination, and study of the precise form

THE ISLAND OF IRELAND

taken by this affords plain indication of the same conclusion.

To begin with, that the idea of one's native land, whether an island or not, is generally associated with the idea of a female being having both virginal and maternal attributes is evident from the familiar fact that most countries are commonly represented in this allegorical form: one has only to think of Britannia, Columbia, Germania, Italia, and the rest. These personages, in spite of their matronly characteristics, never have any husband. The thesis here maintained, however, goes beyond this simple fact: it is that the association mentioned above is much more strongly forged and much more strongly invested with feeling if the homeland is an island. It will, I think, be generally agreed that the conception of Britannia has much more significance to us than has that of Columbia for citizens of the United States.

Most of what is here quoted from the second group of evidence, taken from popular and literary sources, will have a direct reference to Ireland, but similar instances bearing on the theme will also be cited from other countries. In the first place it may be doubted if any other country has such a variety of feminine names. In addition to the customary one of Erin (Ivernia), which would content most countries, Ireland is also called by, amongst other names: Cáitlin Ni Houlihan, Morrin Ni Cullinan, Roisin Dubh (little black Rose), Shan Van Vocht (old woman), Seau Bheau Bhoct, Dark Rosaleen, and by the names of three queens of Tuatha Di Danann—Eire, Bauba, and Fodhla. References to Ireland as a woman, and especially as a mother, are innumerable in poems, speeches, and writings: the following may serve as typical examples.[1]

[1] For these I am indebted to Miss Violet Fitzgerald.

99

I am Ireland.
I am older than the Old Woman of Beare.
Great my glory,
I that bore Cuchulainn the valiant.
Great my shame.
My own children that sold their Mother.[1]

And Mother, though thou cast away
The child who'd die for thee,
My fondest wishes still should pray
For cuisle geal mo croidhe.[2]

Thou has slain me, O my bride, and mayst serve thee no whit,
For the soul within me loveth thee not since yesterday, nor to-day.
Thou hast left me weak and broken in mien and in shape
Betray me not who love thee, my Little Dark Rose.

Had I a yoke of horses I would plough against the hills,
In middle-Mass I'd make a gospel of my little Dark Rose.
I'd give a kiss to the young girl that would give her youth to me
And behind the kiss would lie embracing my Little Dark Rose.

The Erne shall rise in rude torrents and hills shall be rent,
The sea shall roll in red waves and blood be poured out,
Every mountain glen in Ireland and the bogs shall quake
Some day ere shall perish my Little Dark Rose.[3]

Fallen her own winsome beauty
From her lovely shapely face,
Full breasted nurse of fair hosts,
No heir is left to her.

[1] P. Pearse, 'I am Ireland'.
[2] Michael Doheny, 'A cuisle geal mo croidhe'. Doheny escaped to America in 1848 after taking part in the O'Brien rising.
[3] Traditionally ascribed to Hugh O'Donnell, 1602 (translated by Patrick Pearse).

THE ISLAND OF IRELAND

She hath no friend, no mate,
No lover in her bed,—
A woman with no strong man's protection!
No man lieth beside her
Of the true blood of her heart's affection.

She hath no hope of any husband
For the true Gaelic blood
Over the stormy white-bayed sea is gone.
For this her mind is heavy.

The gentle widow shall not find
A lover or a friendly mate
Until the true Gaels come again—
With freemen's shouts inspiring dread,

No wonder that the isle of strengths,
Once beloved, should now repine
For the Gaelic race of noble deeds,
Who once cherished her full well.

The nurse of the fosterling though she be
Widowed of every husband
O Mary, how pitiful her fate,
Bereft of all her ancestral beauty!

Without protection against the island's evil
Alas, the deformity of her condition
Those who possessed her thus,—
The ancient mother of the sons of Mileadh.

A harlot without respect or honour
In this land of Partholon's stronghold.
Her reason hath withered without reward,
And her seed is subject to savages![1]

[1] Geoffrey Keating, 'My Pity How Ireland Standeth', 1644 or 1650 (translated by Pearse).

'Yet I do not give up the country. I see her in a swoon, but she is not dead: though in her tomb she lies helpless and motionless, still there is on her lips a spirit of life, and on her cheek a glow of beauty.'[1] 'Nurse of our bringing up is she, and when you have looked at her she is not unlovely.'[2] But perhaps the most moving description of all is to be found in W. B. Yeats's play *Cathleen ni Houlihan*, where the spirit of Ireland is depicted as a poor wandering old woman whose sorrows impel the young men (the scene is cast in 1798) to forsake all else, even their brides on their wedding-day, and follow her call. The young hero in the play does this and the play closes with a question put by his family to a young boy who has just entered: 'Did you see an old woman going down the path?', to which he answers 'I did not, but I saw a young girl, and she had the walk of a Queen'. We get here the identification of maiden, old woman, and queen (*i.e.* mother) so characteristic of the unconscious conception of the mother.

We now pass to, apparently, a different theme, the connection of which with the previous one, however, will be pointed out later. In every region of the world the belief may be found that there exists somewhere, usually in a western sea, a magical island which is identified with heaven. In Europe it goes under various names: Meropis, the continent of Kronos, Ogygia, Atlantis, the Garden of the Hesperides, the Fortunate Isles, and so on. The actual position of the island was depicted on many mediaeval maps, such as the one made by Lambertus Floridus in the twelfth century, now in the Bibliothéque Nationale, Paris, the Hereford map of the thirteenth century, and the

---

[1] Anti-Union speech by Grattan, May 26, 1800.
[2] O'Grady, Catalogue of Manuscripts in the British Museum, 1894, No. 385.

twelfth-century map of the world in Corpus Christi College, Cambridge.

There are three features regularly attaching to this concept: (1) in that land all wishes are fulfilled; (2) from it new souls emanate; (3) it is the land to which the dead depart. These three features will be considered in order. With the *first* of them psycho-analysts are very familiar. The phantasy of a life where all wishes are easily fulfilled, the unconscious 'omnipotence of thoughts', represents the desire to live over again the once-tasted experience of such an existence. The notion that such a life is possible is not so fantastic and pretentious as it may appear; we all actually experienced it at one period and we simply desire to return to this experience. I refer, of course, to the period of complete gratification passed through during intra-uterine life, the perfection of which gradually 'fades into the light of common day', as Wordsworth put it, in the succeeding stage of infancy and childhood. It is true that the joys to be tasted in the Fortunate Isle are depicted in more adult terms than this humble origin would suggest, a comprehensible enough fact, but it is noteworthy that the part played by feeding, the chief pleasure in infancy, is remarkably prominent in most of the descriptions. Few of these islands are without their fountain of life and eternal youth as well as a bounteous supply of golden apples, in which symbols it is not hard to recognize the mother's milk and breast; fruit, particularly apples, are a constant symbol of the breast in the unconscious. So natural, indeed, did the idea of luscious feeding seem to be in connection with the concept of a Fortunate Isle that the mediaeval caricatures of it—Cockaigne and Schlaraffenland, for instance—deal with little else; roast geese parade the streets, adding the finishing touches to their condition by continually turning as they walk; wine flows in rivers, and so on. There can be little doubt that unconscious memories of the mother's womb and breast contributed to the formation of this phantasy of a wishless Paradise. The relation of it to the memory of the mother was plainly brought out in Sir James Barrie's play, *Mary Rose*. It will be remembered that the Peter-Pan-like heroine of the play, who quarrels with her husband and is afraid of her father but is devoted to her mother and her child, *i.e.* has an intense maternal fixation, is charmed away by the irresistible spell of a magic island, which is depicted in the form of a woman with wooing music. Incidentally, music, *i.e.* the mother's soothing lullaby, extensively associated with the ideas of children and the third of our themes, death. Throughout Northern Europe children were cautioned not to hearken to the sweet songs of the Elves (the music of which is known in Germany as *Alpleich* or *Elfenreigen*, in Sweden as *ellfr-lek*, in Iceland as *liuflíngslag*, in Norway as *Huldreslát*) lest they be spirited away by Frau Hölle, and Baring-Gould[1] has interestingly traced the same idea in many of our Dissenting hymns, *e.g.* 'Hark! hark, my soul! Angelic songs are swelling', 'Sweet angels are calling to me from yon shore'.

The *second* feature, that the island is where children originate, is the one that most unambiguously points to a maternal source. A place where children are born evidently can be nothing else but a symbol for the mother's womb. Largely through Otto Rank's detailed work,[2] we have become familiar with the extraordinary extensive part played by the idea of water in myths and beliefs relating to birth, so that it is not surprising to find a place so closely connected with water as an island functioning as a com-

[1] Baring-Gould, *Curious Myths of the Middle Ages*, p. 425.
[2] Otto Rank, *Die Lohengrinsage* (1911), pp. 26-32, etc.

mon womb symbol; in individual psycho-analyses one is familiar enough with this. The frequent unconscious process of inversion, of course, aids this (a place contained by water instead of a place containing water). As is well known, in folklore and mythology babies mostly come from a river, a well, a pool, or the sea, at all events from a watery place where they are stored. In Wordsworth's poem quoted above, 'Intimations of Immortality from Recollections of Early Childhood', after speaking of the boy's birth from 'that imperial palace whence he came', he goes on to say:

>Hence in a season of calm weather,
>Though inland far we be,
>Our souls have sight of that immortal sea
>Which brought us hither,
>Can in a moment travel thither,
>And see the Children sport upon the shore,
>And hear the mighty waters rolling evermore.

The meaning of the *third* feature, that the Fortunate Isle should also be the abode of the dead—they are often for this reason called the Isles of the Blessed—is less obvious, and only becomes intelligible when one remembers the idea, again commonly found both in folk belief and in the individual unconscious, that in dying one simply returns to the place whence one came: 'dust thou art and unto dust thou shalt return'. The unconscious mind cannot apprehend the idea of annihilation and substitutes for it that of return to the Nirvana existence of pre-natal life. It is probable that on this is largely founded the belief in re-birth and reincarnation.[1] From this point of view it is quite comprehensible that what might be called the uterine conception of death is again closely associated

[1] See chapters xxxviii and xxxix of my *Papers on Psycho-Analysis*, 1918.

with the idea of water.[1] That souls of the dead have to cross water before arriving at their final abode is an idea of which thousands of examples could be quoted, from the Greek Styx to Böcklin's Toteninsel. It is curious to note that remains of this pagan belief are to be found in many English hymns:

> Shall we meet beyond the river,
> Where the surges cease to roll,
> Where in all the bright Forever
> Sorrow ne'er shall press the soul?
>
> Shall we meet in that blest harbour,
> When our stormy voyage is o'er?
> Shall we meet and cast the anchor
> By the fair celestial shore?

The following lines occur in the Lyra Messianica, in a poem on 'The Last Voyage'.

> On! on! through the storm and the billow,
> By life's chequer'd troubles opprest,
> The rude deck my home and my pillow,
> I sail to the land of the Blest.
>
> Ye waters of gloom and of sorrow,
> How dread are your tumult and roar!
> But, on! for the brilliant to-morrow
> That dawns upon yonder bright shore!
>
> Now, ended all sighing and sadness,
> The waves of destruction all spent,
> I sing with the children of gladness
> The song of immortal content.

[1] See Otto Rank, *op. cit.* and *Psychoanalytische Beiträge zur Mythenforschung*, 1919.

THE ISLAND OF IRELAND

Or I may recall the familiar stanzas of Tennyson's 'Crossing the Bar':

> Sunset and evening star,
>   And one clear call for me!
> And may there be no moaning of the bar,
>   When I put out to sea.
>
> But such a tide as moving seems asleep,
>   Too full for sound and foam,
> When that which drew from out the boundless deep
>   Turns again home.

We thus see that all aspects of the idea of an island Paradise are intimately connected with womb phantasies, with our deepest feelings about birth, death, and mother. Now the point I wish to make here is that this connection, although common enough elsewhere, is extraordinarily close in Irish thought. Without fear of contradiction it may be said that there is no culture so impregnated throughout with the various beliefs and legends associated with the idea of an island Paradise.[1] The number of Erse names for it is in itself indicative evidence of this. Thus: Thierna na oge, the Country of Youth; Tir-Innambéo, the Land of the Living; Tirno-nog, the Land of Youth; Tir Tairngire, the Land of Promise; Tir N-aill, the Other Land; Mag Már, the Great Plain; Mag Mell, the Agreeable Plain. The Gaelic Flath Innis, the Noble Isle, to which the souls of the departed go, is evidently a variant of the same idea. The beliefs are made up of the elements we have considered above. We find there the fountain of

---

[1] The fullest accounts are collected in Jubainville's *L'Épopée celtique en Irlande*, 1892, and in the 'Essay upon the Irish vision of Happy Otherworld and the Celtic Doctrine of Re-Birth', by Alfred Nutt, the greatest authority on this subject, in vol. ii of Meyer's *Voyage of Bran*, 1897.

life, the golden apples, children come from it and the dead return to it. Heroes set out to secure the wonderful Cauldron of Re-Birth, a typical womb symbol, just as elsewhere they did for the Holy Grail. Altogether the idea of re-birth in relation to the island of the Other-World plays a quite extraordinary part in Irish mythology.[1] The Fortunate Isles of the Irish were invariably in the west. From the *Odyssey* (xx, 356) onward the west has always been associated with the idea of death, and long before the war the usual expression in Munster for dying was 'to go west'.

We thus see, first, that the idea of Ireland has been intimately associated with the ideas of woman, mother, nurse, and virgin,[2] and, secondly, that no other country has shown such an extensive and tenacious belief in the conception of a Western Isle possessing the uterine attributes of happiness, birth, and death. It is no very far step to infer that the two themes are connected, that the Magic Isle was a glorified idealization of the Irishman's own birthplace, Ireland; indeed the Norse, who adopted many Irish beliefs before their Leinster kingdom was destroyed at Clontarf in 1114, actually called it by the name of Ireland hit Mikla (Greater Ireland). It is therefore quite comprehensible that the average Irishman should react to the idea of foreign invasion in a different manner from the conscientious objectors when faced with the usual question in their trial: What would you do if a German assaulted your mother? The primordial nature of the response that most men make to such a situation is due, as psychoanalysis has amply shown, to the deeply rooted Oedipus

[1] See Alfred Nutt, *op. cit.*
[2] It is of interest that several writers have connected the national musical instrument of Ireland, the harp, with the sistrum of Isis, a well-known emblem of virginity.

complex, to the sadistic conception formed by most boys of the cruel and violent nature of the father's love demonstrations towards the mother.

Granted that this may have been true of the Irish in the past, have we any evidence that such ancient beliefs should have lingered on unconsciously and affected the people in modern times? Quite apart from the general expectations based on the permanence of the underlying complexes, there is a wealth of evidence indicating an affirmative answer to this question. It seems almost impossible for Irishmen to express their feelings on political subjects without using imagery similar to that described above, and they have shown by their conduct that this imagery is pregnant with meaning to them. It is no chance that Ireland, alone of the constituent elements of the British Empire, refused in the sixteenth century to relinquish the Catholic cult of the Virgin-Mother, and that virginity is nowhere held in higher esteem. And it is perhaps more than a coincidence that some of the most implacable leaders of the Republicans, such as De Valera, Erskine Childers, etc., are Irish only on their mother's side.

Let us take, as an example, the first of the modern leaders, Charles Stewart Parnell, so long the adored chief of the Nationalist Party. 'The Parnells were supposed either to have concealed Fenians in their house, or documents of a compromising kind, or weapons. At all events a search party arrived, insisted on going through the house, would not be denied entrance anywhere, actually would penetrate to Mrs. Parnell's bedroom and turn possible hiding-places upside down there with sacrilegious hand. That at least is how the young man at Cambridge received it when all was related to him. It was rank sacrilege and violation of what should have been the sanctity of his mother's room. . . . He brooded upon it probably more than a little morbidly. It grew to seem a monstrous thing. Its memory and its infamy influenced his whole nature. It turned him into a hater, a hater of the England by whose order this thing had been done. . . . The men of the search party that had invaded his mother's bedroom do not seem to have found anything . . . unless it were a sword belonging to Charles which they took away with them. What he wanted with, or what right he had to the sword I do not know, but probably the taking of it from him was another coal laid on the fire of his wrath.'[1] Or I may quote the following passage from Killiher's *Glamour of Dublin*, 1920: 'Alone amidst the gross batterings of material things, she stands patient with her old sacred civilization—a reverence for youth, a worship of womankind unique in an age of apostasy, a devotion to lost causes that are so often but virtue herself in distress—all these the stigmata of her martyred but indestructible soul.

> And we love thee, O Bauba![2]
> Though the spoiler be in thy hall,
> And thou art bereft of all,
> Save only that Spirit for friend
> Who shapes all things in the end:
>
> Though thine eyes are a sword that has slain
> Thy lovers on many a plain,
> When glad to the conflict they pressed
> Drunk with the light of thy breast
> To die for thee, Bauba!'

I will finish with a few passages taken from speeches made in the spring of this very year. De Valera in a speech on February 1922, said: 'There were people who held Ire-

[1] Hutchinson, *Portraits of the Eighties* (1920), pp. 30, 31.
[2] One of the many feminine names for Ireland.

land was a mother country, and would never consent to making her a kind of illegitimate daughter. . . . Ireland, being a mother country, had a right to be in a position worthy of the dignity of a mother country.' In the same month Michael Collins wrote in a similar strain: 'At a conference in London with the British representatives I made it quite clear that Ireland was a Mother country, with the duties and responsibilities of a Mother country'. On April 30 De Valera said of the Free Staters: 'They wanted them to come and hold Ireland while the shackles were being put upon her'. So the oldest and the youngest records of the Irish concur in resenting with the bitterness of despair, and now at last of triumph, the rape and violence offered to their beloved mother-land.

The point of view brought forward in this essay is—I will not say too slight—but too isolated for one to draw safe practical conclusions from it. But I may perhaps be permitted to suggest that possibly history would have been different if England had had more inkling of the considerations here mentioned and had, instead of ravishing virgin Ireland as though she were a harlot, wooed her with the offer of an honourable alliance. That this was the only hopeful attitude was not seen until the chief power in England was in our days entrusted to a citizen of another small Keltic land.

Postscript.—Subsequent history seems quite in accord with the suggestion made in this essay, and the old sullen suspicion of England's intentions have not diminished with Ireland's republican status. The recent outburst of bitter resentment at Great Britain's refusal to help Eire in driving Northern Ireland out of the United Kingdom against the wishes of its inhabitants was quite in the traditional manner. Peninsulas, such as the Iberian and

Scandinavian ones, tolerate quite well a division of the same race into two communities, and even allow the development of somewhat differing languages for them. But Ireland is not a peninsula; it is a complete insula. So the majority feel it unbearable that it should be divided, however great the economic, religious, and even racial differences of the two parts may be. To them the settlement of Ulster is an abiding rape.

IX

THE RELATION OF ABNORMAL PSYCHOLOGY TO SOCIAL PSYCHOLOGY[1]

In any record of Morton Prince's contributions to psychological science the fact will always deserve mention that he was one of the first to perceive the intimate connection between social psychology and psychology of the abnormal, and to proclaim this by issuing a *Journal* devoted to these two studies. The purpose of the present essay is to inquire into the significance of the various points of contact between the two.

The title itself he has proposed for the latter of these branches of study does not seem to have been very happily chosen, to judge from the reluctance of other workers to adopt it. Apart from linguistic objections to it,[2] it would appear to lay unnecessary stress on the difference between the fields of the normal and the pathological. Without wishing to attach too much importance to the question of nomenclature, which, after all, is largely a matter of expediency and opinion, I should myself, for reasons that will presently be indicated, have preferred to use the term 'clinical psychology'. In England 'medical psychology' is the term most widely used, but it is possible that professional prejudice may have much to do with this preference. In this connection an interesting suggestion made

[1] Contribution to the Morton Prince Commemoration Volume, 1926.
[2] Few workers have been willing to reconcile themselves to the admission that their psychology is abnormal, and still less to the risk of being themselves designated as 'abnormal psychologists'

some years ago by Wilhelm Specht may be recalled. He proposed to restrict the term 'psycho-pathology' to the study of abnormal mental phenomena carried out from a purely medical point of view, *i.e.* the investigation of the causes, pathological significance, and modes of treatment of such states; and to use the term 'pathopsychology' for the investigation of the same data purely from the point of view of general psychology. Certainly this distinction is well worth noting, for much of the interest attaching to the intensive study of pathological mental states that has been carried out in the past quarter of a century is clearly due to the startling extent to which knowledge gleaned in this field has been illuminating for other fields as well.

The etymological association between the word 'clinical' and beds has long ceased to operate. The feature of clinical medicine that distinguishes it from other forms of medical study is not that it is carried out at the bedside, for most often it is not, but that it represents a special mental attitude in the investigator. His attention is concentrated, that is to say, not so much on the elucidation of a particular disorder or the investigation of any given system of the body, as on the scrutiny of an individual human being considered *as a whole*. Now it seems to me that this is the very feature that most sharply distinguishes the medical psychologist from his more academic colleagues and also the one to which the fruitfulness of his results may fairly be attributed. One of the outstanding conclusions to which this methodological mode of approach has compelled assent is that the various forms of mental functioning are extraordinarily interrelated and mutually dependent, so that justifiable scepticism arises in regard to much experimental work which professes to isolate such processes as intellectual or memory ones from the rest. This is only one of the many respects in which the clinical method has come into some degree of conflict with the older methods, though the history of science gives every reason to believe that such conflicts can only represent a transitional stage in the development of psychology as a whole.

A reconciliation between the results achieved by different methods of investigation will only be possible when these methods are granted equal recognition and compared side by side. With this aim in view it would seem a reasonable extension of the term 'clinical psychology' to apply it also in other fields than that of pathology. This would, it is suggested, be done when one intends to emphasize the special attitude of mind and mode of approach that we call 'clinical' towards any psychological problem. In the present paper the term will be used partly in this sense and partly in its original, more restricted sense.

Before inquiring into the relation of this branch of psychology to the other branch called social psychology, it will be necessary to enter to some extent into its characteristics. In seeking to define what are the most distinctive features of clinical psychology I shall probably find general agreement up to a certain point and then considerable disagreement after. This is inevitable with a writer representing the psycho-analytical school, for this school has developed the characteristics of the clinical method further than any other workers in clinical psychology.

The first characteristic, already mentioned above, is an aversion from, on the one hand, the generalities so common in the older psychological writings, and, on the other, the tendency to consider mental problems apart from the life of any actual individual. Put in an obverse way, this amounts to a preference for relating such problems to the life of the personality as a whole. This in itself would stamp clinical psychology as a branch of individual psychology, and it certainly is that, though it is also much more besides. It may appear odd that the branch of psychology which most devotes itself to the study of the individual should come to be also the branch which is establishing the closest contact with social psychology, but some of the reasons for this will appear presently.

The decision to make an intensive investigation of a (necessarily small) number of individuals proved to be a much more fateful one than it must have appeared at first. The motive impelling the pioneers to make this decision was the necessity of doing something when confronted by the terribly urgent problem of suffering, and this motive enabled them to overcome just the obstacles that had hitherto been imposed in the way of any penetrating investigation of the mind. The history of the investigation of the body was repeated in the sphere of the mind. To examine the inside of the body had, for centuries, been forbidden as something taboo, not nice, not proper, and not right. But the extreme desirability of learning something about what, why, or when men suffered from disease at last broke down this prohibition. Examination of the inside of the mind was still longer held up, and mainly by similar obstacles. Even now discretion soon imposes a limit of permissibility on any psychologist who may seek to explore the mental processes of his subjects. The curious result has been that psychologists have, till lately, been compelled to study anything rather than human beings. They could investigate vision, hearing, speech, but only a careful selection of the things seen, heard, or said—still less what the mind actually thought of these things; what animals do when they are angry or starved, but not what human beings do in similar circumstances.

With this tradition most clinical psychologists have definitely broken. Faced with the grim tragedies of neurosis, they have had perforce to come to close quarters with the intimacies of emotional life, and, much to the horror of their contemporaries, including the more conservative members of their own profession, they have proceeded to examine dispassionately the facts in this way brought under their notice and even to publish the conclusions to which their investigations have led them. Their justification has been that the relief of suffering, on the one hand, and the march of knowledge, on the other, are more weighty considerations than excessive regard for wounded susceptibilities.

When now the study of the mind is approached in this way, with a propensity to consider every problem in reference to the whole personality and with the resolve not to shrink from exploration of the inner mental life, however intimate, wherever necessary, experience shows that it will result in certain characteristic views being taken of mental functioning. These, then, come to be rather distinctive attributes of the clinical method. Four of them may be selected for special emphasis; they may each be memorized by a single word: genetic, dynamic, unconscious, and instinctual, respectively. A few words will be said about them in this order. It will be noticed that academic psychology gives its assent in general terms to three of them, to all except the idea of the unconscious, but they are all taken much more seriously and applied much more rigorously in clinical psychology.

Everyone would, of course, agree with the statement that the mind develops, but a great deal more than this is meant when it is said that clinical psychology views the mind *genetically*. Here the continuity of the mind at different ages is regarded quite literally. It is held that the significance of any given current mental process is not completely known unless the full genesis of it is also known, unless its predecessors can be traced back in an unbroken chain to the beginnings of mental life in the infant. It has been found that many of the older elements of the genesis, and often the most important of these, are not completely transformed into or replaced by their successors, so that a certain amount of their original significance is still retained. The practical effect of this is that many of our impulses, interests, and ideas carry with them an extrinsic significance based on their genetic history; that they represent more than what they purport to. In extreme cases, of which unconscious symbolism is the most striking example, the subject is totally unaware of this surplus significance. The state of affairs just indicated is most pronounced in pathological conditions, the essence of which is that the patient is dominated by a still too living past, a past which, though forgotten, refuses to fade or to submit to transformation. The most advanced school of clinical psychology, following Freud, carries this genetic principle to its logical conclusion and maintains that all our later reactions in life are really elaborations of simpler ones acquired in the nursery. The power to modify the more fundamental types of reaction becomes rapidly less as the child grows, and some of us even think that no fundamental change in character can take place after the fourth year of life.

In its *dynamic* view of the mind, clinical psychology comes into decided opposition with the old associationist psychology. When one mental element occurs after another, it is no longer possible to think we have explained this by saying that the second element, having been attached to the first through temporal contiguity, or inherent similarity was aroused by the presence of the first. Dynamic factors such as those designated by the words motive, tendency, purpose, impulse, are sought for in every single instance, however minute, and no explanation is regarded as adequate unless a factor of this kind is demonstrated. This holds even with mental events, such as slips of the tongue and the like, that previously were supposed to 'happen' without any ascertainable reason, and certainly without any motivation. Yet the older views die hard in some fields of work—for instance, in regard to dreams. Many psychologists are still fully satisfied if a dreamer says: 'I was talking French in the dream, probably because my father, who appeared earlier in it, has just returned from France, so that the thought of him would make me think of the French language'.

A thorough-going dynamic conception of mental events as essentially the expression of the interplay of various forces[1] leads to many important consequences. One comes, in this way, to realize that a great number of mental processes come about as compromise-formations, various conflicting forces having contributed to the end result The extent to which conflict between opposing tendencies takes place in the mind, and the importance of such conflicts, is a matter on which there is not universal agreement among clinical psychologists at present, but that intrapsychic conflict is of far greater significance than used to be thought is becoming very generally recognized. It is particularly hard to overlook its significance in neurotic disorder, for the manifestations of this are nothing else than the expression of such conflicts. Freud himself has applied his 'wish' theory of the mind in a great many different fields and, however much or little anyone may agree with the details of these applications, there can be little doubt, as Holt has well pointed out, that this line of

[1] I am, of course, aware that 'force' is one of those words not to be used in strict scientific speech, and only write it here as a convenient and easily comprehensible shorthand for more cumbrous periphrases.

work has given a considerable impetus towards the appreciation of the extensive part played by conative trends in regions of mental functioning, such as, for instance, dream formation, where their existence had been hardly suspected.

The subject of the *unconscious* mind is so vast—it is quite possible that in the future it may be ranked as the most important discovery of the past half-century—that no discussion of it here would be in place. One word must suffice in reference to the empty objection that, since the word 'mental' is equivalent to 'conscious', no unconscious mental processes can be allowed to go on. *Ça n'empêche pas d'exister.* Its reality is attested by the work of many authorities, any one of which would suffice for the purpose; one may mention the observations of Binet and Janet, and the experimental work on dissociation by Morton Prince, quite apart from the huge literature of psycho-analysis. Apparently the critics would have us write such phrases as: 'the neural dispositions and synaptic changes, all of which are quite unknown, with which the corresponding mental processes, if they occurred in consciousness, would be expressed by the wish to murder a brother-in-law'; whereas we are content with the less cumbrous phrase: 'the unconscious wish to murder a brother-in-law'. In the present state of our knowledge the whole question is a mere verbal quibble. When neurologists know enough to describe conscious processes in terms of cerebral physiology, then they will have no difficulty in doing the same for unconscious processes, and everyone will be happy; but the essential point is that the two kinds of mental processes are absolutely on the same footing in this matter. Nor can I repeat here the respects in which Freud's particular conception of the unconscious differs from that of other writers, fundamental as I hold them to be.

As befits a discipline of medical origin, the clinical attitude is close to the biological one, and most clinical psychologists feel that one of the chief goals of their work is to be able to state their mental data in biological terms, *i.e.* in terms of the *instincts*. The interesting contributions that have appeared in the *Journal of Abnormal Psychology and Social Psychology* of late only go to show how complicated and obscure are the problems relating to the instincts, and it cannot be said that clinical psychology has yet been in a position to elucidate finally any of them. But it has advanced two steps at least in this direction. It has cleared the ground by showing that a number of supposedly inborn instincts with which other psychologists had operated are complex products, and so are capable of resolution into more primary elements. This remark applies, for instance, to many in the list of instincts propounded by McDougall in his popular *Social Psychology*. In the second place, the analyses effected by clinical psychologists, particularly by Freud, of the conative aspects of the mind, have revealed much of importance concerning the development, manifold fate, and products of the instinctual side of mental life, and it is reasonable to expect that further research along these lines will bring us nearer to the ultimate sources of mental impulse.

After this sketch, imperfect as it is, of the features characterizing the clinical approach to psychology, let us turn to social psychology and try to ascertain something of the relationship between the two. Social psychology itself has evidently been in great part developed because of the peculiar straits in which sociologists and all serious students of social problems find themselves. It is impossible to proceed far in the study of social institutions without perceiving that the only work of a non-psychological kind that can be done in this field must remain on a purely descriptive or classificatory level. The simple reason for this is that no problem can be raised concerning the origin, function, or significance of any one of these institutions that does not immediately involve some psychological consideration.

The sociologists who have recognized this state of affairs have naturally turned to psychology for assistance and co-operation. They must, in the past, have been somewhat bewildered at the response, for until late years this has been decidedly a negative one. The notorious lack of interest of most psychologists in such mundane topics as motive and meaning prevented a wide response of any kind, and the few who occupied themselves with the sociological data, such as notably Wundt, confined themselves either to the classificatory studies of the kind already familiar to sociologists or else to the vaguest generalities.

Three explanations have been proffered for this curiously unresponsive attitude on the part of psychologists. The most charitable is that suggested by writers of the class of Le Bon, who suppose that the side of man from which light is needed to explain sociological phenomena, the side about which psychologists have been able to say so little, is perhaps one which is not present in the material studied by the psychologist, *i.e.* in man considered as an individual. They have put forward the view that the mental tendencies concerned with social institutions are dormant in the individual and are stirred to activity only when he comes into close contact with a group of his fellows. They thus postulate a special class of instincts—the herd, gregarious, or social instincts—which are manifest only in the relation of the individual with the group.

Of the many criticisms that can be made of the view just enunciated, one only may be mentioned here. The hypothesis would seem to attach far too great importance to the mere factor of number in human psychology. It would be very remarkable if instincts which are supposed to play no part in a man's relations to those nearest him—friend, enemy, wife, and family—should suddenly emerge the moment he comes into contact with a larger number of people. At what point do they appear, and what is the magic number that has this effect?

The second hypothesis, put forward by Wilfred Trotter, avoids this particular difficulty. He supposes that what psychologists have not borne sufficiently in mind is the biological history of man. He insists that man is throughout a gregarious animal, and agrees that we should postulate a special group of instincts, which he sums up under the name of 'herd instinct', in accordance with this consideration. But he maintains that these instincts play an important part also in the simpler and individual relations of life, not only where group contact is present. According to him, man is at every moment, even in the privacy of his chamber, nothing but a gregarious animal, and much of his most individual behaviour is dictated by the indirect effects of his social instincts.

The third explanation of the general psychologist's lack of helpfulness in the social domain is that proffered by the psycho-analytical school of clinical psychology. It would agree with the two previously mentioned ones that something essential must have been overlooked by the general psychologist, and also with the second explanation that this something is, nevertheless, to be found in the study of the individual. But its indictment of the general psychologist is more far-reaching than either of the others, being to the effect that he has extensively ignored highly important aspects of his own field. As was already indicated above, we mean by this the intimate regions of the mind, those in which the final answers to most psychological problems are to be found.

To many it will seem an overweening pretension to maintain, as has been done in this paper, that the branch of psychology which is most concentrated on the study of man as an individual, and predominantly with the morbid states of the individual, should be regarded as the branch which has most to offer the student of socio-psychological problems. And yet these two grounds for objection are the very reasons why one ventures to put forward this pretension. For morbid states have special and overwhelming claims to importance as fields of psychological investigation. Individual suffering has momentous consequences for both the investigator and the subject which are paralleled by no other psychological situation. As regards the former, experience has shown that no other motive, not even scientific curiosity, is strong enough to overcome the various motives (largely of personal origin) which compel him to desist from intruding into the intimacies of another person's innermost life. And, similarly, no other motive than suffering has yet been found, except in the rarest cases, to induce a human being to submit to any really searching investigation of his own mind. The academic psychologist is thus, in regard to his study-material, at a permanent and unalterable disadvantage as compared with the clinical psychologist.

The second objection indicated above challenges the right to transfer to normal psychology conclusions arrived at through study of the abnormal. Such a critic, however, is being misled by the word 'abnormal' and is evidently unaware of the real nature of neurotic suffering. As is now becoming more widely recognized, this is not due to disease in the ordinary sense of the word so much as to the adoption of a particular method of dealing with a social situation. The idea, which we owe mainly to Freud, that neurosis is one of man's ways of meeting various difficulties in his relation to his fellow-man, *i.e.* to social difficulties, has revolutionized our conception of psychopathology in the past quarter of a century.

If neurosis represents a solution, however unsatisfactory, of various social difficulties, then it is impossible that an exceedingly intensive investigation of it, such as is necessary for therapeutic purposes, should be undertaken without throwing light also on the inner nature and meaning of the social institutions themselves in regard to which the difficulties have arisen. And there are ample indications in the literature of the past fifteen years that this expectation is being fulfilled, though even yet psycho-sociological studies proper are only in their infancy.

It will thus be seen that there are two fundamental points of contact between clinical and social psychology. In the first place, the study of social relationships and social institutions demands that special attention be directed to the questions of meaning, motive, significance, and the like; in short, to the interpretation of the dynamic aspects of the mind. Now these are the aspects with which clinical psychology is perforce peculiarly concerned, certainly more so than any other branch of psychology. Further, clinical psychology is not in a position to be content with the superficial interpretations of motive that are customary. The correctness of its conclusions are constantly being checked by results, and to secure these it is necessary to deal with the real actual motives operative in a given case, not with the ostensible ones. In other words, it has to penetrate to the sources of motive in the unconscious, to the fundamental roots of all our impulses, emotions, and conduct.

In the second place, as was hinted above, it so happens

that the subject-matter itself is far more nearly identical in the two branches of psychology in question than might at first sight be supposed. The social institutions studied by the one discipline are the products of the same forces that create the neurotic manifestations with which the other is concerned; they are simply alternative modes of expression. Let us consider for a moment a few of the chief topics that are the object of socio-psychological investigation. One problem is the organization of societies, the inner structure and external relationships of groups, clans, and nations, with all the concomitant questions of government and authority. Another is the vast domain of sex relationships, the complicated questions surrounding the marriage and family bonds, the accompanying institutions of prostitution and concubinage, and the endless variety of ritual, folklore, and superstition that invest the themes of love and birth. A third is that of religion in all its forms and manifestations: theology, ritual, ethics, and morality, and the conduct of life in general. One can safely say that every one of these problems has, at times, to be made the subject of a penetrating investigation during the elucidation of some neurotic manifestation. Many a neurotic symptom represents the individual's attempt to deal with the complicated relationship between son and father, a problem which, on the other side, connects with the great questions of government, leadership, authority, submission, and so on. That religion represents essentially a mode of appeasing the sense of guilt arising from various anti-social tendencies is becoming more and more widely recognized, and every clinical psychologist knows that conflict over these same anti-social tendencies may lead to neurotic or even psychotic disorder, so that his work is very largely taken up with the elucidation of them. That many clinical psychologists have also shown considerable intrepidity in investigating the manifold problems relating to the sexual life is familiar enough to the readers of Dr. Prince's *Journal*.

It is impossible, in a short contribution such as the present one, to do more than call attention to some of the main points of contact between the two branches of psychology under consideration. The preceding remarks on the identity of content in the two cases may appear unduly categorical, but it would need a volume even to illustrate such an enormous theme. Fortunately, all that has been said here can be supported by reference to an already extensive literature on the subject, and I may conclude with the simple statement that most of the keys to socio-psychological problems will be found in the realm of clinical psychology.

X
THE INFERIORITY COMPLEX OF THE WELSH[1]

THIS is the first article by a psycho-analyst to appear in any Welsh periodical. It is perhaps a matter of some interest that, although it was a Welshman who introduced the subject of psycho-analysis to this country, more than twenty years ago, the subject has been almost completely ignored in Wales.

Your Editor has asked me to say something on the inferiority complex of the Welsh, thereby indicating that he shares the common opinion that this is a typical Welsh feeling. I am inclined to agree with him in this, but it is necessary to qualify any such general statement so as to avoid misunderstanding; indeed, perhaps it would be wiser never to enter the thorny field of national psychology without surrounding oneself with reservations. What exactly is meant by a typical national trait? Certainly not necessarily one that is especially common in that country. That may or may not be so, but the word 'typical' in this connection refers rather to a trait that is sufficiently distinctive, either in its nature or its manifestations, sufficiently pronounced or sufficiently frequent, to become particularly associated in men's minds with a given country. As is well known, these associations are seldom the same, or at all events are seldom expressed in the same terms, in the minds of the inhabitants of the country concerned and in those of strangers. When foreigners comment on the alleged hypocrisy of the English or the

[1] Published in *The Welsh Outlook*, March 1929.

thriftiness—let us call it—of the Scotch, these people will be more likely to recognize the same virtues under other names, for instance, a common-sense capacity for compromise in one case and a capacity for cautious self-control in the other. Coming to the present case in point, I should not have thought it would occur to the average Englishman to say of the Welsh that they exhibit feelings of inferiority—posssibly even the contrary—though he might well mention attributes which a psychologist would recognize as proceeding from such feelings. Perhaps this is not very surprising in this instance, for efforts are usually made to conceal these particular feelings, certainly from the outer world and as much as possible from oneself, and it is the subject himself who is best qualified to speak on the matter. What proportion of Welshmen would confess to such feelings when he compared his own nationality to others I cannot at all say, but I should know that the number, as in any group of men, would surely be less than that of those afflicted by them.

Now what is meant by the expression 'inferiority complex'? Really nothing more than the words imply, namely, that the person concerned has an undue tendency to compare himself unfavourably with other people, to despise himself, to be oppressed by a sense of inferiority. These feelings arise from within and have little or nothing to do with any actual inferiority even when they appear to be connected with this. They may, in certain people, reach agonizing degrees of intensity, and they then come under the notice of the medical psychologist. A man's life may be made so miserable as to be ruined over his distress at something that other people would regard as utterly trivial, a retreating chin, a large nose, a tendency to blush; and what is still more puzzling, as I hinted already, the defect in question may not be present at all in actuality.

Such feelings may attach themselves to any sphere of life, physical, intellectual, moral, aesthetic, and so on; I use the words 'attach themselves' because they never originate in respect of the ideas in question but only become secondarily attached to them.

Psycho-analysis has found out a number of interesting things about these feelings. In its exploration of the deeper and previously inaccessible regions of the mind to which we give the name 'unconscious', psycho-analysis discovered, as is widely known, that the heart of man contained a number of things repellent to the conscious mind, crude and primitive tendencies, the existence of which was not even suspected by consciousness. It is not so widely known, however, that psycho-analysis has also discovered that the heart of man always contains the very opposite of this, namely, that everyone is far more moral in his unconscious mind than he has ever suspected. It is as though good and bad—to use popular terms—with which we are familiar in our conscious minds, are both of them prolonged below the surface of the mind, or, to put it more correctly, that they proceed from much more massive amounts of both goodness and badness that exist in the unconscious, in that region where the most intense conflicts are fought out without our ever being aware of them. The results of the disturbances underneath leak through from time to time and the feelings of inferiority with which we are concerned constitute only one of many forms in which this may occur. Perhaps the most interesting thing psycho-analysis has discovered about these particular feelings is that, whatever the form may be in which they show themselves whether in reference to physical, intellectual, or any other matters, they always proceed from one source, and that is from a sense of *moral* inferiority. Such a person has a part of the mind that is intensely discontented with the moral standard he has attained and is ceaselessly criticizing him for his comparative failure in this respect; thus inferiority really means guiltiness. Whether this is justified or otherwise is another matter: it is often the saints of this world who are least satisfied with their moral stature.

Misfortune and suffering often have the effect of evoking a sense of inferiority, but not in the simple way one might imagine. It is not that the defeated man feels inferior because he has been defeated, but he will feel inferior if he thinks that the defeat has been his fault, for instance, if he thinks that his misfortunes are a visitation from the Almighty as an expression of His wrath at his sins. It follows that religiously minded persons are more prone to suffer in this way than others, for they interpret misfortune in moral terms. It is well known that they are prone to searchings of heart on such occasions and ask, 'What have I done that this should happen to me?' The Old Testament is replete with examples of this. One would expect, therefore, that a religiously minded people whose history is one of defeat and suffering will be more prone than others to develop a national sense of inferiority, however much they may try to conceal this beneath trumped-up boastings of their good qualities.

There are few nations to whom these remarks apply more strikingly than the Welsh and the Jews, two peoples who have a great deal in common in their psychology as well as notable differences. It would be tempting to investigate the past history of the Welsh from this point of view. One has the impression that the trait in question is one of relatively recent growth, certainly since the Middle Ages. Their contempt for the Saxons was well known, but with the advent of the Normans the situation changed. Much might be said in this connection about their peculiar religious history since the time of the Reformation and the overwhelming importance of Nonconformity, for good or ill, in regard to Welsh characteristics, but I have perhaps said enough to indicate that the problem of national traits is much more complex than might appear, and is one that will one day prove to be a fascinating study.

XI
MENTAL HEREDITY[1]

Ever since Mendel's work it has been evident that in estimating the relation of heredity to environment in respect to any character, we have first to ascertain the component units in that character; in other words, what actually constitutes an individual gene. The work on the inheritance of eye colour illustrates very well the difference between the pre- and post-Mendelian points of view. This criterion, however, has hitherto been applied in mental fields only very inadequately. It is a consideration that forces itself on the attention of the psycho-analyst, much of whose work consists in dissecting mental attributes into their component elements. He is constantly dismayed at the glibness with which generalizations are made concerning various mental attributes, knowing as he does that such labels commonly cover a quite heterogeneous composition. This is strikingly true of most discussions on mental heredity where the speakers do not seem to have at all appreciated the primary importance of reducing their material to terms that cannot be further analysed, and the enormous difficulty of doing so. Psychoanalysts would maintain that fruitful studies in the field of mental heredity are to be expected only after the mental elements have been isolated in a pure state. They themselves are engaged on this difficult and obscure task. So far, the most promising of their results in this connection would appear to be the correlating of various mental attributes with varying capacity for excitation of different

[1] Contribution to a symposium on Mental Heredity held by the Eugenics Society, January 29, 1930.

zones of the body. It would seem likely that the excitability of these zones represents a mental element incapable of further analysis, and therefore one to which the next study to be applied would be one in the field of heredity.

XII
PSYCHO-ANALYSIS AND BIOLOGY[1]

IF psychology is regarded as a part of biology, and surely it must be, then it is possible to maintain that Freud's work, that is, the creation of psycho-analysis, signifies a contribution to biology comparable in importance only with that of Darwin's. I, for one, am prepared to maintain that this is not an exaggerated assertion. On the other hand, one may make the interesting reflection that to-day is the first occasion on which this work, inaugurated nearly forty years ago, is being presented before an assembly of biologists. The contrast between these two statements is so startling that it should prove instructive to dwell on it for a moment. No one has ever suggested that biologists are less alert than other workers in taking note of any progress that concerns their special field of interest—the gradual and rather uninspiring advance in their own work during just these forty years has probably, on the contrary, disposed them rather to look with welcome for any signs of fresh vision—so how is it to be supposed that such a revolutionary contribution as is here suggested should have escaped their notice? Would it not appear more likely that those psychologists are right who regard the revolution in question as a mere storm in a tea-cup about which biologists do not need to trouble themselves?

Although these questions can be answered, what weight

[1] Read before the Second International Congress for Sex Research, August 7, 1930.

will the answers carry? We inevitably touch here on the divorce that unhappily has existed hitherto between psychology and biology, indeed between psychology and all the rest of science. The fundamental reason for this divorce is undoubtedly the difficulty that has existed in applying biological principles to the study of the mind. Dimly perceived barriers erect themselves in the mind against the attempts to do so. Attitudes of a philosophical, or perhaps even religious, order, attitudes always implicit and sometimes explicit, interpose themselves and impede objective judgement. The result has been a widely spread scepticism about the possibility of ever creating a scientific psychology, and this has not been lessened by the spectacle of innumerable 'schools' of psychology, the only common link among whom has often been the banality, not to say the sterility, of their conclusions. Biologists, being also human, must presumably have fallen back on the same impression as that harboured by the man in the street, one composed of the dual belief that it is inherently impossible for the mind to investigate itself and that it is so easy for any mind to investigate itself that any expert contribution to the task is superfluous.[1] The antinomy contained in this belief does not seem to trouble the man in the street, since both sides of the contradiction harmonize in the satisfying conviction that there is nothing to be feared from the psychologist. Once reassurance has been obtained on this point, professional psychologists could safely be installed in the various universities of the world. To do them justice, they have very faithfully

[1] This was well illustrated recently by H. G. and F. L. Wells and Julian Huxley, who in their *The Science of Life* did not hesitate to present the subject of modern psychology, contemptuous of all errors in the presentation, without feeling the need to consult anyone with a first-hand knowledge of it.

observed the implied contract by confining their attention to those aspects of the mind where there was no risk of ruffling the feelings of anyone. Freud's work has disturbed this peaceful state of things. It might have been more of a bombshell than it was, had there not been to hand very potent methods for damping the powder, methods by means of which the significance of his findings could be denied or in the worst case blurred and dimmed.

The essence of Freud's discovery was the existence and nature of the unconscious mind, and we shall see presently how the study of its functions forged for the first time an intrinsic link between biology and psychology. Freud derives the greater part of what we ordinarily call the mind, *i.e.* the conscious mind, from certain primitive impulses, expressions no doubt of the primary instincts themselves, the direct manifestations of which have been so checked as to result in the retention of the impulses in the unconscious mind. He maintains that the origin of our conscious interests, mental activities, strivings, and feelings in these 'repressed' impulses is unknown to us because of powerful forces operating in the mind to ensure the unconsciousness of these impulses, and, of course, of the connection between them and our conscious mind. More than this, the existence of the 'repressing' forces themselves are also unconscious, so that normally one has no suspicion of what is 'repressed' or even that anything is 'repressed'. The instinctive response to such statements can, therefore, in the nature of things, only be a quite sincere incredulity, for the individual has no means of detecting within himself the operation of any such conflicts as Freud describes. This negative response can be amply fortified by a variety of considerations, pseudo-philosophical objections to the very concept of an unconscious mind as a contradiction in terms, aesthetic and moral objections to the content of this supposed unconscious as described by psycho-analysts, logical objections to the numerous paradoxes revealed by them, common-sense objections to the improbability of the whole set of ideas and the incompatibility of them with all previous conceptions man has held of his nature, and so on.

The psycho-analyst, on his side, must admit the force of all these objections, which have to be dealt with and not ignored, and yet the mass of data he has at his disposal leaves him no escape from accepting the validity of his conclusions. To the outside observer who has not had access to these data he can only advance two main considerations. On the one hand, he can point to a number of phenomena hitherto inexplicable and discounted, such as the complicated processes of dreaming, of psycho-neurotic activities, and of other malfunctioning of the mind, all of which become intelligible on the basis of his conclusions and on no others, and he can show how a large number of imperfectly understood phenomena, for instance, of mythology, of religion, of anthropology, can be further illuminated by applying the conclusions derived from investigation of the unconscious mind. On the other hand, he can assure such an outside observer that the forces preventing any possibility of objectively appreciating the significance of unconscious mental activities are much more formidable than he can have any notion of without investigating them at first hand. Finally, he can give a satisfactory explanation of the striking fact that the endeavour to apply scientific principles to the study of the mind has hitherto been so much less fruitful than other scientific endeavours. The problem of bringing together those who have studied a subject at first hand and those who have not is never an easy one: in the case of psycho-analysis, the difficulty, enormously heightened for the reasons just indicated, has up to the present proved quite refractory.

I intend to persist in spite of this difficulty, and in doing so will ask for your indulgence while I lay before you a number of considerations of a purely psychological order, the bearing of which on biology it will be possible to point out only after they have first been expounded. Although I have designated psycho-analysis as the study of the mind from a biological point of view, it should at once be said that this does not mean any deductive application of biological principles to such a study. On the contrary, Freud's investigations were of an unusually empirical nature, dictated first by therapeutic rather than by purely scientific motives, and it was only gradually that the general bearing of them, and particularly their biological import, became manifest. His work began with the endeavour to understand, and in this way effectively to cope with, the very puzzling and distressing phenomena of psychoneurotic disorders. He found that these differed in their meaning from 'normal' mental activities, which we regard as rational and intelligible, in being disguised presentations of unconscious primitive impulses, whereas the latter activities represent transformations and developments of these impulses. Once the disguise could be penetrated, it was thus possible, from investigation of the psychoneuroses, to obtain a view of the original impulses which is far harder to obtain from any study of the 'normal'.

I want to make this matter as plain as possible, since you might very well wonder why one should devote so much attention to, and build a whole theory of the mind on, what perhaps appears to you as unusual and aberrant, indeed diseased, conditions. Well, the first point to insist on is that neuroses are not at all diseases in the sense of being conditions produced by the action of pathogenic agencies on an otherwise 'normal' organism. On the contrary, they arise from within the very nature of the personality and represent merely one of the various ways of reacting to situations that are in themselves normal or, at all events, universal. While we can say a great deal about the nature of these important situations and also about the various modes of reaction towards them, we are not yet in a position to pass an exact comparative judgement on the differences between the neurotic and the so-called normal development. We have grounds for thinking that what passes for mental normality may represent a much less straightforward and healthy line of development than is generally assumed, that some of it is perhaps forced and distorted; but much of its development is very obscure and as yet imperfectly understood. What is unmistakably plain to us, however, is that a neurotic constitution stands much nearer to the original basis of the child's mentality than does normality. It is far less altered, and indeed from one point of view it would be correct to say that it signified a failure in development. With the neuroses the primitive mentality of the child has remained embedded, so to speak, and merely covered over, whereas with the normal it has undergone a complicated evolution, or even distortion. This, as has already been remarked, affords us an unequalled opportunity to ascertain the nature of the primitive mentality from which all the later stages proceed, and I shall point out later that the knowledge thus acquired unavoidably raises in the mental sphere the old biological problem of the relation between ontogeny and phylogeny.

We are here concerned essentially with the findings

that have been made by means of the method of psychoanalysis, and with the bearing they may have on our comprehension of the biological instincts. This is not the place to describe the method itself or the fine network of mental processes it sets out to unravel. It is, however, impossible to omit all reference to purely psychological matters, though I will try to make my remarks in this sphere as brief as I can. It will be easier to understand them if one keeps constantly in mind the fact that beneath the surface of consciousness there is a state of conflict far more constant and intense than one would have supposed likely. What these conflicts are over, and what are the forces engaged on the different sides, are, of course, matters we shall have to consider later. Freud has found it convenient to envisage the mind as being divided, more or less sharply, into three parts, but this division does not bear a simple relation to that into consciousness and the unconscious. There is, to begin with, the mass of primitive and infantile impulses to which he has given the impersonal name of the *id* (German *Es*). Already in the first year of life there is beginning to develop out of this what may properly be termed the ego, and from the beginning the ego shows the characteristic of exercising selection. Among the immense quantity of incoming material presented to it from within and without, perceptions, stimuli, needs, impulses, and so on, it selects some which it decides to regard as belonging to itself, having what we call the quality of 'ego-syntonicity', while it rejects others. The distinction it thus effects by no means corresponds with the actual difference between stimuli proceeding from within and those proceeding from without. Those of the rejected ones which emanate from the *id*, and which, therefore, are part of the individual organism although they are denied union with the sense of personality that characterizes the ego, are by definition incompatible with the ego, and have to pursue their future path on lines independent of it or even in opposition to it. They are 'ego-dystonic'. A further complication comes in through the building out of the ego of a third institution, the 'super-ego', which performs special functions such as the warning and guarding of the ego against the dangers arising to it from activity on the part of the repressed id. The id is essentially unconscious, though not entirely so; the super-ego is mainly unconscious; and even a large part of the ego itself belongs to the region of the unconscious. If this description is correct it will be seen that the region of the mind of which we are aware, *i.e.* consciousness, plays a much more modest part in our total mental activities than has previously been suspected.

Freud's conception of the mind is fundamentally a dynamic one. He views all mental processes in such terms as aim, purpose, striving, tendency, impulse, or—to use his favourite expression—wish. Ideas are mostly but the spearhead of wishes; as the old saying has it, the wish is father to the thought. Emotions are dynamic reactions to thwarted wishes. A very great part of mental activity consists of the endeavours on the part of the primitive and repressed id impulses to find expression in spite of the opposition of the ego. They succeed in making their existence felt in a variety of ways. Often the character of the personality has to be profoundly modified, indeed distorted, in building up special 'reaction formations' to keep in check particular tendencies on the part of the id; examples of these reaction formations are pity and horror as protections against cruel tendencies, modesty against those of display, disgust against those of uncleanliness, and so on. More positive manifestations of the id impulses can be achieved by either disguising them, as happens in the neuroses, or by transforming them, as in the more 'normal' course. An example of the latter is the mechanism known as 'sublimation', whereby a given sexual impulse is desexualized in nature and meaning, and the energy belonging to it is directed to a non-sexual aim; pederastic and feminine tendencies, for instance, can in this way be converted into pedagogic interests, ungratified maternal desires into philanthropic activities, and so on. Whichever of these two processes, namely, disguise and transformation, is at work, the important underlying principle is that before any derivatives of a primitive id impulse can be accepted by the ego and admitted to consciousness it has to fulfil certain conditions. It then becomes what is known as *bewusstseinsfähig*, 'capable of consciousness'. In its passage from the deeper to the more superficial layers of the mind it undergoes a variety of changes; examples of the mechanisms concerned in these changes are those designated by the names of displacement, condensation, substitution, reversal, compromise, symbolism, compensation, and so on, into the details of which we need not enter here.

Another way of regarding mental activity is in terms of certain principles that would appear to regulate it. Unconscious processes, for instance, are entirely regulated by the 'pleasure-pain' principle, the meaning of which explains itself. It is characteristic of the earliest stages of human development, both in the individual and in the race. Its main attribute is a never-ceasing demand for immediate gratification of various primitive desires and the avoidance at any cost of unpleasant experience. It is thus exquisitely egocentric and asocial. It bears an important relation to the matter of psychical tension, the precise nature of which, however, is not yet clear. The attempt to correlate high tension with 'pain' and the relief of tension with pleasure has succeeded only over part of the field, and it is becoming plain that the relationship is a more complicated one, unknown qualitative factors probably playing an important part. The thought processes corresponding to the pleasure-pain principle proceed by the use of analogies and superficial associations, treat resemblances as equivalent to identities, ignore the laws of formal logic, and make no distinction between a phantasy and an actual situation in life. There is reason to think that a need is first met by conjuring up a hallucinatory or imagined gratification, and it is only the failure of this to procure lasting alleviation of the need that brings other mechanisms into play. The tendency just described then comes into conflict with what is known as the 'reality principle', one which genetically is derived from the earlier one; this is closely cognate to what in biology would be called the principle of adaptation, of utility, or of survival. Its function is to adapt the organism to the exigencies of reality, to subordinate the imperious demand for immediate gratification and to replace this by a more distant but more satisfying and permanent one. It is thus influenced by social and other considerations that are ignored by the earlier principle. It can, however, only guide and control the pleasure principle; it can never abrogate its activity. In the course of development the early conflict between the two principles is in a varying degree resolved; the pleasure principle obtains free rein in phantasy and dream life, and otherwise achieves its gratification along the lines laid down by the reality principle. Often enough, however, the conflict between the two lasts into later life and complicated pathological results ensue. Some ten years ago Freud suggested that there might be still a third principle directing mental activity, one more fundamental even than the other two. This he calls the 'repetition compulsion', meaning by it the tendency to repeat certain experiences apparently for the mere sake of repeating and quite independently of any such function as obtaining pleasure or dealing with reality. It is harder to demonstrate the separate existence of this principle than that of the other two, nor is it clear what its actual significance and function may be. Freud surmises that the repetition serves the function of enabling the difficult experience to be assimilated, but that the tendency to repeat is itself a deeper one than anything to do with this particular function; indeed, that it is the most fundamental principle of all mental activity, the conservative tendency to hark back to the past and reinstate a former condition.

Throughout his work Freud has been searching for some broad generalization under which could be summarized the various forms of conflict with which investigation of the deeper mental layers is predominantly concerned. It is plain that the most satisfactory generalization for this purpose would be one expressed in terms of the instincts proper, and there is here a field of fruitful co-operation between biologists and psycho-analysts. Unfortunately the various lists of instincts that have been drawn up by different authors, however satisfying for their immediate purpose, do not prove very useful in the deeper analysis of the mind. They mostly suffer from the defect of not representing analysed data: it commonly happens, for example, that what has been labelled as an innate instinct turns out on analysis to be a quite complicated product of more primary tendencies. Freud, therefore, renounced the use of the conventional classifications and contented himself with seeking first of all for two broad groups, the minute classification of which could be left till later. Even this preliminary sketching out of the field has proved to be more difficult than might perhaps have been anticipated, and he has had to pass by degrees from his first attempts to increasingly modified schemes. His success here has been distinctly more questionable than with most of his other generalizing work, *e.g.* with psychoneuroses, dreams, etc.; and this fact is itself an indication of how hard is the task. It is one I am dwelling on here because of its specially close connection with general biological problems. As Freud (1930) himself says: 'The whole of analytic theory has evolved gradually enough, but the theory of instincts has groped its way forward under greater difficulties than any other part of it. And yet a theory of instincts was so indispensable for the rest that something had to be adopted in place of it.' He began with the rough-and-ready division of the instincts into those concerned with self-preservation, of which hunger may be taken as the most typical example, and those concerned with preservation of the species, all of which he termed sexual instincts; the energy pertaining to the latter he designates as Libido. There was thus a contrast between the ego instincts and the libidinal instincts directed towards objects. Historically, the nature of the repressed impulses was examined by psycho-analysis before that of the repressing forces. Closer acquaintance with the latter made the conclusion unavoidable that the ego itself was also invested with libido. Freud termed this narcissistic libido to distinguish it from object-libido, but the two are interchangeable in fact and probably identical in nature. The complication thus introduced somewhat confused the previously clearly cut distinction between ego and object instincts. Jung solved the difficulty by refusing to recognize any distinction between different instincts, and applied the term Libido to all mental energy. Freud, however, did not believe that all instincts could be of the same nature, being probably influenced in this attitude by the deep impression he had received from the facts of mental conflict. He therefore sought for a wider conception than his earlier dichotomy and achieved it in a very original manner, which is still the subject of much dispute; it represents Freud's personal views and has not yet been confirmed and accepted by the general body of psycho-analysts. Certain clinical observations made him suspect that the function of all instinctual activity is to bring about the reinstatement of an earlier condition; this he termed the 'repetition compulsion'. Taking together this conclusion and the correspondence between the pleasure-pain principle and the Fechner stability law, he drew the logical inference that the ultimate goal of instinct must be to reinstate the earliest condition, namely, inanimate matter. From this general law, however, of instinctual activity tending to dissolve the complex into the simple, and ultimately the living into the dead, the organic into the inorganic—a law which could perhaps also be followed into the realm of physics itself—he exempts one set of instincts, the sexual. He thus reaches a new dualism in the contrast between instincts tending towards death and those tending towards more life. Freud then uses this conception to explain many puzzling phenomena of both social and sexual life. He supposes that the death instinct, which is originally concerned with the individual, becomes directed outwards as an impulse towards destruction. Actually this is always fused with one particular, masterful component of the sexual instinct and the combination is familiar clinically in the mysterious tendencies called 'sadistic'. It is, indeed, possible that the directing outwards is brought about by the Eros or life principle as a means of overcoming, or at least countering, the dangerous death instinct (Thanatos). Whatever may be the final conclusion about the biological status of the supposed death instinct, there is ample evidence to show that the conflict between aggressive or destructive impulses on the one hand and those of friendliness and social cohesion on the other—shortly put, between hate and love—is by far the most important and fateful for human life. It is with the unravelling of the buried tendencies of these two sets, and the relation between them and the complexities of consciousness, that psycho-analysis is mainly concerned, and it has accumulated a vast mass of evidence to show how extensive are the ramifications of the conflict in question. It is plain that all this knowledge is a direct contribution to biology, for ultimately this conflict, and similar ones, must be reduced to purely biological terms. Further, if Freud's conception of a death instinct is substantiated, and it has previously been adumbrated also by biologists, *e.g.* Ehrenberg, then it cannot fail to be a signal contribution to the riddles of life.

While it cannot be said that psycho-analysis has proffered as yet an entirely satisfactory solution to the vexed problems concerning the nature and classification of the instincts, it has certainly provided a valuable method for the study of these problems and has already made important contributions in this field. The part of the field that was first explored by psycho-analysis was the sexual instinct, the reason for this being its central importance for the therapeutic problems of psychopathology. Probably it is through its contributions to sexuology that Freud's work is best known. Both the extensiveness and the startling nature of these contributions have brought them into such prominence as not only to obscure Freud's contributions in other fields but also to confuse the idea of his whole theory. Overlooking the central importance he attaches to the doctrine of conflict, critics commonly charge him with what is called 'pansexualism', *i.e.* with teaching that the mind contains no other motives or elements than sexual ones. To describe, or even to mention, his theory of sexuality is to invite the recrudescence of this panic-stricken accusation, but in this respect I find myself to-day in a fortunate position, for if there is any place where psycho-analytical views on sexuality may safely and legitimately be imparted it is surely before a Congress for Sex Research.

Perhaps the most important novelty in Freud's work on human sexuality was his discovery that it passes through a complicated development at two different periods of life. This entirely contradicts the popular view previously accepted by all psychologists to the effect that the sexual instinct suddenly appears in a fully fledged state at the time of puberty. Extensive investigations have shown, on the contrary, that the sexual instinct is not a simple thing that makes its appearance in a finished form, but that it has to undergo most surprisingly elaborate phases of development—not only once, but twice. The first time it does this is in early childhood, in the period reaching from the beginning of life to the end of the fourth year at latest. After this, relatively little further change takes place during what is called the latency period, from the fourth year to the time of mental puberty. At mental puberty the individual once more passes through a cycle of development on another plane, but the characteristic features of this cycle, the endless variations and modifications possible in it, are all repetitions of corresponding features in the first cycle. The individual features of the first cycle are produced by the interaction of the inborn constitution and the environmental influences, whereas the second cycle is much less influenced from without, being, as was just remarked, predetermined by the course of the first one.

With other animals than man the sexual instinct may become manifest early or late, but I think it would be hard to find among them any parallel for the extraordinary human feature I have just mentioned of a double development of the instinct. What the meaning of this distinctively human feature may be, and how far it may go in explaining the mental differences between man and other animals, are matters that open up fascinating problems.

A corollary of the conclusion just mentioned is that the first, fateful cycle of development occurs in relation to the immediate environment, and is therefore essentially an incestuous one. It is not surprising to hear that this consideration is closely connected with the deep conflicts, with the repression and the splitting of the mind to which I drew attention earlier in this paper, and also with the fact that the greater part, and often the whole, of this first sexual development becomes completely forgotten in later years. From the observations of comparative ethnology, the history of the development of law, the study of religions and many other sources, it is abundantly clear that the strongest and deepest taboos to which mankind is subject are those concerned with incest. There is good reason to think that the question of incest lies at the centre of all problems of guilt, of remorse, of condemnation, of sin, and ultimately of the whole of morality and religion. To those investigators who had recognized this it had long been a puzzle how incest could play this important part in generating so many reactions when there was so little evidence of any conflict on the matter. The complicated laws and moral reactions were of such a kind as to postulate the strongest temptation towards incest which had to be kept sternly in check, and yet little could be observed of any such temptation—on the contrary, there seemed to be either indifference or a natural aversion which would render the existence of all these moral reactions superfluous. Freud's finding that the first cycle of sexual development is essentially incestuous, and that it leads to the strongest possible mental conflict, completely solves this puzzle by showing that the positive urge towards incest which any unbiased thinker—had such a person existed—would have had to postulate from the known facts of moral condemnation, does really exist, but in a form invisible to consciousness.

It would be natural to think that the repression into the unconscious of these early incestuous trends was due to the condemnation, either inherent or traditional, that attaches to them. The matter proves, however, to be not so simple. There is reason to suppose that the condemnation itself arises in relation not to incest *qua* incest, but to a peculiar feature that necessarily accompanies any incest situation. I refer to the rivalry with the parent of the same sex over the loved object. It is this rivalry that has such fateful consequences and which makes incest so different from other forms of sexuality. One has to remember that it takes place at a time of life when the rivalry has features never present in any later situation. These are as follows: in the first place the rival enormously surpasses the infant in all possible manifestations of power, so that the latter is, in the nature of things, doomed to defeat; secondly, the rival is also a loved object, and one on whom, moreover, the infant depends for the fundamental necessaries of existence; in the third place, the infant's sexual impulses and other instincts happen at this time to be in a stage characterized by insatiable sadism and aggressivity, so that the retaliatory punishments it fears are of a correspondingly terrifying nature. Further, the child's physical state and imperfect sexual organization in themselves exclude the possibility of its desires being gratified even if the external situation were more favourable to them, and this simple fact unites with that of the external rivalry in various complicated ways. Investigation of the hidden part of the child's mental life makes one realize that it is faced with well-nigh insoluble problems, and just at an age when it is least capable of dealing with them. It is a biological problem of the first order to explain how it comes about that human offspring should be born with adult desires and with less capacity for gratifying them than any other animal, so that it has to distort its mind in the endeavour to deal with them and to learn painfully to repress them and to postpone for many years their re-emergence, only to find itself even then presented with a fresh set of difficulties.

The precise nature of the development of the early sexual cycle is a much more complex affair than might be supposed, and I propose here to call attention only to certain outstanding features in it. The development can conveniently be described either in terms of the relation between subject and object or in terms of the impulse itself. From the former point of view one distinguishes three main phases, the auto-erotic, the narcissistic, and the phase of object love. The auto-erotic phase is characterized by an absence of any relation between subject and object, for both the sources of stimulation and of gratification are mainly confined to the infant's own body; it is improbable that the infant distinguishes even between those emanating from its own body and those really emanating from without, for the feeling of undivided selfness must dominate its conception of the world at this stage. In the narcissistic stage that supervenes on the auto-erotic, a certain organization is beginning to appear, and the infant takes its own body as a definite object on which to expend its desires and affections. The final phase, that of object love, is itself divided into two, according as the attitude to the external source of interest is a partial one, confined to the sexual organs, or a total one in which the personality of the other person is taken into account.

In describing the development in terms of the impulse itself, one would point out that it is, to begin with, much more diffuse than the adult one, and that it seems to arise first in conjunction with the great primary needs of life, being, in fact, stimulated by the functioning of these. Thus the earliest manifestation of all is to be found in connection with the act of feeding, particularly at the breast, and this itself has two fairly distinct phases, the sucking and biting phases respectively. The next stage in development is also associated with a primary bodily function, that of excretion. Any serious investigation of childhood will reveal the important part excretory acts play in infantile sexuality, but it was reserved for psychoanalysis to demonstrate not only its complexity, but more especially the astonishing influence the manifold reactions to it have in determining later character traits. Side by side with these sensory contributions to sexual excitation go those provided by the special senses. Here, however, the earlier ones, proceeding from the senses of smell, taste, and hearing, are soon eclipsed by the powerful ones derived from the sense of vision, which then bifurcate into the pleasure in seeing and the pleasure in being seen. It will be noticed that in this description one is dissecting the sexual instinct, or—more accurately—one is regarding it as being built up out of a number of components which can, to a great extent, be viewed as distinct units. There are reasons for surmising that these units, even if not absolutely primary in nature, are independently variable and that probably they are hereditary. Perhaps the most interesting of these component impulses, as they are called, and certainly the one that gives rise to the most trouble in the course of development, is the sadistic one. The origin of this is probably in muscular activity, including muscle sensations. Indications of it can plainly be traced to the second phase of the oral stage, so that the name of 'cannibalistic' has been given to it. It becomes much more prominent during the following, excretory stage, at which other sexual interests and impulses are so subordinate that it is commonly known as the 'anal-sadistic stage'. The precise relation between this sadistic component of erotism and the aggressive, hate or 'death' instincts furnishes one of the most obscure and fascinating problems of psychoanalysis. The relationship is undoubtedly an extremely close one, so much so that a considerable amount of actual fusion takes place between the two instincts, making often the discrimination between them a matter of the very greatest difficulty.

So far, no mention has been made in this account of the genital organs themselves, and indeed the evidence goes to show that they play relatively little part until the second year of life. It is not until the third, or even the fourth, year that they attain the primacy they normally maintain thereafter. The first phase of genital development is called the phallic one, because of the prominent part that the penis, or in the female the homologous clitoris, plays in it. The masculine attitude implied by this would appear to be normal in both sexes, though undoubtedly it is commonly reinforced in the female by purely neurotic reactions. The second phase is the fully developed one and, as was mentioned above, no further changes of importance take place until the age of puberty, when a second course of development is entered on that follows in a modified form the path of the first course with its individual variations.

PSYCHO-ANALYSIS AND BIOLOGY

I should like to preface what I have to say on the vexed question of bisexuality and homosexuality with the remark that the experience of psycho-analysis shows it to be by far the most difficult problem to envisage impartially of any in the whole field of depth psychology. Even the resources of psycho-analysis, with its unique power of undermining bias and also of obtaining otherwise inaccessible data, have not yet been equal to achieving conclusions that are satisfactorily objective, and as for workers in other fields—sociology, ethnology, and so on—one can only say that their attempts at sex impartiality are often quite lamentable. The memory of several important books on genetics impels me to express the friendly advice to biologists that generalizations on the subject of sex differences, particularly among humanity, are the surest invitations to subjectivity that exist. One fundamental difficulty here is the obvious consideration that every one of us is either male or female, is from the beginning an interested observer in a matter that is fraught with the deepest prejudices. Broadly speaking, and with many exceptions, the tendency of men is to lay stress on the extent of sex differences, and for women to minimize them. Freud himself postulates an original bisexuality in both male and female, but, while most psycho-analysts have uncritically accepted this hypothesis, there is reason to think that it deserves more scrutiny and definition than it has hitherto received. What I think can be asserted with sureness is that in the deeper layers of the mind far more bisexuality exists than is generally supposed. But the difficulty in the way of making a final estimate here is the indubitable fact that so much of this deep bisexuality, or—to speak more accurately — of the homosexual part of it, is quite secondary in nature. In the tremendous conflicts over the infantile incest, familiarly known as the

Oedipus complex, the most potent defence against the dangers associated with it is the development of what may be called an inverted Oedipus complex; that is to say, the boy develops a feminine attitude in respect of his parents, and the girl a masculine one. For certain reasons, ultimately connected with physiological differences, the inversion produces more positive and visible effects among women and is much more readily accepted by their ego, but this is by no means the same as saying it is more extensive with them than with men. In neither sex is the correlation between the amount of mental inversion present, and the signs of physical hermaphroditism at all close, a fact which is also suggestive of the secondary nature of much of the inversion.

At present the most important work being carried out in psycho-analysis is the endeavour to elucidate the precise connections between sexuality on the one hand and the attitudes of fear, guilt, and hate on the other.[1] The interrelationships here are quite extraordinarily involved, and it is impossible for me to present such obscure problems in the space at my disposal. I mention them only to indicate how much psycho-analytic work deals with the unravelling of the instincts. It has been established that, of the attitudes in question, that of guilt is the least primary, but even here the possibility of an inherited tendency is not to be altogether excluded. That the non-gratification of sexual impulses is inherently connected with reactions of fear and hate is also quite certain, though the precise chronological relationship and also the physiological correlates remain to be elucidated.

After presenting this exceedingly sketchy account of psycho-analytic work, I shall now ask you to consider a

[1] See my paper, 'Fear, Guilt, and Hate', chapter xiv of *Papers on Psycho-Analysis*, 5th edition 1948.

few of the respects in which the conclusions reached by means of it would appear to have a bearing on ordinary biological problems.

The most obvious are those respects in which psycho-analysis has made direct contributions to the biology of the mind, *i.e.* to our understanding of the biological forces operative in the mind. This is a question of an enormous mass of detailed work on the complex action and interaction of the deeper instinctual strivings from which our manifold conscious mental processes are derived. More important even than this detailed work, however, is the promise psycho-analysis can hold out of future developments, from which it is reasonable to hope that we shall be in a position to describe the whole of the mind in terms of processes derived from tendencies and reactions already known to be operative among the 'lower' animals. No informed person doubts any longer that the processes at work in the human body are of the same kind as those belonging to other animals, and that a continuity of development must exist between both. Those who have instinctively resisted this conclusion—and I am sure that unexpressed reservations exist in respect of it more commonly than is sometimes supposed—have been able to find support in the fact that hitherto no serious attempt has been made to apply the doctrines of evolution to the mind as a whole. In Darwin's day there was not sufficient knowledge to sustain his tentative efforts in this direction, and Huxley, on being faced with the problem of ethics, definitely recoiled from the task. When, some twenty years ago, I termed Freud the 'Darwin of the mind'[1] I meant by this to convey my opinion that in his investiga-

---

[1] I am far from being alone in this estimate. Geoffrey West, for instance, in his *Charles Darwin* (page 317) has the passage, 'In the very deepest sense, Darwin was Newton's successor, as Freud his'.

tions the genetic principles of evolution were for the first time being worked out in the sphere of the mind. The great strongholds of the opponents have always been the seeming fact that religion and morality, and to a less extent the manifestations of awe, wonder, and aesthetics are distinctive characteristics of man that fundamentally separate him from the rest of creation. Psycho-analysis, however, has already been able to throw such light on the genesis of these mental attitudes as to make it probable that, before long, we shall be able to demonstrate a complete continuity between them and the instinctual reactions from which other more mundane mental processes are already seen to be derived. We are beginning to understand how even the most complex of our mental processes are nothing but elaborated reactions to stimuli, proceeding either from the environment or from inner vital needs which can be shown to represent the inherited instincts.

In the second place, I am persuaded that the application of psycho-analysis in the way of practical personal experience would be a form of training that would equip a biologist for his work in a peculiarly valuable degree. All our thinking is hampered and deflected by the influence of quite unconscious processes, and it is safe to predict that the first competent biologist who takes the trouble to purify his thinking from these influences by means of psycho-analysis will be in a unique position to further the science of biology. I have mentioned above two respects in which it is specially difficult to secure unbiased thought in biological work, namely, in problems to do with incest, *i.e.* inbreeding, and with sex differences; but the same principle is in more subtle ways valid over a much larger field.

In the third place, and finally, one may raise more diffidently the question whether any of the conclusions reached by psycho-analysis in the mental sphere are susceptible of direct transference to the somatic sphere with which biologists are usually concerned, or whether they may not at least serve as suggestions for possible investigation. Ferenczi (1924), for instance, in a stimulating—though at times over-speculative—book which deals with the application of psycho-analysis to biology, has pointed out that the extraordinary plasticity of the mental manifestations of instinctual activity as revealed by psycho-analysis cannot but make one think that the same may be true of its somatic manifestations. By plasticity in this context is meant the displacements and transferences of mental energy that play such an astonishing part in the unconscious mind. The phenomena of hysterical conversion have shown us that this displacement can take place not only from one mental process to another, but also from the psychical to the physical. Ferenczi, in his conception of 'amphimixis', has extended this conception to the transferences and fusions of energy that appear to take place between two or more erotogenetic zones of the body, and he has plausibly suggested that similar displacements may occur within the purely somatic functioning.

Brun (1923), in an important work based on experimental observations, chiefly on ants, has reviewed a great part of the psycho-analytical theory from the point of view of biological parallels. He discusses also the facts of displacement, compares the phenomenon of regression—that reversion to earlier modes of function so common in the unconscious—with that of atavism, and raises the whole question of conflicts between instincts that is the central point of the psycho-analytical theory. With such conflicts he was able to establish the same law as holds good in the mind, that—provided there is no quite exceptional stimulation of the latter—it is the newly acquired instincts that normally obtain a supremacy over the older ones, an unexpected discovery for which the theoretical explanation is still lacking; we must have here the biological precursor of what in psycho-analysis is called 'repression'. Miss Searl (1930) has recently carried his work further by reviewing the broad conflict between ego, *i.e.* reality, and libido forces throughout a wide range of biological facts, and has drawn an instructive contrast between the two ways in which animals have sought to achieve supremacy of the former over the latter—the method of canalizing the libido into fixed seasons as compared with that of utilizing a part of it to strengthen the ego in the manner so distinctive of human psychology; she connects the greater emancipation of man, as compared with woman, from the earlier method with differences in the ego development in the two sexes.

From the field of heredity I will select two considerations. The investigation of the enormously important question of mental inheritance has always been hampered by the difficulty of knowing with certainty whether the thing measured is a primary mental element or a complex product of developmental processes, and the endeavours to enlist mathematics as a device for circumventing the difficulty do not carry entire conviction. By means of psycho-analysis one is enabled to dissect and isolate mental processes to an extent not previously possible, and this must evidently bring us nearer to the primary elements, to the mental genes in terms of which genetic investigations can alone be carried out. So far, the simplest processes we have reached are the activities of the various erotogenic zones of the body; it is certain that these vary with different individuals, and there is some evidence hinting that this variation is hereditary. The other consideration is that when psycho-analytic methods are applied to data obtained from savage races and from mythology and archaeology, it becomes difficult to resist the conclusion that there is an extensive resemblance between the phantasies and mental peculiarities of our young children and what one must infer to have been characteristic of the race as a whole in primitive times; the ideas of cannibalism, of incest, and of father-murder are prominent among the many I am referring to. Freud himself views these conclusions, perhaps rather uncritically, in the Lamarckian manner, but plainly it is for the biologists to furnish a final explanation of them. The important point is that we have extensive evidence strongly suggesting a connection between infantile mental development and early racial experiences. I am well aware that the old Haeckelian formula of ontogeny repeating phylogeny is much too simplistic for current biological thought, but the facts themselves remain in wait of some explanation. Altogether the extent to which the mind is dominated by the past is an impressive finding in psycho-analytic work; it is not merely that the mind reverts with astonishing ease to older habits and modes of functioning, but that these past activities still remain active beneath the layers of more developed forms of thought. We are persuaded that this is true not only of the past of the individual, but also of the race, and it may well prove, as Ferenczi has suggested, that somatic processes also are dominated to a much greater extent than we now know by their ancestral history; in pathology, for instance, the reversion of tissues to embryonal types is familiar—the grim secret of cancer must evidently lie here; but that the whole process may prove to be ultimately a physico-sexual one is a suggestion that psycho-analysis cannot refrain from offering on the basis of its experience with the mind.

Perhaps, however, the most far-reaching consideration

for biologists that emerges from psycho-analytical work is the possibility of having to supplement the principle of survival value as the sole criterion of living processes. I am aware that many biologists have themselves questioned the monopoly of this principle, and even its very validity, but I am concerned here only with possible contributions from the side of psycho-analysis. From three points of view Freud has suggested that principles may be at work in living organisms quite independently of utility or survival value to either the individual or the race. In his principle of repetition-compulsion, for example, the idea is that there exists a tendency towards the repetition of previous experiences and the reinstatement of earlier conditions which is of no obvious value to the organism and which serves no function of heightening pleasure or avoiding pain. He even thinks it likely that this principle may be at work in every instinct, side by side, of course, with its other functions. Personally I find it difficult to isolate this principle completely and to be sure that one has excluded all possibility of other functions being subserved by the processes he cites as examples of it; it is, in any case, a matter in need of further elucidation. A similar remark applies to the supposed death instinct, which was considered earlier in this paper, and also to the relationship between it and the repetition-compulsion.

We appear to stand on firmer ground in a third case, that of the pleasure-pain principle. This case has been well argued by Brun, in what was the first specific contribution to the relation between psycho-analysis and biology, and also by Ferenczi in the book already referred to. Biologists have endeavoured to subordinate the data of the pleasure-pain series to the utility principle by pointing to the more successful performance of a function when it is accompanied by pleasure, as well as to the undeniable fact that most examples of the pleasure-pain series occur in direct association with functions of value to either the individual or the species. But it is very doubtful if this covers the ground. In the first place, one is justified in exercising scepticism in this sphere because of what one knows of the extremely subtle ways in which puritanical motives can discredit the importance of pleasure if any possible utilitarian explanation can be found. To make my meaning clear, I will take a crass example. In the endeavour to paint the sexual impulses as nothing but an urge towards reproduction, it is customary to gloss over a number of very awkward facts. The sexual nature of the manifestations that do not fit into the theory can be extensively denied, as with the sexuality of childhood, which is so obviously remote from reproductive motives, or else dealt with by abusing the concept of 'play'. Or, as with so-called perverse impulses, they can be ascribed either to 'disease', whatever that may mean in this context, or to original sin, in both of which cases the biologist is exempted from considering them in connection with the functioning of instincts. In extreme cases the world is even exhorted to substitute the decision to procreate for the desire to obtain pleasure. But, as I say, while it is relatively easy to exclude motives acting so crudely as this, it is far from easy to exclude more subtle and unconscious influences of a similar origin. To return to the facts. There can be little doubt that it is exceedingly hard to bring under the head of the utility principle many of the examples of functioning that have been revealed by psychoanalysis, and it has furnished enough evidence at least to justify the reopening of the question whether the pleasure-pain principle may not be a completely independent one. Ferenczi has argued that this must apply to somatic processes as well as to mental ones, and Brun has sought for confirmation of the principle within the field of animal biology. Basing himself on Wasmann's work, in spite of Wheeler's critical objections to Wasmann's conclusions, he considers that the observations and experiments in the field of symphilia among ants prove the existence not merely of acquired habits but of definitely inherited instincts the functioning of which is dictated solely by the search for pleasure. Not only are these symphilic instincts of no value to either the individual organism or the species, but they are so dangerous to welfare as actually to threaten the extinction of various species; how many of the innumerable species of animals have died out as the result of similar disharmonies between the pleasure and the reality impulses can, of course, never be known, but that many may have is a possibility well worth considering.

I will bring this paper to an end by repeating the thesis with which I began, namely, that psycho-analysis has at long last forged a link between psychology and biology, and by expressing my conviction that this link will in the future prove to be of inestimable practical as well as theoretical importance.

REFERENCES

BRUN, R. (1923). 'Selektionstheorie und Lustprinzip' (Betrachtungen anlässlich der Lektüre von Erich Wasmanns Monographie über die Gastpflege der Ameisen), *Internationale Zeitschrift für Psychoanalyse*, vol. ix, p. 183.

— (1926). 'Experimentelle Beiträge zur Dynamik und Ökonomie des Triebkonflikts (Biologische Parallelen zu Freud sTrieblehre)', *Imago*, vol. xii, p. 147.

FERENCZI, S. (1924). 'Versuch einer Genitaltheorie', especially pp. 111-113.

FREUD, SIGM. (1930). 'Civilisation and Its Discontents', English Translation, p. 94.

SEARL, MISS. (1930). 'The Roles of Ego and Libido in Development', *International Journal of Psycho-Analysis*, vol. xi, pt. 2, p. 125.

XIII

THE PROBLEM
OF PAUL MORPHY[1]

A CONTRIBUTION TO
THE PSYCHOLOGY OF CHESS

PAUL MORPHY was born at New Orleans on June 22, 1837; he had a sister six and a half years older than himself, one two and a quarter years younger, and a brother two and a half years older.[2] His father was a Spaniard by nationality, but of Irish descent; his mother was of French extraction.

When Paul was ten years old his father, who was himself no mean player, taught him chess. In a year or two he proved himself the superior of his elder brother Edward, his father, his mother's father, and his father's brother who was at that time the chess king of New Orleans. A game is preserved which, according to an eye-witness, he is said to have played victoriously against his uncle on his twelfth birthday while blindfolded. At the same age he played against two masters of international renown who happened to be in New Orleans at the time. One of these was the famous French player Rousseau, with whom he played some fifty games, winning fully nine-tenths. The other was the Hungarian master Loewenthal, one of the

[1] Read before the British Psycho-Analytical Society, November 19, 1930. Published in the *International Journal of Psycho-Analysis*, January 1931.
[2] As the dates of their birth are not given in any of the biographies, I may usefully mention them here: Mahrina, February 5, 1830; Edward, December 26, 1834; Paul, June 22, 1837; Helena, October 21, 1839.

half-dozen greatest living players; of the two games played the young Paul won one and the other was drawn. After this period, little serious chess was played for some eight years while he was pursuing his studies; his father allowed him to play occasionally on Sundays, but with the exception of Judge Meek, the President of the American Chess Congress, against whom he played and won six games when he was seventeen years old, he encountered only much inferior opponents. His uncle had by then left New Orleans for the West, Rousseau was otherwise absorbed, and Paul's brother, father, and grandfather had abandoned chess when he was in his teens, so the statement that has been made is probably true that in these years he never met anyone to whom he could not give a rook, consequently no one from whose play he could learn anything. In 1851 the first International Chess Tournament had taken place, at which Anderssen emerged as victor, and in 1857, when Morphy was just twenty years old, one was held in New York. He easily gained the first place, losing only one game out of seventeen, and during his stay in New York played a hundred games with the best players there, losing only five of them. In circumstances which will engage our attention presently, he visited London and Paris in the following year and his prodigious feats there read like a fairy tale. He not only defeated every champion he could induce to meet him, including Anderssen himself, but also gave several astounding exhibitions of simultaneous blindfold play against eight picked players, winning the large majority of the games. Towards the end of his stay in Paris he defeated blindfold the whole of the Versailles Chess Club playing in consultation. On his return to New Orleans he issued a challenge to play anyone in the world at odds. On receiving no response to this he declared his career as a chess player—which had lasted barely eighteen months, comprising actually only six months of public play—finally and definitely closed.

Of the actual quality of Morphy's play we shall have something to say later, but for the moment it will suffice to say that many of the most competent judges have pronounced him to have been the greatest chess player of all time. After his extraordinarily premature retirement he took up the practice of law, his father's profession, but although he possessed much skill in the work he was unsuccessful in practice. He gradually relapsed into a state of seclusion and introversion which culminated in unmistakable paranoia. At the age of forty-seven he died suddenly of 'congestion of the brain', presumably apoplexy, as his father had before him.

The evident problem arises of what relation, if any, his tragic neurosis bore to the supreme activities of his life, activities for which his name will always be remembered in the world of chess. It was popularly believed that the excessive preoccupation had affected his brain, but his biographers, who were naturally chess enthusiasts and zealous for the credit of their beloved pursuit, asserted with conviction that this was in no way responsible. Nevertheless, with our present knowledge we should find it impossible to believe that there was not some intimate connection between the neurosis, which is necessarily concerned with the kernel of the personality, and the superb efforts of sublimation which have made Morphy's name immortal. In contemplating this problem, let us begin with some reflections on the nature of the sublimation in question.

The slightest acquaintance with chess shows one that it is a play-substitute for the art of war, and indeed it has been a favourite recreation of some of the greatest military leaders, from William the Conqueror to Napoleon. In the contest between the opposing armies the same principles of both strategy and tactics are displayed as in actual war, the same foresight and powers of calculation are necessary, the same capacity for divining the plans of the opponent, and the rigour with which decisions are followed by their consequences is, if anything, even more ruthless. More than that, it is plain that the unconscious motive actuating the players is not the mere love of pugnacity characteristic of all competitive games, but the grimmer one of father-murder. It is true that the original goal of capturing the king has been given up, but from the point of view of motive there is, except in respect of crudity, no appreciable change in the present goal of sterilizing him in immobility. The history of the game and the names for it are of confirmatory interest here. Authorities seem to be agreed that the game originated in India, passed from there to Persia, whose Arabian conquerors transmitted it to Europe nearly a thousand years ago. Its first name, from which all others are derived, was the Sanscrit one of *chaturanga*, literally four members. This was also the Indian word for 'army', probably because of the four components of elephants, chariots, horse, and foot. The old Persians shortened the name from *chaturanga* to *chatrang* and their Arabian successors, having neither the initial nor the final sound of this word in their language, modified it into *shatranj*. When it re-emerged into later Persian the unconscious must have been at work, for it had by then been shortened to *Schah*, an assimilation having evidently taken place with the Persian *Shah* = King; 'chess' thus means the royal game, or the game of kings. *Shah-mat*, our 'check-mate', German 'Schachmatt', French 'échec et mat', means literally 'the king is dead'. At least so the Arabian writers on chess thought, and most European authors copy them in this. Modern Orientalists, however, are of opinion that the word 'mat' is of Persian, and not of Arabian, origin, and that 'Shah-mat' means 'the king is paralysed, helpless, and defeated'. Again, from the point of view of the king it makes very little difference.

In the Middle Ages an interesting innovation was introduced into the rules of chess which deserves incidental mention. By the side of the king stands another piece who was originally his counsellor, Persian *firz* (Turkish *vizier*). As his main occupation was supposed to be, not fighting, but advising and defending, he was in action the weakest piece on the board, his only move being one square diagonally. In the Middle Ages he gradually changed his sex, thus passing through the same evolution as the Holy Ghost, and came to be known as the regina, dame, queen, and so on. It is not known why this happened. It was suggested by Freret, an eighteenth-century writer on chess, that a confusion must have arisen between the words 'fierge', the French for *firz*, and 'vierge'. It has more generally been thought that as this used to be the only piece for which a pawn could be exchanged on reaching the eighth square, when it was sometimes called 'un pion damé', this circumstance led to its being given the same name as the French one for draughts, *i.e. dames*. About the middle of the fifteenth century this change in sex was followed by a great increase in power, so that the piece is now stronger than any other two together. Whatever may be the truth, therefore, about the linguistic speculations I have just mentioned, it will not surprise the psycho-analyst when he learns the effect of the change: it is that in attacking the father the most potent assistance is afforded by the mother (= queen.)

It is perhaps worth remarking further that the mathematical quality of the game gives it a peculiar anal-sadistic nature. The exquisite purity and exactness of the right moves,[1] particularly in problem work, combine here with the unrelenting pressure exercised in the later stages which culminates in the merciless *dénouement*. The sense of overwhelming mastery on the one side matches that of unescapable helplessness on the other. It is doubtless this anal-sadistic feature that makes the game so well adapted to gratify at the same time both the homosexual and the antagonistic aspects of the son-father contest. In these circumstances it will be understood that a serious match places a considerable strain on psychical integrity and is likely to reveal any imperfections of character development. All games are apt at times to be marred by unsportsmanlike behaviour, *i.e.* by the sublimation undergoing a regression to its asocial origins, but with chess the strain is exceptionally great and is complicated by the circumstance that a specially high standard of correct demeanour is exacted.

It is interesting to compare with these psychological considerations some historical data on the way in which the game has been variously received by religious authorities. Van der Linde and Murray, the two greatest authorities on the history of chess, discuss sympathetically the Indian tradition that the game was invented by the Buddhists. It is certainly suggestive that the first mention of it occurs in connection with a stronghold of Buddhists. According to their ideas, war and the slaying of one's fellow-men, for any purpose whatever, is criminal, and the punishment of the warrior in the next world will be much worse than that of the simple murderer; hence—so runs the story—they invented chess as a substitute for war. In this they would appear to have anticipated William James's suggestion of providing war-like substitutes, one quite in

[1] Chess may well be called the art of the intellect.

accord with the psycho-analytical doctrine of the displacement of affects. In a similar vein St. J. G. Scott narrates a Burmese story to the effect that chess was invented by a Talaing queen who was passing fond of her lord and hoped by this distraction to keep him out of war. Ambivalence runs through the whole story, however, for the view has also been put forward that chess was invented by a Chinese mandarin, Han-sing, who wanted to amuse his soldiers when in winter quarters. A Ceylon legend has it that the game was invented by Ravan, the wife of the King of Lanka, in order to distract that monarch when his metropolis was being besieged. On the other hand, about the year 1000, a puritanical regent of Egypt, usually known as Mansar, issued an edict forbidding chess. In mediaeval times chess became widely popular, and the ecclesiastical attitude towards it appears to have been mainly negative. The statutes of the church of Elna, for example, lay down that clergy indulging in chess shall be *ipso facto* excommunicated. At the end of the twelfth century the Bishop of Paris forbade the clergy even to have a chess-board in their house; in 1212 the Council of Paris condemned it utterly; and, some forty years later, St. Louis, the pious King of France, imposed a fine on whoever should play the game. John Huss, when in prison, deplored having played at chess and thereby run the risk of being subject to violent passions.

In returning to the problem of Paul Morphy I shall begin with giving some description of his personal attributes and the characteristics of his play. In appearance he was small, only five feet four in height, with preternaturally small hands and feet, a slim, graceful figure, and a 'face like a young girl in her teens' (F. M. Edge). Falkbeer, who knew him, observed that he appeared younger than he really was, adding: 'One would certainly have taken him rather for a schoolboy on his vacation than for a chess adept who had crossed the Atlantic for the express purpose of defeating, one after another, the most eminent players the world then knew'. He had a very pleasing manner and a delightful smile. His demeanour was strikingly modest. On only two occasions was he known to invite anyone to play with him, and, with an uncanny intuition, he chose for these exceptions the two men, Staunton and Harrwitz, who were to exercise such a baleful influence on his life. He bore himself, even in the unpleasant controversy we shall presently relate, with the greatest courtesy and dignity. While playing he was very impassive, with his eyes fixed steadfastly on the board; opponents got to know that whenever he looked up, which he did without any exultation, it meant he could foresee the inevitable end. His patience seemed inexhaustible; Edge, his first biographer, records having watched the famous Paulsen spend an hour or two over a single move while Morphy sat calmly looking on without the slightest movement of uneasiness. He seemed insensitive to fatigue, and I will recall a story which illustrates his powers of endurance as well as two other features: his astounding memory—which, incidentally, he possessed also for music—and his capacity for sensorial imagery, a quality which links chess players with musicians and mathematicians. It is narrated by Edge, who was at the time acting as his secretary, and concerns an exhibition he was giving when just twenty-one at the Café de la Régence in Paris, then the Mecca of chess players from all over the world. He played blindfold eight games simultaneously against powerful opponents who, incidentally, were freely helped by advice from a crowd of expert players. It was seven hours before the first of them was defeated and the match lasted ten consecutive hours, during the whole of which time Morphy abstained from taking either food or even water. At the close there was a scene of terrific excitement, and Morphy had the greatest difficulty in extricating himself from the ovation in the streets and escaping to his hotel. There he slept well, but at seven in the morning he called his secretary and dictated to him every move in all the games, at the same time discussing with him the possible consequences of hundreds of hypothetical variations. It will be agreed that only a mind working with exceptional ease could have accomplished such an astounding feat. Nor was it an isolated achievement sustained by excitement. There are few more exhausting occupations than serious chess, and the number of those who can continue for more than three or four hours on end without feeling the strain is not very great. Yet Morphy has been known to play continuously from nine in the morning until midnight on many successive days without his play weakening in the least and without his showing any signs of fatigue. In psycho-analytical terms this must signify a very exceptional level of sublimation, for a psychological situation of such a degree of freedom can only mean that there is no risk of its stimulating any unconscious conflict or guilt.

It is not easy to describe Morphy's qualities as a player in other than general terms without presupposing a knowledge of chess technique. I hope that the generalizations I shall venture on will be in some measure trustworthy; we possess, at all events, ample data on which to found generalizations, for there survive some four hundred of Morphy's games, and an extensive literature has grown up of critical comments subsequent authorities have made on the individual moves.

To begin with, there are different styles of chess which depend partly on the temperament and aim of the player and partly on the conditions under which he is playing.

Speaking very roughly, it depends on whether one sets more store on winning or on not losing. In tournaments, for instance, where defeats are heavily penalized, it may pay to aim at a few victories and a number of draws rather than at more victories but more defeats. The two extremes are represented by a slashing but risky attack on the one hand and a tediously defensive stone-walling on the other. Naturally the ideal player combines the best from each attitude. He spends some time in fortifying his army, not so much for defensive reasons as to get them into the strongest position from which to deliver an attack. A player may excel in either of these activities, or his fortifying may have an almost purely defensive aim in which any opportunity for an attack comes rather as a piece of luck. In chess there are—if we omit the recent 'hyper-modern' play—two well-known styles, known as the combinational and the positional, which are sometimes said to correspond with the romantic and the classical temperaments respectively. At the period we are concerned with, about the middle of the last century, only the former existed and, indeed, the latter is essentially the product of the last fifty years. The main difference between the two methods, at least in its extreme form, may be likened to that between a cleverly designed attack in battle and a steady siege. The aim of the combinational method is to plan a skilful grouping of the pieces to make a co-ordinated onslaught on the king, whereas that of the positional method is the more cautious—but in the end sounder—one of gradually building up a fortified position and taking advantage of the slightest weakness in the opponent's position, wherever this may happen to be.

Now Morphy certainly possessed in the highest degree the gifts necessary for a master of combinational play, those of foresight, calculation, and power of divining his opponent's intentions. Some of his games are masterpieces in this respect which have rarely been equalled and, indeed, the popular impression of his style among chess players is that of vehement and victorious onslaught. One would therefore have anticipated with assurance that someone possessing such gifts, and whose brilliant performances were at such an early age, would have owed his success to an unusual genius in the qualities of intuition and adventurousness that might naturally be expected to appeal to youth. Yet the interesting thing is, and one that throws a good deal of light on Morphy's psychology, that he passed beyond this style and, in fact, ranks as the first pioneer of positional play—though it was Steinitz who later developed the principles of it. It was a fortunate coincidence that the only player in history whose genius in combinational play has equalled Morphy's was not only just at that time at the height of his career, but actually met Morphy in combat: I refer to Anderssen, till that moment the foremost player of the day and virtually the world's champion—though this title was not formally employed till a decade later. Murray says of the two men: 'Both were players of rare imaginative gifts, and their play has never been equalled for brilliance of style, beauty of conception, and depth of design. In Morphy these qualities blazed forth from sheer natural genius; in Anderssen they were the result of long practice and study.' Reti, in his *Modern Ideas in Chess*, has instructively explained that Morphy's famous victory over Anderssen was due, not to greater brilliance in the sense just indicated, but to his establishing the method of brilliance on a basis of the more mature positional play. It must have been a memorable scene to witness this slim youth overpowering the huge, burly Teuton of forty, not in the traditional fashion of the young hero overcoming a giant by more audacious imagination—for in this quality they were equally matched and equally unsurpassable—but by more mature depth of understanding. The interest of this observation for our purpose is the indication it gives that in Morphy's mind chess must have signified a fully adult activity, and success in it the serious occupation of a man rather than the rebellious ambition of a boy. I shall submit later that being shaken in this matter was one of the factors that led to his mental catastrophe.

Morphy was master of all aspects of the game in such a high degree, and was so free of mannerisms and individual peculiarities of style, that it is not easy to single out any particular characteristics. Chess, it is true, like all other games, is replete with unconscious symbolism. One could, for instance, comment on the skill he showed in attacking the king from behind or in separating the opposing king and queen; the latter, by the way, is illustrated in the first of his games ever recorded, which was played against his own father. But such details are not to our purpose, for pre-eminence in chess depends on a broad synthesis of exceptional qualities rather than on skill in any particular device or method. Careful consideration of the whole of Morphy's manner of play yields, I think, the indubitable conclusion that the outstanding characteristic he exhibited in it was an almost unbelievably supreme *confidence*. He knew, as if it was a simple fact of nature, that he was bound to win, and he quietly acted on this knowledge. When the Americans who had seen him play prophesied that, on meeting any European champion, he would, in the manner of Andrea del Sarto to Raphael, 'bring the sweat into that brow of his', chess players in Europe scoffed at the prediction as mere American bombast, and the only question in their minds was whether it was worth their leaders' while to play such a youngster. To anyone who knows what years of assiduous practice and rich experience go to attaining any degree of prowess in chess, nothing could seem more utterly unlikely than that a beginner embarking on this arduous path, as Paul Morphy was, should have the career he actually did on reaching Europe. Yet before he left his native town he calmly predicted his coming victories with the completest assurance. Such presumption might reasonably be regarded as megalomania were it not for the awkward fact that it was justified. On his return home, far from being flushed with pride, he remarked that he had not done so well as he should have, and in a sense this also was true, for when playing on a few occasions in a state of indisposition he was guilty of some weak moves that fell below his usual standard of play and even cost him a few games. It is not surprising that, endowed with such confidence in his powers, his play was marked by a boldness and even audacity in his moves that give at first the impression of being over-adventurous, and perhaps even of hazarding risks, until one perceives the sureness of the calculation behind them. His intrepidity was naturally more manifest when he had to do with relatively inferior players. Here he could behave with apparent recklessness, extravagantly flinging away one after another of his pieces until, with an unsuspected movement, his small remaining force would suddenly deliver the *coup de grâce*; on one such occasion he achieved the extraordinary feat of effecting a mate by simply castling. His boldness and his sense of how important position is in chess-playing are shown in two other characteristics for which he is well known: the extent to which he appreciated the value of developing the pieces early and continuously, and his willingness to make sacrifices to gain a better position. There is a story, perhaps apocryphal, that when he was a child he was so eager to bring his pieces forward that he regarded his pawns as a nuisance to be got rid of as soon as possible: how different from the great Philidor, who had declared pawns to be the very soul of chess! It is, at all events, quite fitting that the name 'Morphy opening' in chess has been attached to the following device. What is called the Muzio opening is characterized by a bold attack in which a knight is sacrificed in the fifth move so as to obtain what is believed to be a commensurate advantage in position. In the Morphy opening the same tactics are followed up by sacrificing a bishop also, so that it is sometimes known by the name of 'double Muzio'. Very few people indeed are to be found confident enough of their attack to be able to risk such grave initial losses. Even the defence named after him, the Morphy defence to the Ruy Lopez opening, one which is so valuable as to have been elaborated since into some twenty named variations, is the most aggressive of the manifold defences to this opening.

With Morphy, chess sense, if one may use such an expression, was far more innate than acquired. He had read a good deal, but gave away the book as soon as he had looked through it. He said himself that no author had been of much value to him, and that 'he was astonished at finding various positions and solutions given as novel—certain moves producing certain results, etc., for that he had made the same deductions himself, as necessary consequences' (Edge). MacDonnell, who watched his play in London, wrote later of it in his *Chess Life-Pictures*: 'I fancy he always discerned the right move at a glance, and only paused before making it partly out of respect for his antagonist and partly to certify himself of its correctness, to make assurance doubly sure, and to accustom himself to sobriety of demeanour in all circumstances'. The following story raises the whole question of the method employed in mental calculation. In the famous seventeenth move in the Four Knights' game with Paulsen on November 8, 1857, Morphy offered to exchange his queen for his opponent's bishop. Paulsen was naturally suspicious of a trap and carefully investigated the possibilities. After pondering on the situation for more than an hour, and detecting no trap, he accepted the offer and after eleven more moves had to resign. Years afterwards, Steinitz carried out a full analysis of the situation and maintained as a result of it that the future possibilities in the game were far too numerous and complicated for it to be conceivable that any human brain could calculate and predict them. It so happened that an onlooker had asked Morphy after the game was over whether he had been able to foresee the end of it from his famous move; to the question he returned the enigmatic answer: 'I knew it would give Paulsen a deal of trouble'. Steinitz was doubtless right in his conclusion so far as consciousness is concerned, but one wonders whether the so-called intuitive chess does not imply a special power of pre-conscious calculation. The experiments Milne Bramwell carried out showed that the subconscious capacity for arithmetical calculation, as tested in hypnosis, far exceeds the conscious capacity, and the same may well hold good for the computation of chess moves.

We may take it that this remarkable combination of capacity and confidence could not occur unless it was a direct representative of the main stream of the libido and was providing the best possible solution of any conflicts in the deepest trends of the personality. It follows that anything interfering with such an indispensable expression the personality would be likely gravely to endanger its integrity, and so indeed events proved. Our knowledge of the unconscious motivation of chess-playing tells us that what it represented could only have been the wish to overcome the father in an acceptable way. For Morphy, the conditions necessary for its acceptability were essentially three: that the act in question should be received in a friendly manner; that it should be ascribed to worthy motives; and that it should be regarded as a serious and grown-up activity. We shall see that each of these conditions was grossly violated on his fateful visit to Europe and shall try to trace the mental consequences of this. It is no doubt significant that Morphy's soaring odyssey into the higher realms of chess began just a year after the—unexpectedly sudden—death of his father,[1] which had been a great shock to him, and we may surmise that his brilliant effort of sublimation was, like Shakespeare's *Hamlet* and Freud's *Traumdeutung*, a reaction to this critical event.

I shall now consider the critical period of Morphy's life in more detail, and for this purpose shall find it necessary, in the first place, to introduce to those of you who are not conversant with the history of chess some of the most prominent figures of the day in that world. Six of these need to be mentioned in this context: four of them became friendly admirers of Morphy, the other two set him a psychological problem to which he was not equal.

First in order of time was Loewenthal, whom Morphy had already successfully encountered when a child. Loewenthal had made further progress since then, and in the Birmingham tournament that took place during Morphy's visit to England, in which the latter did not participate, he won the first place, although both Staunton and Saint-Amant were also competitors. In a match arranged between the two, Morphy decisively beat him, and Loewenthal became a firm friend and admirer, taking his side in the unfortunate controversy to which we shall

[1] This occurred on November 22, 1856.

presently have to refer. He foretold that, after Morphy's games were published—a task which he himself successfully undertook later—the chess world would rank him above all other players living or dead. The stakes in the Loewenthal match were £100, and after winning, Morphy immediately presented Loewenthal with some furniture costing £120 for a new house he was taking. We shall repeatedly have occasion to note how fastidious Morphy was over the subject of money. Before he left America, for instance, when the New Orleans Chess Club offered to subscribe money to enable him to participate in the Birmingham tournament, he had refused—not wishing to travel as a professional chess player. Next comes Paulsen, an American, famous at that time for his amazing exhibitions in blindfold chess and later for winning two matches against Anderssen as well as for his important contributions to chess theory. He was Morphy's only serious rival at the New York tournament, and, from reading a couple of his published games he predicted on that occasion that Morphy would beat him; just before the tournament they played three games, blindfold, of which Morphy won two and drew one. Paulsen also became a devoted friend of Morphy. Saint-Amant was at that time the foremost player in France. He did not play any single-handed games with Morphy, but lost five and drew two of seven consultation games against him. He also became a fervent admirer, and said of his blindfold play that it was enough to make the bones of Philidor and La Bourdonnais rattle in their grave, without doubt the handsomest compliment a Frenchman could pay. The genial Anderssen we have already met. He was the best player living and was generally recognized to be the world's champion until his defeat by Steinitz some years later; he obtained a prize at each of the twelve tournaments he took part in and won the first place in seven of them. Mongredien, the president of the London Chess Club, said of him that he was, 'except Morphy, the most splendid and chivalrous player whom I have ever encountered', and his treatment of Morphy certainly confirms this estimate of him. Although his colleagues brought the greatest possible pressure to bear to prevent his impairing German prestige by going abroad to play a match with a youngster of no official standing, and in spite of his having no opportunity to practise beforehand, Anderssen made no excuses but travelled to Paris to meet his fate at Morphy's hands. Reproached afterwards for not having played so brilliantly as he had in his famous match with Dufresne, he made the generous rejoinder: 'No, Morphy wouldn't let me'.

Morphy's relations with these four men contrast sadly with his experiences of the two who will next concern us. Of these the more important was Staunton, and to explain his significance for Morphy a word must be said about the position he occupied. He was a man with a greater prestige than his tournament record would lead one to suppose. It is true that, by his victory over Saint-Amant, Horwitz, and Harrwitz in the 'forties, he could claim to be considered the leading player in the world, but he was not able to sustain this position, being beaten, for instance, in the London tournament of 1851 and the Birmingham one of 1858. He was, however, a great analyst; and the standard text-book that he wrote, together with his position as one of the first chess editors, made him the *doyen* of the English, if not of the European, chess world. In the middle of the last century England was easily paramount in chess, and perhaps this contributed to the reasons that made Morphy select Staunton as the antagonist he most wanted to meet; it was the wish to play against Staunton that was his main motive in crossing the Atlantic. In psycho-analytical language we may say that Staunton was the supreme father *imago* and that Morphy made the overcoming of him the test case of his capacity to play chess, and unconsciously of much else besides. A piece of evidence is extant which goes to show that this choice of father *imago* was far from being a recent one. At the age of fifteen Morphy had been presented with a copy of the games played at the first International Tournament of 1851, of which Staunton was the secretary. He took it on himself to write on the title-page: 'By H. Staunton, Esq., author of the *Handbook of Chess, Chess-Player's Companion*, etc. (and some devilish bad games)'. After Morphy's victory at the New York tournament some enthusiasts mooted the possibility of a European champion coming to America to play him. On hearing of this Staunton published a deprecatory paragraph in his weekly chess column and remarked that 'the best chess players in Europe are not chess professionals but have other and more serious avocations'. To hint that Morphy's chess was either a juvenile pastime or else a means of making money were innuendoes that must have wounded him to the quick, for there is ample evidence that he was morbidly sensitive to either suggestion. His New Orleans friends nevertheless issued a challenge to Staunton to come to America, which he not unnaturally refused, dropping, however, a broad hint that Morphy would find him at his disposal were he to come to Europe. Morphy crossed four months later, and, on being introduced to Staunton, at once asked him for a game. Staunton pleaded an engagement and followed this by a course of such ungentlemanly behaviour as to be explicable only on the score of neurotic apprehension; it was in fact said of him that he suffered from what was called 'nervous irritability'. For three months, during his stay in England and after, Morphy endeavoured, in the most dignified manner, to arrange a match, to which Staunton replied with a series of evasions, postponements, broken promises, and pretexts that his brain 'was overtaxed by more important pursuits'—not that the latter prevented him from participating in the Birmingham tournament in the very same month. Foiled in his hopes, Morphy laid the whole matter before Lord Lyttelton, the President of the British Chess Association, who made a sympathetic reply, and the matter rested at that. During this time, however, Staunton kept up in his chess column a steady fire of criticism of the man he avoided meeting, depreciating his play, hinting that he was a monetary adventurer, and so on. One sentence may be quoted from Morphy's final letter to him: 'Permit me to repeat what I have invariably declared in every chess community I have had the honour of entering, that I am not a professional player—that I never wished to make any skill I possess the means of pecuniary advancement'.[1] The whole episode led to an acrimonious wrangle in the chess world in which the large majority supported Morphy, and subsequent opinion almost unanimously regards Staunton's behaviour as totally unworthy of him. The effect on Morphy was immediate, and it showed itself in a strong revulsion against chess. As Sergeant, Morphy's latest and best biographer, writes, 'Morphy sickened of chess tactics—off the board. Is there any wonder?'

Towards the end of this episode Morphy crossed to Paris, where he at once approached Harrwitz, *le roi de la Régence*. This gentleman also does not appear in an amiable light in his dealings with Morphy, which were marked by morbid vanity and a total lack of chivalry (Sergeant). We need not go into the sordid details, which have been fully described by Edge, but the upshot was that Harrwitz with-

[1] F. M. Edge, *Exploits and Triumphs of Paul Morphy*, 1859.

drew from the match when he was being decisively beaten. Morphy at first refused to accept the stake, a sum of 290 francs, but on its being represented to him that other people would lose money unless his victory was officially sealed in this way, he assented, but devoted the sum towards defraying Anderssen's travelling expenses to Paris. Morphy's neurosis increased after this, and it was only temporarily abrogated by the pleasant episode of the match with Anderssen, the final flare-up of his chess fever.

Something should now be said about the reception Morphy's successes met with, for they were of such a kind as to raise the question whether his subsequent collapse may not have been influenced through his perhaps belonging to the type that Freud has described under the name of *Die am Erfolge scheitern* (those wrecked by success). I alluded earlier to the scene at the Café de la Régence on the occasion of the brilliant *tour de force* when Morphy successfully encountered eight strong players at once when blindfold; it was so tumultuous that soldiers ran up in the expectation that there was another revolution. Morphy became the lion of Parisian society, was entertained everywhere, politely allowed himself to be defeated at chess by duchesses and princesses, and finally left France in a blaze of glory, the culmination of which was a banquet at which his bust, made by a famous sculptor, was presented to him crowned with a laurel wreath. His reception on his return to New York, where patriotic fervour was added to the other enthusiasms, may well be imagined. It was widely felt that this was the first time in history in which an American had proved himself, not merely the equal, but the superior of any representative in his field drawn from the older countries, so that Morphy had added a cubit to the stature of American civilization, In the presence of a great assembly in the chapel of the

University he was presented with a testimonial consisting of a chess-board with mother-of-pearl and ebony squares and a set of men in gold and silver; he also received a gold watch, on which coloured chess-pieces took the place of the numerals. An incident that occurred at this presentation may be mentioned as illustrating Morphy's sensitiveness. Colonel Mead, the chairman of the reception committee, alluded in his speech to chess as a profession, and referred to Morphy as its most brilliant exponent. 'Morphy took exception to being characterized as a professional player, even by implication, and he resented it in such a way as to overwhelm Colonel Mead with confusion. Such was his mortification at this untoward event that Colonel Mead withdrew from further participation in the Morphy demonstration' (Buck). At the Union Club of New York he was presented with a silver wreath of laurels. He then proceeded to Boston, where a banquet was given in his honour at which were present, among others, Agassiz, Oliver Wendell Holmes, Longfellow, and Lowell; in a speech at this banquet Quincey made the witty remark: 'Morphy is greater than Caesar, because he came and without seeing conquered'. Shortly after this he was presented with a golden crown in Boston.

Adulation of this degree showered on a young man of twenty-one inevitably imposes a severe strain on his mental integrity, and one may well ask whether it did not play some part in the tragedy that followed. In this connection I should like to quote an interesting passage from the obituary notice written years later by Morphy's boyhood friend Maurian. Maurian ascribes the revulsion against chess—which, by the way, he does not associate with the subsequent mental derangement—to the completeness of Morphy's success, but in quite the opposite sense to that we have just indicated. He writes: 'Paul

Morphy was never so passionately fond, so inordinately devoted to chess as is generally believed. An intimate acquaintance and long observation enables us to state this positively. His only devotion to the game, if it may be so termed, lay in his ambition to meet and to defeat the best players and great masters of this country and of Europe. He felt his enormous strength, and never for a moment doubted the outcome. Indeed, before his first departure for Europe he privately and modestly, yet with perfect confidence, predicted to us his certain success, and when he returned he expressed the conviction that he had played poorly, rashly—that none of his opponents should have done so well as they did against him. But, this one ambition satisfied, he appeared to have lost all interest in the game.'

Before attempting to answer the question just raised, I think it well to finish the story itself and give some account of the later mental developments. On settling down in New Orleans Morphy's intention was to devote himself to the profession of law, of which he had an excellent knowledge. He found, however, that his now unwelcome fame as a chess player prevented people from taking him seriously as a lawyer, and this injustice preyed greatly on his mind. Buck, who had the assistance of Morphy's relatives in compiling the story of his later years, states that 'he became enamoured of a wealthy and handsome young lady in New Orleans and informed a mutual friend of the fact, who broached the subject to the lady; but she scorned the idea of marrying "a mere chess-player" '.

Within a year or two of his establishing himself in what he intended to be his serious permanent profession, the Civil War broke out, and Morphy was faced with the prospect of a real war interfering with his endeavour to substitute a peaceful occupation for his pastime of mock war.[1] His reaction was characteristic of the man who had built his mental integrity on converting hostile intentions into friendly ones—he hastened to Richmond, and in the midst of hostilities applied for a *diplomatic* appointment. This was refused, and soon after his return to New Orleans, his mother-town, it was captured by the Federal enemy. The Morphy family fled on a Spanish warship to Cuba, thence to Havana, Cadiz, and Paris. He spent a year in Paris and then returned to Havana until the war was over.

Already at that time his mental state could not have been at all satisfactory, for within a couple of years of returning to New Orleans his mother persuaded him to spend eighteen months in Paris, his third visit there, in the hope that the change of environment would restore him. His aversion to chess was by now so complete that he did not go near the scenes of his former triumphs.

Before long there manifested itself unmistakable evidence of paranoia. He imagined himself persecuted by people who wished to render his life intolerable. His delusions centred on the husband of his elder sister, the administrator of his father's estate, who he believed was trying to rob him of his patrimony. He challenged him to a duel, and then brought a law-suit against him, spending his time for years in preparing his case; in court it was easily shown that his accusations were quite baseless. He also thought that people, particularly his brother-in-law, were trying to poison him, and for a time refused to take food except at the hands of his mother or his (younger, unmarried) sister. Another delusion was that his brother-

[1] In the discussion of this essay Dr. Bryan and Miss Searl attached great importance to the effect of this episode on Morphy's mind, and I am inclined to agree with them; it may even have been the precipitating cause of the psychosis, as the London experiences certainly were of the neurosis.

in-law and an intimate friend, Binder, were conspiring to destroy his clothes, of which he was very vain, and to kill him; on one occasion he called in the latter's office and unexpectedly assaulted him. He was given to stopping and staring at every pretty face in the street, which I should ascribe to feminine identification. He was also passionately fond of flowers. I will quote one habit from this time, on which, however, I am unable to throw any light. During a certain period, according to his niece's account, he had a mania for striding up and down the verandah declaiming the following words: 'Il plantera la bannière de Castille sur les murs de Madrid au cri de Ville gagnée, et le petit Roi s'en ira tout penaud'. It sounds like a quotation, but, if so, I have not been able to trace it, nor can I explain the allusion. His mode of life was to take a walk every day, punctually at noon and most scrupulously attired, after which he would retire again until the evening when he would set out for the opera, never missing a single performance. He would see no one except his mother, and grew angry if she ventured to invite even intimates to the house. Two years before his death he was approached for his permission to include his life in a projected biographical work on famous Louisianians. He sent an indignant reply, in which he stated that his father, Judge Alonzo Morphy, of the High Court of Louisiana, had left at his death the sum of 146,162 dollars and 54 cents, while he himself had followed no profession and had nothing to do with biography. His talk was constantly of his father's fortune, and the mere mention of chess was usually sufficient to irritate him.

The problem we have set ourselves at the outset is: what relation did Morphy's chess career bear to his later mental disorder? Sergeant is at pains to demonstrate that mere preoccupation with chess could not be held responsible, and every medical and psychological expert can only confirm this opinion. His summary of the pathogeny of the disorder is so clear as to merit full quotation. 'Firstly, Morphy had some reason to be disgusted with, not chess, but chess-masters, whom he found of a very different character from himself. He set out, very young, generous, and high-spirited, recognizing, as he said himself, no incentive but reputation, and met not fellow-knights but tortuous acrobats of the pen, slingers of mud, and chess-sharpers. Granted he also met very decent gentlemen such as Anderssen, Loewenthal, and the majority of the leading amateurs in London and Paris. But the mean wounds inflicted by the other sort did not readily heal. Secondly, he always kept himself pure from any taint (as he rightly or wrongly imagined it to be) of professionalism in chess, yet was constantly being, if not called, at least looked on as a professional. And, lastly, he was ambitious in the career he had chosen for himself in life, and, failing in that through an unfortunate combination of circumstances, laid the blame upon chess. The disappointed ambition was assuredly a cause of Morphy's sad fate. . . . A supersensitive nature like his was ill-fitted to stand such trials.' How much Morphy strove to conceal his wound from himself may be seen from the following passage from his speech at the presentation made to him on his return to New York: 'Of my European tour, I will only say that it has been pleasant in almost every respect. Of all the adversaries encountered in the peaceful jousts of the checkered field, I retain a lively and agreeable recollection. I found them gallant, chivalrous and gentlemanly, as well as true votaries of the kingly pastime.'

Let me put the problem in another way. Was Morphy's mental derangement brought on by his very success or by his failure and disappointment? Was his situation that of

THE PROBLEM OF PAUL MORPHY

Browning's Pictor Ignotus, from whom the approach of supreme fame brought forth the cry:

'The thought grew frightful, 'twas so wildly dear!'?

Did he say to himself, like Andrea:

'Too live the life grew, golden and not grey,
And I'm the weak-eyed bat no sun should tempt
Out of the grange whose four walls make this world'?

Did he withdraw from the world with the disdainful consolation:

'At least no merchant traffics in my heart'?

Couched in more psychological language, was Morphy affrighted at his own presumptuousness when the light of publicity was thrown on it? Freud has pointed out that the people who break under the strain of too great success do so because they can endure it only in imagination, not in reality. To castrate the father in a dream is a very different matter from doing it in reality. The real situation provokes the unconscious guilt in its full force, and the penalty may be mental collapse.

I do not think the full explanation can lie here. We have to remember that in the aim most vital to Morphy he had not succeeded, but failed. We have seen how Staunton must have been to him the arch *imago*, and he had not managed to bring him to book. It was all very well to have shown himself to be the best player in the world, with a good presumption that he could have defeated Staunton also. But the cold fact remains that this arch-opponent eluded him. The dreaded father was not merely still at large, but had himself shown signs of unmistakable hostility. Morphy's aim had miscarried of dealing with this repressed hostility towards his father—and the fear of his father's towards him—by converting this into a friendly homosexual encounter. The following consideration gives, I think, a hint that Morphy himself was partly conscious of the failure of his aim. When he returned to New York he declared he would not play any American again except at odds, and this was doubtless justified in the circumstances. But when, a few weeks later, he reached the safety of his home in New Orleans he issued a challenge to play anyone in the world at odds of pawn and move, the only instance in his whole chess career of his probably over-estimating his powers.[1] I read this as indicating a psychological compensation for the underlying sense of having failed, and the anxiety this must have stirred in his unconscious.

There was, however, more than this. When Staunton eluded him he did so in a way that must have suggested to a sensitive person, as Morphy assuredly was, that his aim was accused of being a disreputable one. We know that mental integrity rests essentially on moral integrity, that mental stability can exist only so long as there is guiltlessness. It is impossible that Morphy could have displayed the capacities he did had not his gifts and mental functioning been free to be wholly concentrated on the tasks he set them. But this was so only as long as he could be relieved from any possibility of the counter-forces in his unconscious being stirred. He was at the mercy of anything that might do this. I have pointed out earlier how abnormally sensitive he was to any hint that his aims might not be received in a friendly manner, *i.e.* that they might be treated as if they were unfriendly themselves; to any suggestion that they did not proceed from the purest incentives, and particularly to the possibility of their being

[1] Against this, I admit, the fact might be brought forward that no less a master than Saint-Amant had maintained that 'Paul Morphy must in future give odds to every opponent'.

THE PROBLEM OF PAUL MORPHY

tainted by mercenary motives; and to any attitude that betrayed disdain for their juvenile nature.[1] Staunton bitterly wounded him in each of these three respects. His treatment of him was certainly the reverse of friendly— it is hardly an exaggeration to call it scurrilous; he practically accused him of being a penniless adventurer; and he finally avoided him on the plea that he had more serious, *i.e.* grown-up, matters to attend to. In the face of these accusations Morphy's heart failed him, he succumbed and abandoned the wicked path of his chess career. It was as if the father had unmasked his evil intentions and was now adopting a similarly hostile attitude towards him in turn. What had appeared to be an innocent and laudable expression of his personality was now being shown to be actuated by the most childish and ignoble of wishes, the unconscious impulses to commit a sexual assault on the father and at the same time to maim him utterly: in short, to 'mate' him in both the English and the Persian senses of that word. Obedient to his actual father's wishes he now engaged in the grown-up profession of law and discarded what he had been told was the childish preoccupation of chess.[2]

---

[1] How beautifully Morphy 'moralized' the pastime may be observed in the following passage from the speech already cited: 'It is not only the most delightful and scientific, but the most moral of amusements. Unlike other games in which lucre is the end and aim of the contestants, it recommends itself to the wise, by the fact that its mimic battles are fought for no prize nor honour. It is eminently and emphatically the philosopher's game. Let the Chess board supersede the card table and a great improvement will be visible in the morals of the community.'

[2] To quote again from the speech mentioned above: 'Chess never has been and never can be aught but a recreation. It should not be indulged in to the detriment of other and more serious avocations—should not absorb or engross the thoughts of those who worship at its shrine, but should be kept in the background, and restrained within its proper provinces. As a mere game, a relaxation from the severe pursuits of life, it is deserving of high commendation.'

But it was too late: his 'sins' pursued him. In the two things that comprise manhood, a serious career among men and the love of women, his chess past dogged and thwarted him. He was never able to escape from the 'sins' of youth and to take his place among the world of men. Little wonder that his abandonment of chess became increasingly complete, until he loathed the very name of it. The only recourse left to him in attempting to deal with his burden of guilt was to project it. In the delusions of being poisoned and robbed we recognize the oral- and anal-sadistic phantasies projected on to his sister's husband. His homosexual friendliness to men had broken down, and the antagonism underlying it lay exposed. This emerged in the direction of his brother-in-law, evidently a substitute for his brother, while the last anecdote of his life related above shows how he clung to the exaltation and veneration of his father, to whom was reserved the patriarchal privilege of 'making money'.

Perhaps a general conclusion emerges from contemplating this tragic story. It would seem to afford some clue to the well-recognized association between genius and mental instability. It may well be that Morphy's case is a general one. Genius is evidently the capacity to apply unusual gifts with intense, even if only temporary, concentration. I would suggest that this, in its turn, depends on a special capacity for discovering conditions under which the unconscious guilt can be held in complete abeyance. This is doubtless to be connected with the well-known rigour, the sincerity, and the purity of the artistic conscience. It is purchased, however, at the cost of the psychical integrity being at the mercy of any disturbance of these indispensable conditions. And that would appear to be the secret of 'artistic sensitiveness'.

The story also lends itself to a discussion of some

important psycho-analytical considerations which I have scarcely time here to adumbrate.

It will have been noticed that, for the sake of simplicity, I have throughout referred to Morphy's gifts as a mark of his capacity for sublimation, and the question may well be asked whether this is a just description of a disguised way of gratifying hostile, *e.g.* parricidal, impulses. In answer I would admit that the impulses behind the play are ultimately of a mixed nature, but the essential process seems to me to be a libidinal one. I conceive that the parricidal impulses were 'bound' by an erotic cathexis, actually a homosexual one, and that this in its turn was sublimated. The enormous value of the process to Morphy's mental health is evident from the considerations adduced above, and this I take to be an example of an important general law, namely, that the process of sublimation has ultimately a defensive function.[1] By discharging id energy along a deflected path, and particularly by transforming a sexualized aggressivity, it protects against the dangers to the ego which we know to proceed from excessive accumulation of that energy.

Finally, it is worth pointing out that when one speaks clinically of the 'breakdown of a sublimation' one really means the cessation of its defensive function. Morphy could play chess as well after as before his mental failure, as may be seen from his occasional games with Maurian; in most such cases, perhaps in all, the actual capacity acquired in the sublimating process remains intact in itself. What is lost is the ability to use this talent as a means of guarding against overwhelming id impulses, and this is really what patients are fearing when they express

[1] Dr. Glover expressed a similar conclusion in his recent paper before this Society: 'Sublimation, Substitution and Social Anxiety,' October, 1930.

the anxiety lest 'psycho-analysis will take their sublimations away from them'.[1]

[1] The original material on which this essay is based can mostly be traced through the bibliographical references given in the *Encyclopaedia Britannica* (11th and 14th editions), and P. W. Sergeant's *Morphy's Games of Chess* (1921). I am greatly indebted to Mr. Sergeant for his courtesy in placing at my disposal much unpublished material, including the manuscript of another forthcoming book by him on Paul Morphy. I am also obliged to Paul Morphy's niece, Mrs. Morphy-Voitier, of New Orleans, for kindly furnishing me with much useful information about him and the family.

XIV
PSYCHO-ANALYSIS AND MENTAL HYGIENE[1]

ADOPTING the view that psycho-analysis must have important bearings on the general subject of mental hygiene, you have invited me to give you some account of it. It is plain that, before discussing the applications of a branch of science, it is essential to know something about it, so I shall mainly confine myself to an exposition of it, the theme of its many applications to mental hygiene—in education, in child clinics, in general knowledge of mental prophylaxis, and probably even in the modifying of some of our social institutions—being too vast for the present occasion.

It has long been dimly realized, especially by moralists, that internal mental conflict is one of the most fundamental influences in man's life. It has often been shortly described as the conflict between the good and evil forces within him. Much, probably most, of the sufferings and unsatisfactorinesses of human existence proceed from this state of conflict, from the disharmony within man's mind. The essential purpose of religion itself is to deal with this conflict so that the better side of man's nature shall conquer the evil side and he thus attain to a state of happiness, clear conscience, and good behaviour. The success of religious endeavours in this direction has, however, been only very partial, and thought has turned—at first tentatively—towards science in the hope of obtaining a better solution of conflict.

[1] Summary of an address delivered before the National Council for Mental Hygiene on December 10, 1931.

By science we can here only mean psychology, the scientific study of the mind. For reasons that I need not go into here, psychology, however, has been in the past timorous and unhelpful in grappling with the problem. It has been reserved for a young branch of psychology, inaugurated by Professor Freud of Vienna, to face boldly the difficult and painful personal problems concerned in this matter of mental conflict. Being occupied, as a physician, with the alleviating of some of its more glaring manifestations, in the form of nervous disorders, he was impelled to seek out the meaning and causes of mental conflict in general. For the purpose of his work he devised a special technique that enabled him to explore hitherto unknown regions of the mind, the deeper layers of the mind which we now call the unconscious; whereupon two important conclusions soon emerged. In the first place, he came to realize that far more of human unhappiness in general and the unsatisfactorinesses of life proceed from this source than had ever hitherto been appreciated, and, in the second place, that the sources of mental conflict go far deeper into the roots of the personality than had ever been guessed.

This brings us to our present subject-matter, and the first question that naturally arises is: What exactly is meant by the word 'psycho-analysis'? It would take me far too long to tell you the numerous things that the word does not mean, but to which it has been wrongly applied. There can be few words which have been more extensively misused—a state of affairs which has wrought much harm. Instead I shall confine myself to what I judge to be the proper meaning of the word. It seems to me proper to use it in any one of the following three senses, but in no others:

1. The first sense in which the word 'psycho-analysis' was used was when it was coined by Professor Freud to

designate a special method of treatment for neurotic disorder. Freud had made the discovery that neurosis was dependent on the forcible separation of one part of the mind from the rest, and that it could be healed by bringing these two parts of the mind into harmony with each other. He uses the word 'repression' to indicate the process whereby one part of the mind is repelled and kept at a distance from the rest, particularly from consciousness. It is a little like the common process known as 'putting things out of one's mind', but it also applies to the *keeping out* of consciousness elements which in some way are dimly felt to be incompatible with it; these last elements, which are the important ones in the present connection, have therefore never been in consciousness.

The impulses repressed from consciousness are instinctively regarded as evil and dangerous. The strongest forces are therefore brought into play to keep them checked. All might be well if these forces of repression succeeded in their object, but unfortunately they do not always succeed. The repressed impulses find all sorts of ways of coming to indirect expression, and in their endeavour to break through they create very disturbing effects both on the individual and on the surrounding world. Neurotic disorder constitutes one of these disturbing forms of indirect expression; its presence indicates that the defences of repression are breaking down. Man instinctively recoils from the idea of opening up the mind and of releasing these repressed impulses into consciousness. He feels that to do so would be tantamount to giving them free rein, with terrible consequences in the way of immorality, licence, and cruelty. To the uninformed, therefore, psycho-analysis sounds like an attempt to take away the only remaining defences against these terrible impulses. In reality its aim is quite contrary to this. We know that, fortunately, there exist far better systems of self-control within the mind than the mechanical expedient of repression clutched at desperately during the painful early stages of development. The aim of psycho-analysis is to transfer the control of the mind from the crumbling and no longer successful defences of repression to the ego itself, and thus to place the individual in a psychological position of far greater security and self-control than he has ever been in.

There are many other methods of treatment than that of psycho-analysis. By whatever form they are called—suggestion, psychological discussion, 'individual psychology', hypnotism, etc.—they all have the central aim in common of maintaining the repressions intact, and, by strengthening or otherwise influencing them, to reinforce their restraint over the unconscious impulses. They therefore act in a diametrically opposite way to psycho-analysis, which recognizes that the limits of the repression defence have been reached and that more secure and suitable ones can be substituted for it.

So far as we can see, there are theoretically only these two alternative methods of treating nervous disorders. There are, of course, many forms of bad psycho-analysis, *i.e.* procedures used under that name which are not actually psycho-analysis at all. The British Psycho-Analytical Society, which trains students in the difficult technique, is confined in membership to persons who are properly qualified to practise psycho-analysis, and the British Medical Association recently decided that the term 'psycho-analytic treatment' should properly be reserved to the special technique used by members of that society.

2. The second legitimate use of the term 'psycho-analysis' is to denote the use of the special technique just referred to, for the purpose of making any scientific

investigation of the mind apart from therapeutic aims. So far, no other method has yet been devised for penetrating into the deeper layers of the mind (the unconscious mind) —layers which we consider are of great importance in their influence on the more accessible layers. These deeper layers are also the older ones, so that it may be said that psycho-analytic investigation is truly an inquiry into the genesis of the mind.

3. The term 'psycho-analysis' is also applied, and I think quite legitimately, to denote the body of knowledge obtained by the use of this method of investigation.

The most comprehensive conclusion reached by the use of psycho-analysis is the existence of a hitherto unknown region of the mind of which the individual is totally unconscious, the existence of which he does not even suspect, and which Freud therefore designated as the unconscious. However ready one may be to accept this conclusion, it is one which cannot be truly appreciated, or even realized in a proper sense of the word, without the person having himself had first-hand personal experience of the actual processes that go to make up the unconscious. I will nevertheless attempt to convey to you something more about the further conclusions reached in respect of this unknown region of the mind.

It would appear convenient to regard the mind as divided into two parts—the ego or self, and the rest of the mind, which is inaccessible to the ego, is out of harmony with it, and is therefore kept at a distance from it. No doubt originally these two parts were one, *i.e.* in the young infant, and there we may regard the mind as essentially a mass of primary urges which at first are of an impersonal nature, so that Freud has designated them by the impersonal term 'id'. As the ego develops, a considerable part of these primary urges are kept in repression away from consciousness, *i.e.* remain unconscious. Later on, another curious and important department of the mind develops, largely from the ego itself. It is called the 'super-ego', and among its many functions would appear to be the necessity of watching over and guarding the ego, so as to prevent it from yielding to any of the primitive id urges which are apprehended as being dangerous. If the child develops normally, the super-ego becomes the conscience, which is a healthy and useful mental institution. More often, however, this development is imperfect, and thus the super-ego retains its primitive character, which is of a savage and cruel nature. It is the effect of this cruel super-ego which gives rise to the morbid feelings of inferiority, impotence, sense of guiltiness, and fear. The sense of guiltiness, which plays a large part in psychology, has little or nothing to do with our social moral code, and may indeed be quite opposed to it. To give an example of this, paradoxical as it may seem, it is probably an excessive sense of guiltiness that often drives people to commit criminal acts, *i.e.* acts which are considered guilty in the usual social sense. Nevertheless, this irrational sense of guiltiness may impose a taboo over what might appear to be most harmless activities, such as speaking, walking, eating, etc., such interference with natural activities constituting neurotic symptoms. The code of the super-ego, derived from very early infantile defences against the fears aroused by id urges, is irrational, cruel, and, above all, punitive. The tendency to what analysts call self-punishment, *i.e.* compulsive behaviour, the effect of which is to thwart or injure our own interests and happiness, plays a far greater part in everyday mental life than can easily be imagined. Regarded as a method of treatment, psycho-analysis aims at substituting for this desperate code another one based upon the moral consciousness of the ego itself.

PSYCHO-ANALYSIS AND MENTAL HYGIENE

From the preceding it will be seen that psycho-analysis attaches the greatest importance to the early development of mental life. We consider that the first few years of life are both much more important than is commonly appreciated, and also present the child with far greater problems and difficulties. It is likely that nothing happening after the age of four years can radically alter the character of an individual, which is fully made up at that age; later events, it is true, may stimulate and bring into activity various aspects of the character, but they cannot create anything new, or effect any real change in the character.

The difficulties just alluded to relate essentially to the child's inner impulses. Many of these are dangerous in their intent, and therefore generate fear within the child. I refer, for example, to such impulses as those to kill or even devour the human beings most nearly in contact with the child. Assailed with waves of fear and terror, it has recourse to the desperate expedient of the super-ego in order to protect itself. As we have seen, however, the super-ego may, in its turn, prove to be a bad servant, and to act tyrannically in its endeavour to protect. The sense of guiltiness is a clumsy device, but the only one accessible at this age.

The environment, as a rule, does little to help the child in its struggles; indeed it does not comprehend them or even know of their existence. Knowledge of them naturally moves one to inquire whether something cannot be done to help the child during this most difficult period of its existence, and thus to lay the foundation for a healthier and happier mental functioning in later life. The problem can be tackled along two lines. In the first place, environmental influences can be made more favourable in the following ways: (1) Respect for the child's developing personality. There should be no endeavour to infuse our own adult emotions and aims into the child. The child should be allowed to develop according to the line which its own personality will lay down. In other words, we have to realize that the child is not, as we sometimes feel, merely a part of ourselves, but a distinct other person with wishes, aims, and feelings of its own. (2) The child should not be over-excited, particularly in ways that give rise to sexual excitation. I have in mind the many forms of undue emotional and physical intimacy with the parents, such as sharing a bed or bedroom with them, and many forms of caresses. (3) One should avoid exciting the child's fears, and, above all, its moral fears, which are in any event great enough. It is perhaps less harmful to punish a child in anger than as the enforcement of a moral principle.

Unfortunately none of these maxims, however conscientiously adhered to, carry us very far in helping the child. One can do more by refraining from harming a child than by actively helping him. It would seem that the child's unconscious, the area of difficulty, is so remote from the world of reality that the latter impinges on it only to a very limited extent. The question therefore arises whether it would not be possible to help the child in the same way as one does a neurotic adult, namely by direct psycho-analysis, which would remove the underlying fear and guilt. There are many difficulties in the way of this, but Mrs. Melanie Klein has developed a special technique of child analysis which overcomes them. She has written a book, published recently, which expounds her methods and results. I am personally convinced that her pioneering work in this field will prove to be of great importance.

Leaving the matter of neurotic difficulties, I should like to say a word or two about the still graver forms of mental disorder. Some recent work, particularly by Mrs. Klein, gives us good grounds for surmising that much of what we call mental deficiency, even in its severer forms, may be the result of extremely deep-seated conflicts within the unconscious mind, and there is even some prospect that psycho-analysis of mentally defective children may prove to have valuable remedial effects. Psycho-analysis has also been used in the treatment of insanity. There, as perhaps might have been expected, its results are not so promising as in the field of neurotic disorder; there are, nevertheless, certain forms of insanity which can be not only helped, but even cured, in this way.

XV

THE INDIVIDUAL AND SOCIETY[1]

THE old problem indicated by the title of my paper has been approached from many angles, political, moral, economic, and so on. Interest in it, however, has been stimulated afresh by the profound discoveries of Psychoanalysis. Psychology inevitably impinges on Sociology via what is called Social Psychology. This is an attempt to estimate the relative influence on man of external and internal factors. The essential question here is: what proportion of man's behaviour is determined by physical factors and by the institutions that constitute his social environment, and what proportion by his individual nature? It is a matter of some interest that bias is usually manifested in approaching this question. It would seem that temperamentally people are divided into those who would wish stress laid on the one set of factors and those who would wish it laid on the other. One might almost speak of there being two views of human nature. One set of people sees a vast number of external influences, climatic, economic, geographical, physical, racial, etc., acting on a relatively uniform human nature, moulding it and modifying it from place to place, from epoch to epoch. The other sees a number of restless internal urges and cravings which seize eagerly on the varying material provided by the outer world and use it for the purpose of self-expression and self-protection.

[1] Read before the Sociology Society, London School of Economics, March 8, 1935. Published in the *Sociological Review*, July 1935.

It would seem wiser to postpone the attempt to answer this quantitative question of relative importance until we understand more about motivation in general from both sides. Since many students are, I imagine, mainly concerned with the first set of factors, which may be called the external ones, I shall not risk tilting the balance unduly by calling attention to some of the considerations on the other side. For anyone who has made himself familiar with the discoveries of psycho-analysis cannot fail to realize that they add importance to the internal factors in human motivation.

Freud, the pioneer of psycho-analysis, was forced by the nature of his work to adopt this attitude of attaching importance to internal factors. As is well known, he began his studies with the endeavour to understand the meaning of certain nervous disorders, in fact all neurotic suffering. Those who have made no special investigation in this field are very prone to ascribe such maladies to current external factors, such as grief, over-work, and other misfortunes. Closer examination soon showed how inadequate is this explanation. Even where the external factor in question might appear to account for the outbreak of the trouble, it in no way explained its nature nor the particular form in which it showed itself. The external factors commonly evoked are both few and banal, whereas the number of possible ways in which a neurosis may manifest itself seems to be quite endless. There must, therefore, be other and more individual factors at work than the external ones. Psycho-analysis of the separate symptoms showed Freud that they consisted of repetitions, in a disguised and symbolic language, of significant experiences in the person's earlier life. Thus, the paralysis of an arm might date from an occasion in which the person had used or attempted to use this arm in a significant experience; for instance, an angry assault. But it was found that, strictly speaking, some only of the elements of the earlier experience were being repeated or reproduced in the symptoms, and the question naturally arose why these elements in particular should be singled out. The choice of them must have been determined by other factors dating from still earlier influences in the person's life. In other words, it is not only the disturbing experience as such that has caused the trouble, but the particular way in which that individual responded to it. He was, to some extent, prepared for it beforehand. Something in his early development had made him specially sensitive to certain aspects of experience and perhaps immune to other, even injurious, ones. And so, in the endeavour to understand the meaning of the symptoms, one is driven to seek farther and farther back in the person's early life. We now know that whether a person will become neurotic or not in later life is already determined by certain features of his early childhood development, and very little by what happens to him later.

I have cited the example of neurosis, not only because it was the first phenomenon to be investigated by the psycho-analytical method, but also because it is a prototype. Neuroses belong to the most mysterious of human happenings, and the light now shed on their nature has proved of exceptional interest. We can say that neuroses represent one of the many ways in which an individual responds to certain difficult social situations through which everyone has to pass. They should therefore be of special interest to students of sociology. The tracing back of their roots to early childhood has made us realize that early human development is a much more tiresome and arduous matter than is generally thought. In its endeavour to become a human citizen the infant is asked to recapitulate 50,000 years of human development in the first five years of its life, and the strain is often greater than it can bear. At the end of this period the personality is made for good or for ill, and little that can happen later can radically change it. Freud maintained that character is made by the age of five, and more recent investigation would seem to indicate that the essential basis is laid down even earlier. We are getting, there, very near to the inherited biological constitution, with which we always have to reckon. The important point is that this inborn constitution of instincts is decidedly malleable in the early years of life and very much less so later. All that would give these early years a peculiarly fateful significance.

Modern psychology no longer regards human behaviour as the product of simply two sets of forces, the internal and external ones I mentioned earlier. It would appear to be nearer the truth to describe it as the result of the interaction of two separate sets of internal forces on the outer world. Psychology has naturally more to say about the two internal sets than about the outer one, and I should therefore continue with some description of them. All this makes the matter a good deal more complicated than it appeared at first sight. Instead of simply speaking of the interaction of man's urges on his environment, one has to recognize that, although these urges do constantly seek for expression, at least an equally great part of man's activity as a whole is concerned with innumerable measures for checking, deflecting, and controlling them.

This double nature of human mentality is the most essential part of psycho-analytical doctrine, as indeed it is of most philosophies and religions. It is a state of affairs that originates during early development, so that only investigation of this can provide us with the understanding of it. It would appear that the infant very soon builds up an ego, the conscious part of which we term the *self*, which contrasts with the undifferentiated and unorganized primitive impulses. Stimulation of the latter invariably evokes fear, which we clinically term anxiety, on the part of the ego, and it defends itself against the supposed danger by a great number of characteristic devices. One of the earliest is simple repression, that is, an attempt to keep the impulses at as great a distance as possible from the ego. In this way arises the unconscious mind of which we hear so much nowadays.

Although it is easy to discuss intellectually the concept of the unconscious, that is, mental activity of which we are not aware, it would appear to be impossible truly to apprehend it without experiencing this unconscious activity by first making it conscious, *i.e.* by psycho-analysis. One cannot convey to anyone who has not had this experience the extent to which one is unconscious of the layer of mind in question. The person has no glimmer or awareness whatever of the mental processes active below the level of consciousness. Dreams and various other phenomena are hints that something is going on which we do not understand, but we have thoroughly learnt how to discount and dismiss them from our attention. Nevertheless, it is this deeper region of the mind that constitutes the core of the personality from which all we know of ourselves is only a series of superficial radiations.

In the unconscious a steady conflict goes on between the two halves of the personality to which I referred a moment ago. Our behaviour and conscious mental attitudes represent a series of compromises and reactions that proceed from this unceasing internal conflict. Normally the conflict itself is successfully kept out of sight by the various mechanisms I have shortly termed compromises, but often enough it rises to the surface in the form of unhappiness, doubt, and lack of confidence; occasionally it may assume more violent forms. It is quite impossible to understand human nature except in terms of this constant profound conflict within the mind.

Let us now consider a little more closely the actual nature of the conflict and the sets of forces on either side. On the one side we may, for the present purpose, group together the primary impulses under the names of sexuality and aggressivity. They are, to begin with, of a diffuse, undifferentiated and chaotic order, but as time goes on some degree of organization is brought about. A remarkable feature about them is the readiness with which stimulation of them generates fear. The fear varies greatly in amount, and attacks of panic and terror commonly enough seize consciousness itself in children. The problem of why there should be so much fear is an interesting and important one. There is good evidence for the view that dread of punishment by no means accounts for all of it. It is rather to be correlated with the intensity of any aggressive impulses that may be functioning. These primary impulses are mainly directed towards the parents; of course, first of all the mother. That tumultuous and obviously incompatible emotions and impulses should be experienced in respect of the same object is what accounts to a great extent for the intensity of the subsequent conflicts.

On the other side stands the ego, which may be roughly defined as the part of our primary nature whose activity does not generate fear. As the ego develops and becomes more organized, it shows great sensitiveness to fear generated by stimulation of the other set of impulses, which we may now call the repressed impulses. The major part of early mental growth consists in developing various devices for strengthening or reassuring the ego on the one hand, and controlling or deflecting the repressed impulses on the other. In this connection I propose to introduce another complication—I hope the last one—in the scheme I am outlining. Our original picture of a simple conflict between the individual and his environment I have already complicated by laying stress on the internal conflict between the two sides of human nature. But even this description does not complete the story. The mind would appear to be divided not simply into two groups of mental forces, but into three. With most people, at least the third group, of which I am now going to speak, assumes an importance comparable to the other two, so that we have finally to view the mind in what schematically might be termed a triangular form. I have already mentioned one of the protective mechanisms of the ego, namely repression, that is to say, the constant endeavour to keep the repressed impulses at a distance from the ego. A more complex device is that the ego takes over a certain amount of energy derived from the repressed impulses, divorces it from them and re-directs it against both them and itself. Put in this condensed way, my statement cannot be very intelligible. Let me put it more concretely. Some of the hurting tendency of the aggressive impulses, which previously had been directed against other people, is taken over and directed against oneself. This is the way in which the conscience begins its development. But I am not speaking of conscience as we know it in adult life, where it is a compound of love for an ideal and self-condemnation when that ideal is departed from. What I am speaking of here is sometimes given the rather paradoxical name of an unconscious conscience. Freud calls it the super-ego because of its capacity to rule the ego.

This primitive unconscious conscience must be clearly distinguished from the later conscious one, since it differs from it very greatly. In the first place, the self-condemnatory aspects of it are far more prominent than any ideal or love aspects. With many people its severity can hardly be exaggerated. What is spoken of as the sting of conscience is nothing compared with the intolerable pain which the primitive super-ego can inflict. The pain can indeed become so unbearable that the ego now has to take measures of defence against the very institution which it had built up for its protection. Another respect in which the super-ego differs from the familiar conscious conscience is in being far more irrational. If our (conscious) conscience has been properly developed its dictates are not only ethical, but are in accord with rational considerations; we can adduce pretty plausible reasons for the various things our conscience believes in. It is quite otherwise with the super-ego. Its criterion is neither that of ethics nor of reason, but solely that of imagined danger. If it fears a given impulse it may adopt a condemnatory attitude towards even harmless derivatives of such impulses. The most extreme form of this is to be seen in a nervous malady known as conversion hysteria. There a person, without having any affection of the eye at all, may be stricken blind simply as a protection against the supposed danger of using the eye for some forbidden purpose. It is as if the irrational super-ego dreads so much the possibility of the eye being used in a forbidden way, for instance, in some erotic connection, that it ensures against that possibility by ordaining that the person is not to use his eyes even for the most harmless purposes. In this fashion the simplest and most harmless activities may be interfered with or even completely inhibited. Refusals to eat certain articles of diet are common enough in children, and in hysteria may extend to all food; similarly, paralysis of the arm or leg is a not infrequent symptom of hysteria. If we were speaking in moral terms we might say that the super-ego has a very evil mind, since it has the power to detect evil activities which the keenest Puritan himself would pass as harmless. But it would be a mistake to regard the matter in such moral terms. As I said before, it is purely the sense of danger that actuates the super-ego. It is constantly saying to the ego, 'Don't allow any part of yourself to think or behave in that way because it terrifies me, and if you do not heed my injunctions I shall punish you ruthlessly'.

When the amount of anxiety is not too great, the severity of the super-ego becomes modified; it is infused with the elements of love, and gradually develops into the conscience, which is the most important part of our character. It is, however, rare for this development to proceed as smoothly and as completely as we could wish. With most people there are to be found remains of the primitive super-ego which is still being regarded in the depths of the mind as a protection essential to life. From that point of view one can understand the sensitiveness of the individual to anything that might tend to impair the standards set up by the super-ego, a sensitiveness which, in many of its manifestations, may assume the form of intolerance. Paradoxically enough, life itself would be freely ventured on behalf of the standards. Such a person would readily die rather than do something which the super-ego imagines would risk his life, just as some people commit suicide so as to escape the intolerable dread of death. On a lowlier plane there are few people who behave calmly when circumstances demand their admitting having been in the wrong, having made an important mistake, and the like. Most people are even sensitive to any criticism of the way they do their hair or the way they pronounce their vowels. It should be evident that these considerations must have an important bearing on the mysterious national and racial antipathies that often prove so disastrous.

Sometimes the ego experiences difficulty in living up to the demands of its super-ego, either because the ego itself is weak or else because the impossible is expected of it. When this is so, the person is likely to suffer from one of the numerous forms of inferiority feelings. He may be anxious and depressed because of a sense of physical inferiority, or this may show itself more in the intellectual or moral sphere. Whatever form it may take, the inferiority complex is always due ultimately to a sense of moral failure, a shame at not being able to fulfil the demand of the unconscious conscience. Often this lack of confidence or sense of unworthiness is dealt with by developing in a compensatory fashion an attitude of over-assertiveness, dogmatism, and the like. It may easily be imagined how often this unstable mental attitude leads to social difficulties. And this is so not only with individuals, for whole countries may be infected by a sense of national inferiority, coupled with the impulse to overcome it by means of loud assertiveness. Here again we see the possibility of throwing light on many social and political problems.

I shall mention only one more of the various devices with which the ego seeks to protect itself, or to obtain reassurance, and, socially speaking, it is perhaps the most troublesome and dangerous of all these intra-psychical devices. I refer to the endeavour to live out the repressed impulses, in whatever form may seem accessible: to repeat the original forbidden acts under the guise of some kind of sanction. In the field of sexuality this often takes the form of perversion or of compulsive sexual functioning. By that I mean that the person indulges in some form of sexual activity not so much from the natural desire for pleasure, but from the defiant motive of proving to himself that it is safe to commit what another part of his mind feels to be forbidden and dangerous acts. Here the ego tries to ally itself with the repressed impulses and in combination with them to defy the super-ego. This can be done only by the person's surrendering control over the impulses and yielding himself to a sense of compulsion. It is a method of reassurance that has many drawbacks. Any reassurance obtained in this way is bound to be only temporary, and the super-ego always finds some way of avenging the affront to it or else exacts a still more extreme form of reassurance; in the latter case, a vicious circle is set up which has no end. Still more serious are the consequences of using the same device in regard to the aggressive impulses. We have here the explanation of that mysterious belief in force which causes so much trouble in the world. It is astounding how deep in the human mind this conviction lies. When fear is aroused, the belief that the only safety lies in violence is stimulated, and there are very few people who then fail to respond to it. One can see why this should be so. If the deepest fear is of one's aggressive impulses, then it is only consistent to think that the greatest reassurance is that obtained when one can persuade oneself that one is being justified in being aggressive. I have termed this principle, which operates with all unconscious impulses, the homoeopathic principle, since it proceeds on the assumption that like cures like. I am not, of course, saying that all aggressiveness in life comes about in the secondary way I have just described; that is, from motives of internal and external reassurance. There are ways of distinguishing between the natural pugnacity and rivalry of man, leading as it may on occasion even to deeds of violence, from the uncontrollable hatred and impulsiveness that is the mark of inner conflict with its need for reassurance. In the latter case the note of malice or viciousness can always be detected, well described in the Litany as 'envy, hatred, malice and all uncharitableness'. In the field of sport, for instance, one can readily discriminate between the primary desire to conquer and the unsportsmanlike behaviour that emanates from this natural desire having been turned into a vital question, a test case, because of some intolerable inner conflict.

Most of our social institutions, government, religion, marriage laws, etc., have come about as an expression of both the sets of opposing mental forces of which I spoke to begin with. *Religion*, for example, although it inculcates positive activity, love, mercy, and charity, is in practice very much occupied as well with exhortations to restrain and check what is sometimes called the natural man or our lower nature. In the history of the world, religion has proved perhaps the most powerful help to human weakness, to man's constant endeavour to cope with his own nature. *Government* also, although it occasionally provides opportunity for positive activities, for example in our motor roads, Serpentine Lido, and the like, is for the greater part engaged in formulating rules that make various activities illegal, and the important social institution of the Law has as its main function the enforcement of these restraining activities.

What I have just said is the chief point I want to make, so perhaps I may lay stress on it by repeating it in a slightly different form. If our primary impulses were free, we should presumably need no social institutions any more than animals do. Our social institutions subserve a double purpose, and so it is to be supposed that they came into being for that purpose. On the one hand, they arrange for some measure of expression for the primary impulses by canalizing them and providing safeguards to obviate any unfortunate consequences. On the other hand, they act in the service of the super-ego by checking and restraining free expression of the primary impulses. I do not think it possible to understand the nature of any social institution without taking into account this double aspect. Thus sociologists who ascribe the visibly restraining effect of social institutions to extra-human sources, *e.g.* economic, climatic, and the like, often overlook the fact that restraint is a process that proceeds from within the mind as well as being imposed on it from without. It is therefore not simply a matter of human impulses conflicting with external barriers, but of their conflicting as well with restraining forces that are present in every mind from early childhood. Obedience to the law, for instance, may appear to be imposed on the individual solely from without, but the need for law proceeds from within. Similarly, religion may proceed from without, *i.e.* the grace of God, but it also proceeds from within, from the need for religion.

I will now illustrate this thesis by considering two social institutions, taking first that of Marriage. There is an almost infinite variety of marriage institutions in the world. One or more wives may be allowed, one or more husbands, according to the locality. Sometimes the marriage has to last for life; sometimes it is easily dissoluble. In most marriage institutions the husband and wife co-habit, but in a good many they do not live together. What we in England consider as marital functions are in some other countries distributed. There are countries where the sole marital function is the sexual one, the other ones, with which we are familiar, of maintenance, companionship, and mutual upbringing of children, being handed over to another relative, usually the wife's brother. Even in our lifetime in England some such functions have been, in the poorer classes, removed from the husband to the state, *e.g.* education and feeding of the children.

All this being so, it is a matter of some difficulty to perceive the essential character of the marriage bond. We cannot, however, be far from this if we take it that what distinguishes marriage from other relationships between the sexes is the fact that with the former the sexual union is officially recognized by the community. This recognition is always signalized by a ritual act, the wedding ceremony, which of course varies enormously in its form from country to country.

Let me now try to throw some light on the social function of this institution by considerations drawn from a rather unexpected quarter. Readers will be familiar with the fact that young girls frequently evince aversion to the idea of marriage and often declare that they will never allow themselves to be married. The great majority of them, however, overcome this attitude before reaching the age when the question mostly arises, so that it is of little social significance. With men it is different. Their declaration against marriage commonly occurs at a later age, and very often lasts throughout the twenties or even later. It is often more vigorous than with girls and is commonly supported by bachelor friends, who then regard the change of heart either as an act of treachery which they deplore, or as a misfortune that has happened to an innocent victim. This resistance against marriage, as we should call it psychologically, is of considerable interest individually as well as socially. It proceeds from the dim perception that the act of marriage has a fateful significance, from which the man commonly flinches. His apprehensiveness is then shown either by the familiar faintheartedness at the altar or is masked by a more or less defiant refusal to marry. What can be the reason for his fears? This question would usually be answered by various rationalizations, such as his objection to assume the maintenance of a wife and probable children, his reluctance to focus his sexual attentions on one individual and thereby to renounce his previous liberty in this respect, and so on. These rationalizations contain, of course, a measure of truth, but they also reflect light on more fundamental considerations about the essence of the marriage institution. The man evidently feels that a sex relationship with a woman is a very different matter according as it is clandestine or is openly recognized by the world. Psycho-analysis of this attitude has revealed that the problem the man is ultimately faced with is that of combining his intimacy with a woman with his relationship to other men. The world, or Society, the other men in question, ultimately represent the other man in a triangular situation, his potential rival. The individual's complexities in this situation go back to the time of his earliest development when he started life in a triangular situation, and when the *tertium quid* was not merely a potential but an actual rival. In other words, we are concerned here with one of the manifestations of the now familiar Oedipus complex of the child, the conflict between his affection for his mother and the presence of a father who is both loved and hated. It is from this complex that the apprehensiveness we are discussing was engendered. In clandestine relationships with women the person remains in the position of a fearful child who avoids the problem of coming to terms with the other man, that is, later with Society, by simply avoiding him. In marriage, on the contrary, he comes face to face with the other man, claims his right to his own woman, and accords other men the right to theirs. It is evident that this represents both a claim and a renunciation. The bridegroom claims the right to sleep with his bride whatever other men may think about it, but at the same time he proclaims to the other men that he will maintain his relationship to their women on a platonic level. Marriage therefore both frees and restricts. It serves the dual purpose of which I have spoken earlier, of catering to both the repressed and repressing forces in the mind.

The difficulties of the timorous bridegroom may proceed from an imperfect development on either of these two sides. The more obvious of the two is that concerning restriction. In the course of his psycho-sexual development the child co-ordinates the various manifestations of his originally diffuse sexuality, much of which, if perpetuated, would constitute what is known in adult life as perverse sexual functioning. This is a cultural task that many find difficult enough. A large number of people never reach the stage in development that we call genital primacy, one in which all extra-genital functioning is quite subordinate. Even when this task of development is achieved, a further one now awaits him. He is now asked not simply to relinquish many forms of early sexual functioning, but also to effect a great restriction in his choice of object. In other words, it is to be from now on localized to one other person. We know that the large majority fail to accomplish this second task completely. In their development they have not learnt to endure restriction with sufficient equanimity to retain at the same time their self-confidence. Such people are often faced with the cruel dilemma between infidelity and impotency. This is because the early restrictions were felt too much in a negative fashion as threats or signs of punishment, so that they became hard or impossible to bear and were accompanied by constant opposition, resentment, or even defiance. It will be seen that this is more apt to be so when a child is already burdened with an uneasy conscience, so that all restraint is interpreted as punishment for his supposed sinfulness. He then finds it hard to acquire restraint as an integral part of his own personality; it remains something alien, something imposed on him and inimical to his vital interests. Such a person will dread what he regards as the final and permanent restriction of marriage, and one may safely predict that his married life will in any event not be a happy one.

More obscure and often more important are the difficulties that arise from the other of the two sides I mentioned above, the claim to freedom. It is evident that this claim can be comfortably supported, in a civilized environment, only when the man has come to some sort of amicable terms with the other man or men. Unfortunately it often happens that the infantile ideas of union with a woman and destruction of the hated rival have become so closely interwoven as to be practically inextricable. In the unconscious mind the one idea immediately evokes the other and cannot be separated from it. Such a person is in an unenviable predicament. On the one hand, he feels impelled to prove his worth and manhood by following his natural desire to approach a member of the opposite sex, but, on the other hand, this to him seems to necessitate a terrible tragedy, the fulfilment of an appalling task that has been laid upon him. In civilized society he cannot behave like the heroes in the stories of old who triumphantly accomplished their task and slew the dragon, lion, or other impediment in the way. The average man to-day who had to follow such a path would probably be pursued by the fate of Oedipus on a similar occasion, ending his days in torturing remorse. More particularly would this be so if the victim of his impulses were someone whom he otherwise respected and loved, a father or his substitute. In extreme instances of this kind, the person often finds a solution in changing his own sex, in becoming homosexual, or in developing some other form of perversion or neurosis. In the best case he remains a sour bachelor.

The history of marriage as an institution shows that it has changed its form endlessly in the course of its evolution. This evolution is still proceeding even in Christian times. The conditions for divorce, for instance, vary greatly from country to country, from Church to Church. And yet marriage has proved such an invaluable aid to man in his endeavour to tame his most refractory instincts that one may have confidence in its future as an institution. Fuller understanding of the functions it fulfils will surely enable us to remedy at least some of its present unmistakable imperfections.

I have chosen marriage among other reasons because it illustrates very well the contrast between the external and internal points of view, what is sometimes rather unfairly called the sociological and psychological respectively. We have the observation that emotional attitudes among the various members of a family are differently distributed in different countries according to the type of marriage system obtaining there. In a matrilineal society, for example, a son may show a steadier devotion to his father and antagonism to his uncle than is customary with us, we being more familiar with an ambivalent relationship between father and son. And conflicts in respect of the mother or mother substitutes may be replaced by similar feelings about the sister. It would almost appear that in such a society in place of the classical Oedipus complex of our civilized nations, with its love for the mother and rivalry with the father, we find instead a different complex in which the boy feels rather love for his sister and rivalry with his uncle. There arises at once the interesting question of whether this striking difference in the boy's attitude, with all its ramifying effects in his psychology, has arisen endogenously or exogenously. Most anthropologists, foremost among them Professor Malinowski, incline to the view that the matrilineal society arose for some unknown external reason, cultural, economic, or what not, whereas psycho-analysts would incline rather to the view that it arose as one of the numerous forms of defence against the embarrassments of the Oedipus complex, a view I have expounded elsewhere in detail. In other words, the one set of thinkers would regard the Oedipus complex as the product of a particular social and family organization, whereas the other set would regard it as the fundamental and universal motor, of which the different social organizations are by-products. This shows very well the kind of problem which can be finally solved only by co-operation of psycho-analysts with sociologists or anthropologists, the necessary prerequisite of which is the rarely obtainable one that they should each have some adequate understanding of the other's discipline.

The other topic I have in mind is that of the causation of war. Here the sociological point of view would appear to be divided between two explanations. I imagine that the majority of politicians and other social workers regard the most important causes of war as being of a materialistic order in which conflicts of economic policy, the ambitions of armament firms, and the general capitalistic structure of society are among the main factors held responsible. On the other hand, it is to be noted that in practice they do not appear to devote their pacifist efforts to altering these factors. When it comes to practice, they seem rather to adopt a psychological explanation, that wars are due to the pugnacity of peoples, and the basis on which they direct their propaganda is to persuade people to renounce their pugnacity and to decide to fight no more. The obvious simplicity of their psychology justifies some scepticism about the profundity of their investigations into the problems concerned. And actually there are few more fascinating problems than these just because of the extraordinary multiplicity of the various factors. To isolate these factors and to ascribe to each its relative importance, ascertaining which are the more primary and which the more secondary, would strike a scientific man as being a problem of the most formidable magnitude necessitating vast researches before any reliable conclusions could be reached. It is significant of the emotional turmoil that lies behind all this interest in the question of war that up to the present no one in any country has had the idea of even initiating the necessary investigations of which I have spoken. Anxiety often stimulates the desire for knowledge, but when it is too great it paralyses it. It is as if people at present were too anxious about war, too eager for certitude as a reassurance, for them to have the requisite patience to search after the truth, to reach the certainty that only impartial investigation can give. They are so anxious to know the result that they cannot afford the time to look for it.

In this field, also, it is certain that many battles will be waged between those who support the exogenous and those who support the endogenous hypothesis about the essential factors that bring about war. Psycho-analysis has already made some notable contributions to this subject, among which I would cite a book by Edward Glover, entitled *War, Sadism and Pacifism*. One of the first conclusions to be reached by this method was that even among the endogenous causes we have to allot importance to both sides of the conflicting forces within the mind of which I have spoken earlier. It is a very simple fallacy to assume that the psychology of combatants is that of people who for some reason have permitted a breakthrough of their latent pugnacious impulses. Perhaps of equal importance to any such process as this is the urge coming from the side of the ego and super-ego where we have to deal with motives of fear, of need for security, of various ideals, in short, of quite non-aggressive factors. One might venture the prediction that the greatest likelihood of war among civilized nations arises when the balance is not stably held between these two different sets of mental attitudes. The complicated inter-relationship between both of them on the one side and the whole group of external, *e.g.* economic factors, on the other, yields a highly involved series of problems on which I do not propose to touch here. I have endeavoured only to convey some hints of the complexity of sociological problems to which psycho-analysis will surely make an indispensable contribution.

XVI

THE PSYCHOLOGY OF CONSTITUTIONAL MONARCHY[1]

What renders the problem of government so very difficult is man's constantly double attitude towards it, the fact that his attitude is always a mixture of two contradictory sets of wishes. On the one hand, he has very deep motives for wishing to be ruled. Feeling unequal to the task of controlling either his own or his neighbour's impulses, and longing to shift the responsibility for so doing, he demands some authority who shall shoulder the main part of this burden. On the other hand, as soon as the restrictions of authority are felt to be oppressive, he is impelled to protest and clamour for freedom. In an ordered society these two sets of impulses have to be co-ordinated, though in a constantly fluctuating rather than in any static form. At times either set may become predominant. When a people's sense of helplessness, of inferiority arising from guiltiness, becomes unbearable, there arises a passionate clamour for a 'strong' dictatorial government, whether of the autocratic or socialistic variety; while, when a thwarting of personal initiative is felt to be intolerable, there is a call for revolution which may attain a murderous intensity.

Modern psychology well recognizes that these shifting attitudes in the outer world mirror the constant conflict and instability in man's inner nature, the to and fro surges between the expressing and the restraining of his fundamental impulses. It is noteworthy that each side of the

[1] Published in *The New Statesman and Nation*, February 1, 1936.

conflict may be depicted in either ignoble or laudatory terms. We may speak of the divine call to freedom, one of the noblest impulses in man's nature, as well as of his tendency to unrestrained and brutal licence. On the other hand, the controlling tendencies may assume the form of sheer persecution and hateful thwarting of life as well as the confident self-control that ranks as one of the highest of our civic virtues or the acceptance of God's will so characteristic of the greatest saints.

It is also well recognized that this dichotomy of man's nature expresses itself most vividly in the child's relation to his parents—the famous Oedipus complex. In the deeper layers of the mind the attitudes persist in their old child-parent terms, though in consciousness they may have been superseded by more complex ones, such as Herbert Spencer's *Man Versus the State*. No psycho-analyst would hesitate, on coming across the person of a ruler in a dream, to translate 'ruler' as 'father', and he would at once be interested in the way in which the subject's conscious attitude towards the ruler was being influenced by his underlying attitude towards his father. Mostly one should replace the last words by 'the underlying *phantastic* attitude towards his father', remembering that in the child's imagination his father is either far more benevolent or far more cruel than most fathers are—and always more magically powerful and wonderful than any father is. It is the persistence in the unconscious of this element of magic belief that accounts for the recurrent irrationalities in people's attitude towards a government, *e.g.* that blames it for all misfortunes and imputes to its wickedness the non-appearance of an immediate Utopia.

Growing up signifies that the early sense of dependence on the parent (let me say 'father', *tout court*), both real and imaginary, is replaced by a proper independence and self-

CONSTITUTIONAL MONARCHY

reliance *without* any need for violent repudiation or destruction; also that the insoluble conflict between affection and parricide is replaced by an attitude of friendliness combined with a preparedness to oppose if need be. And any satisfactory solution of the general problem of government must include, among other things, a corresponding advance in the relations between governing and governed. I hope now to be able to show that, whatever its deficiencies may be, the success of the constitutional monarchy experiment is essentially due to the respects in which this advance has been achieved.

The experiment, or idea, starts with the assumption that, just as princesses cannot be abolished from fairy-tales without starting a riot in the nursery, so it is impossible to abolish the idea of kingship in one form or another from the hearts of men. If people are emotionally starved in this way they invent sugar kings, railroad kings, or magic 'bosses'. The idea then boldly proposes: let us reserve a king particularly to satisfy the beneficent elements of the mythology in man's ineradicable unconscious that will enable us to deal with the more troublesome elements. This is how it is worked out.

The essential purpose of the device is to prevent the murderous potentialities in the son-father (*i.e.* governed-governing) relation from ever coming to too grim and fierce an expression. To effect this the idea of the ruler is 'decomposed', as mythologists call it, into two persons—one untouchable, irremovable and sacrosanct, above even criticism, let alone attack; the other vulnerable in such a degree that sooner or later he will surely be destroyed, *i.e.* expelled from his position of power. The first of these, the king, is the symbolic ruler, one not directly responsible to the people; the second, the prime minister, is the functional ruler, exquisitely responsible. With these precautions a safe outlet is available for the parricidal tendencies; they may come into action (*a*) in a form that excludes physical violence, and (*b*) so long as they respect the taboo. Charles II would appear to have foreseen the coming arrangement when he wittily warded off the criticism of his epitaph-writing courtier with the words: 'i' faith, that's true, since my words are my own, but my deeds are my ministers''.

In return for the concession made by the populace in mollifying their parricidal tendencies, the government also, by always being ready to accept the verdict of an election, renounces the application of physical force. Under a constitutional monarchy no minister labels a cannon, as Louis XIV did, *ultima ratio regum*. The important point of this consideration is that the institution of limited monarchy, so far from being simply a method of dealing with potentially troublesome monarchs, is really an index of a highly civilized relation subsisting between rulers and ruled. It could not survive, or even exist, except in a state that has attained the highest level of civilization, where reasoned persuasion and amicable consent have displaced force as a method of argument.

When Thiers shallowly thought to define a constitutional monarch completely with the words, *le roi règne mais ne gouverne pas*, he was making a very considerable mistake. In a very deep sense such a king truly represents the sovereign people. I am not here referring to any personal influence of a particular monarch, such as Mr. Gladstone had in mind when he said that knowing Queen Victoria's opinion told him the opinion of the English people. But what of the members of Parliament, the accredited spokesmen of the people? They are temporarily so, and they may err. But when the significant words, *le roi le veult*, have been pronounced, it means in most cases that a permanent representative of the people agrees that their sovereign voice has been at least not grossly misinterpreted. The king is carefully shielded from all personal responsibility and yet he represents the final responsibility—and at critical moments may have to bear it.

An odd instance of the far-reaching influence of this sense of finality came within my experience some years ago. I was talking to the medical superintendent of a Canadian asylum in his room when a woman entered and demanded that her husband, a patient there, be discharged. The doctor, knowing the patient's dangerous tendencies, demurred, and a situation arose which it would have been quite easy to resolve with ordinary tactfulness. To my great astonishment, when the woman went on to say querulously, 'What right have you to keep my husband?' the doctor made a histrionic gesture and declaimed the words, 'I do so in the name of the King!' The woman subsided, though it was not quite clear whether it was surprise or awe had overcome her at the conjuring up of the supreme imperial authority.

The mysterious identification of king and people just hinted at goes very far indeed and reaches deep into the unconscious mythology that lies behind all these complex relationships. A ruler, just as a hero, can strike the imagination of the world in one of two ways. Either he presents some feature, or performs some deed, so far beyond the range of average people as to appear to be a creature belonging to another world. We do not know if the Spanish were really impressed on being told that their Queen could not accept a gift of silk stockings because she had no legs; but it is easy to think of less absurd examples, from the deeds of the Borgias to the impertinences of *Le Roi Soleil*. Einstein has furnished us with a current example of another kind. In the face of such phenomena one gapes with wonder or with horror, but one gapes; one does not understand. Or, on the contrary, he may capture the imagination by presenting to us, as it were on a screen, a magnified and idealized picture of the most homely and familiar attributes. It is here that the child's glorified phantasies of himself and his family find ample satisfaction. When the sophisticated pass cynical comments on the remarkable interest the majority of people take in the minute doings of royalty, and still more in the cardinal events of their births, loves, and deaths, they are often merely denying and repudiating a hidden part of their own nature rather than giving evidence of having understood and transcended it. With the others there is no trace of envy, since the illustrious personages are in their imagination their actual selves, their brother or sister, father or mother. In the august stateliness and ceremonial pomp their secret daydreams are at last gratified, and for a moment they are released from the inevitable sordidness and harassing exigencies of mundane existence. When to this is added the innumerable 'homely touches' of royalty, the proof that they are of the same flesh as their subjects, together with signs of personal interest and sympathy with their lot, loyalty is infused with affection. And a constitutional monarch, so guarded from adverse criticism, has to have a pretty bad character before he arouses any. An autocratic monarch may be selfish and cruel, but kindliness and friendliness are the natural appurtenances of a constitutional monarch.

The psychological solution of an antinomy which the experiment of constitutional monarchy represents, is also illustrated in the mode of accession of a new monarch. Is this ruler of his people, at the same time their highest representative, chosen by the people to fulfil his exalted office, or does he reign by virtue of some innate and transcendent excellence resident in him from birth? Do the people express freedom in choice or do they submit to something imposed on them? The Divine Right of kings was definitely ended in this country three centuries ago, but what of the right of birth? Here again a subtle compromise has been found. By virtue of an Act of Parliament, *i.e.* an agreement between people and monarch, the Privy Council, with the aid of various unspecified 'prominent Gentlemen of Quality', take it on themselves to announce that a son has succeeded to his father, and their decision is universally acclaimed. It is as near the truth as the people's supposed free choice of their functional ruler, the prime minister. In neither case do they actively select a particular individual; what happens is that in certain definite circumstances they *allow* him to become their ruler. Their freedom lies in their reserving the right to reject him whenever he no longer plays the part allotted to him.

We have thus learned how to prevent monarchy from degenerating into tyranny; and we are rapidly learning how to prevent timocracy from degenerating into plutocracy. But we have still to learn how to prevent democracy from degenerating into ochlocracy, or aristocracy into oligarchy.

XVII

HOW CAN CIVILIZATION BE SAVED?[1]

I SHALL best be able to approach the problems we have before us to-day if you will allow me to do so by rather a personal route. I would describe myself as a humanist with a primary interest in science and belief in its value to mankind. By science I essentially mean clear thinking, a definition you might not all of you accept. Philosophers and logicians, for instance, might claim a monopoly of clear thinking. Laboratory scientists, on the other hand, might disclaim clear thinking as being the most characteristic part of their work and might assert that it is their principal business to ascertain facts and let the facts speak for themselves rather than thinking too much about them. Facts may, it is true, speak, but they do not always do so clearly and they very often mislead, or rather the minds on which they impinge often see to it that they receive a distorted impression.

I make these preliminary remarks to indicate my mode of approach to the topics under consideration. So definitely implanted in me is this mode of approach that I must confess had I known what the title of the present symposium was going to be, 'How can Civilization be saved?', I should have had no wish to participate in it. This is not said by way of any reproach to your secretary, but only to indicate my point of view. What he had told me was that you were going to have a discussion on international problems and

[1] Read at a symposium held by the Federation of Progressive Societies, November 27, 1938. Published in the *International Journal of Psycho-Analysis*, vol. xxiv.

HOW CAN CIVILIZATION BE SAVED?

that you would like to hear me say something about the psychological approach to them. Now the actual title seems to me most question-begging, so that it is not evident what is the problem under discussion. We are not told what civilization is to be saved from, and the great assumption is made—one which I do not myself share—that civilization is in danger of destruction. As I say, I am not myself aware of any grounds for this assumption. However, I am perspicacious enough to guess at what is intended by the title. I imagine it must refer to one of two things. It may be the belief that a world war is likely and that this would destroy our civilization, to which I would answer that, in my judgement, our civilization would survive any war, however devastating and widespread, and further that, if such a war is imminent, there is little we common folk can do to prevent its occurrence. Or the title may refer to the belief that the increasing restriction of individual liberty and of the cultural values that go with this constitute a dangerous threat to the continuance of our civilization. This is, of course, a belief that many people do not share. In Germany, for instance, it is widely held that the increase in national freedom of action achieved through a totalitarian rule more than compensates for the disadvantages of any diminution in individual freedom. In Russia, again, it is believed that a gain in economic freedom, so that everyone is free to choose the kind of work he likes and secure in the knowledge that he can obtain it where and when he wishes, offers a similar compensation.

The fear lest man's increasing powers may prove destructive to what he has created, or even to himself, is an old one. Nearly two thousand four hundred years ago, Sophocles, in his *Antigone*, descanted on the extraordinary powers of man, his amazing inventions in locomotion (!) and destruction, in conquering the dangerous forces of nature, and in establishing his mastery over all other forms of life, but we read, in conclusion, 'what matters is not the power: what matters is How the power is used, for good or for evil, for the help of human brotherhood or its destruction'. Civilization has so far survived increases in power far beyond what Sophocles could imagine, but with the imminent tapping of atomic energy they will be immeasurably enhanced. On all sides the cry is raised that man's intellectual progress is dangerously outstripping his moral progress, which indeed has hardly advanced beyond the ethical level of the early Egyptians of five thousand years ago.

Whatever is actually intended by the title of the symposium, it must relate to some feeling of deep uneasiness about the state of the world and the safety of our social institutions—what we may call a serious dis-ease, in the original meaning of the word. With this, probably, goes a state of mental tension, or rather apprehensiveness, and an urgent need for protective action, what is called a need to do something about it. If I now translate the word disease into the current medical meaning, it reminds me that besides being a psychologist I am also a physician. Very early in my medical career I learned to distinguish between good and bad physicians. The latter, I found, were those who are constantly preoccupied with the therapeutic aspects of a situation, who when confronted with a sick patient immediately ask themselves what they can do to relieve him. The good physicians, on the other hand, were those who, while no less desirous of helping the sufferer, are not so obsessed by the question, are able to restrain their impulse to help until they can first answer the question of what is the matter with him. I observed that the prescriptions the latter class provided, though far less frequent, were of much better quality than those provided by the other class, and I had no doubt myself in whose hands I would rather be a patient. While the good physicians were more often willing to admit that there was nothing very important they could do, one was a good deal more sure that whatever they did was likely to be useful.

I cannot refrain now from applying this attitude to the international sphere. There also, I think, I can observe good physicians and bad physicians. There are those who are very ready in their promises that if such and such a course of action were taken, all would be well with the world. Such people, no doubt, do much to ease the minds of those in distress, but it is open to question whether the confusion they produce by concentrating on one supposed solution does not create in other forms as much fresh disease as that which they alleviate. The few good physicians that exist are able to restrain their need for salvation through a quickly found solution and are preoccupied rather with the wish to establish more permanent forms of security by ascertaining the inner meaning of the disease and dangers in question. They are, in other words, diagnosticians rather than therapists. In mathematical language, they hold that certainty is a function of knowledge. Having the self-control with which they can stay their hand while they acquire this necessary knowledge, they are able to perceive that the factors concerned in social and international problems are far more complex and interrelated than is generally supposed.

I am trying to distinguish between two modes of approach, which I have called the diagnostic and therapeutic respectively, and I would ask you to allow me to exaggerate somewhat in order to make my point clear. One might say, for instance, that, broadly speaking, there are two sources of human power: that proceeding from emotion and that proceeding from knowledge. Religion and science would represent a corresponding contrast. The achievements of science, particularly in the physical world, are around us to see and I need not expatiate on their value or on their reliability. A man can send a message across the Atlantic or cross it himself with a degree of certainty that has enormously increased in the past century alone. Emotion, for its part, has also worked mighty and revolutionary changes. It has destroyed empires and it has forged bonds between the most diverse peoples. There is, however, one striking difference between the two sets of effects. In the case of those based on knowledge, it is usually possible to predict and understand the effects, however extensive they may be. In the case of those based on emotion, this is true to a far less extent. Its results are very much more variable. When Christianity was introduced into Rome, for example, it would have been utterly impossible to predict the extremely complicated results that followed. I think there is a definite reason for this difference. Knowledge, in its scientific sense, undergoes a very rigid testing by the facts of reality, so that its conclusions are more closely related to objective reality and are influenced to only a relatively small extent by personal and subjective factors. Emotion, on the other hand, proceeding from within, has, as its main function, the relief of acute mental tension and is commonly dictated to a great extent by subjective wish-phantasies. It is much less likely to proceed along rational lines. An extreme example, which will illustrate the point, is the extraordinarily ill-adapted conduct that so often follows on a state of panic, when people, in a wild belief that they can in that way save their lives, embark on the most violent and ill-considered acts that commonly defeat their own purpose. There are, of course, exceptions to this rule. If emotion is sufficiently defined and concentrated, it will

HOW CAN CIVILIZATION BE SAVED?

achieve its purpose quite adequately and will confine itself to the achieving of it. When, for instance, the sight of boy chimney-sweeps became intolerable to the people of London in the last century, they took effective steps to abolish the sight, and there were very few remoter consequences of their action. Usually, however, social emotions arise from a more complex state of affairs, and they then set in train a whole series of beliefs and wishes which may have a very imperfect relation to reality. We come here to the familiar field of the various political slogans and panaceas, to that of the social agitators who assure us that, if only their particular nostrum is swallowed, all sorts of desirable results will follow. Being very familiar with similar procedures in the field of medicine, I am often reminded of quack remedies when I encounter promises of this kind. In both cases they are open to two sets of criticism. The evidence that they will achieve the specific effect promised is often defective or altogether lacking, and it commonly happens that the effects actually produced are such as have not been at all foreseen. The procedure, that is to say, has not been subjected beforehand to the rigid scrutiny which is demanded in scientific work. There are two reasons for this. The need to assuage the inner tension is so urgent that those concerned cannot afford to embark on the thought processes which scientific examination of the proposition necessitates. This is, of course, generally recognized. A more recondite reason, however, and one not at all generally known, is that the wishes and beliefs initiated by the need to relieve mental tension are of a very peculiar kind. The tension itself reanimates certain primordial processes in the unconscious mind, which are themselves quite divorced from reality, so that the wishes for action that finally emerge are in fact more or less rationalized expressions of very primitive impulses. It is not too much to say, in consequence, that for a slogan to move a multitude emotionally it must of necessity contain important irrational elements, *i.e.* elements which have only a remote relationship to external reality. An impassioned leader has, therefore, to be a little mad, and the harder his task, the madder he has to be.

In the field before us here, the science concerned is that of sociology, but unhappily it is one that has made little more than a beginning. I would ascribe its slow progress to the unfortunate and unscientific prejudice so many sociologists entertain against making a study of psychology. Although their material is obviously concerned mainly with human nature, they are apt to hold the queer view that human nature is a totally different thing in mass from what it is in the individual, and therefore to disdain the opportunities of acquiring a detailed and exact knowledge of it which only study of the individual can provide. Psychology itself, on the other hand, although it has advanced further than is generally known and has also made important contributions to our knowledge of mass sociological phenomena, suffers under the great disadvantage that a profound knowledge of it is confined to an extraordinarily small number of people and that there exist extremely serious difficulties in the way of communicating its results to others.

In so far as I am speaking as a true psychologist, *i.e.* a man of science, you will not, after what I have already said, expect from me anything in the nature of a nostrum or panacea, the application of which will quickly resolve the visible ills from which mankind is suffering. If you press me on the point, the nearest I can produce in this direction is the conclusion that what mankind chiefly lacks is an educated and widespread tradition of respect for knowledge, particularly, in the present context, psychological knowledge. A simple example here will illustrate what I mean. A great deal has been written of late concerning the importance of the psychological factors in the causation of war, and indeed, since war proceeds from a clash of human emotions and wills, the importance of such factors should be sufficiently obvious. Now mankind has, in spite of any temptations in the other direction, an intense aversion to the destructiveness of war, and the nations of the present day are devoting enormous energy to the aim of preventing it. Thousands of millions of pounds are spent annually on armaments which have the avowed intention of preventing war by making potential enemies afraid to attack. Vast sums of money, and a still greater amount of mental energy, are also being devoted to other forms of prevention by various kinds of propaganda. Yet, so far as I know, in the whole world, no one has thought of spending sixpence on making any study of the psychological causes of war. I am persuaded that the reasons for this glaring fact are not merely that people feel there is no time for such studies, the situation being so urgent, but much more that they are animated by intense, and largely irrational, beliefs in other forms of salvation than that of knowledge.

Although I would maintain that what I have up to now said is in the long run constructive, you will doubtless expect that I should have something more specific to say about the psychological study of the international problems with which we are here concerned. The field is a vast one, and I can do no more than select two or three aspects of it on which to comment. I need hardly say that I do no intend to enter on any political discussion, so that my remarks will be equally applicable to different political sides and tendencies. In considering such problems a psycho-analyst would try to see how far he could apply certain basic knowledge he has about the foundations of the human mind, and I shall have to spend a moment or two in expounding these before taking up the question of their application. The driving force of the human mind, the psycho-analyst terms, *tout court*, wishes. They are the beginning of everything. He knows, however, that many of the most primordial human wishes, when they are set in action, engender anxiety or fear, and this for purely internal reasons which I do not propose to expound here. Now man is peculiarly intolerant of anxiety, and has devised a great variety of interesting defences against it. These three things, wishes, anxieties, and defences, go far to explain in an infinite variety what we call human character and human conduct. They are the three things that a psycho-analyst would try to ascertain about any individual or any nation with the investigation of whom he was concerned. They represent the basis of our knowledge from which we start before proceeding to the bewildering variety of effects that emanate from it.

One more point in this connection. For reasons that I cannot explain here, the internal anxiety in question is very apt to become transformed into a feeling of guiltiness or unworthiness, and the unconscious mind is able to apprehend this feeling only in a concrete form. We have to translate this curious state of affairs into conscious language by saying that, when anxiety is engendered, the unconscious mind imagines that it, or rather the body of the person concerned, has inside it an evil and dangerous object, one which, in its turn, is visualized—on cannibalistic lines—as a part or the whole of a foreign human body. I am sure that at this point I am already leaving your comprehension, and so will repeat in simpler language the point I am making. It is merely that fear and bad conscience are two closely related manifestations. They have indeed a reciprocal relationship. It is not only that, as Hamlet said, 'Conscience does make cowards of us all', but further that fear does in itself give rise to a bad conscience. The latter point, though less familiar, can nevertheless be illustrated from common knowledge. You will remember how the Jews of the Old Testament, whenever they were terrified by a fresh misfortune, immediately searched their hearts and had recourse to sackcloth and ashes.

There are very many defence mechanisms, as we call them, which serve the function of protecting against the deep anxiety and guilt. I will mention two of them at this point because of their special importance. One is termed introjection, in which something which is believed to be good and strong is absorbed from the outer world, that is, from another human being, and incorporated within. There it is meant to counteract the power of the evil object equated with the anxiety and guilt, to neutralize it or dissolve it into nothingness. This process, which at its simplest level is conceived of in cannibalistic terms, plays a great part socially in the constant search for a good and trustworthy leader or prophet or even for abstract ideas to which one can pin one's faith. The opposite mechanism to this is termed projection, whereby an effort is made to get rid of the internal evil object by expelling it, projecting it on to another human being and ascribing to the latter the qualities of evil and danger in question. The most vivid and painful example we have of this at present is Germany's desperate efforts to get rid of the bad in her system which she ascribes to the section of her population called Jews. Why she should at present feel so afflicted with a sense of internal badness, and how it comes that she can so successfully project it on to her Jewish population, are interesting and important problems in themselves about which I may be able to say something later.

A sinister feature of both these mechanisms is their tendency to be expressed in absolute terms. The persons and ideas with which they deal have to be *wholly* good or *wholly* bad, a feature which at once removes them from the field of reality. In the case of introjection this feature is a great hindrance to attainable improvements and progress; in fact, it is in large part what is behind the prevailing disbelief in progress. The French proverb, '*le mieux est l'ennemi du bien*', would make better psychology if it were reversed into: the good, that is the absolutely good, is the enemy of the better. The absolute conceptions connected with projection are similarly defiant to rational estimates. It is hopeless to discuss with a full-blooded Nazi the extremely variable qualities possessed by the different members of their Jewish population, because by definition they are all to him wholly and completely and unalterably bad. Without this presupposition the mechanism which he feels to be so necessary to German salvation would be ineffective.

Let us now try to apply these basic considerations to some of the more striking political phenomena of the present day. I will begin by considering what lies behind the word propaganda. In medico-psychological circles of forty or fifty years ago, the conception of suggestion played a tremendous part. The word suggestion became so all-explaining that scepticism was finally aroused by this very quality. Ideas that explain everything usually explain very little. Psycho-analysts were for years accustomed to having their therapeutic results ascribed to 'suggestion' and to have all their observations and conclusions put in doubt by the dictum that they were probably all due to 'suggestion'. In our daily work, on the contrary, we were rather impressed by the relative weakness of what is called the suggestive process, into the definition of which I do not wish to go here. We gradually lost our initial respect for it by finding that, if a suggestion made to a patient did not fulfil certain conditions, that is, did not correspond with certain motive forces already at work in him, the effect of it was extremely transitory and easy to estimate. When, on the other hand, it produced a striking effect, this was brought about essentially by the forces at work within the patient and only to a small extent by the existence of the uttered suggestion. Generalizing from this, we became rather sceptical about the sociologists' outcry concerning the power of the Press, and felt that it was greatly exaggerated. Recent events in Russia and Germany, however, have made me, for a moment, question the former psycho-analytical attitude. The devastating way in which all common sense can be dissipated and replaced by fantastically unreal beliefs has been extremely impressive. Nevertheless, so far as I have been able to make a closer examination of the problem, I have found no good grounds for altering my earlier views, and I am inclined to think that the only reason why such tremendous effects have been possible by the use of the Press, the wireless, and other means of propaganda, is that they were well aimed at a body of highly charged emotion which was already present in a latent form in the victims. What that propaganda has done has mainly been to provide a welcome sanction for emotional wishes already simmering below the surface. Let us consider a concrete example of this. Millions of respectable Germans, who were previously ordinary citizens of their country and of the world, have been induced to believe that they are members of a chosen race, which by its unique gifts was designed by fate to dominate all others, but that unfortunately they were surrounded by an envious and hostile world who hated them to the core, and who not only would take but had already taken every opportunity possible to ill-treat and subject them. I am not, of course, maintaining that the whole of these two beliefs are purely delusional and have no relation whatever to reality. All I am concerned to point out is that the absoluteness of the terms in which they are cast would arouse a psychiatrist's suspicions and that, if he were a good psychiatrist, he would wish to inquire further into the previous state of mind that made the emergence of these beliefs possible. He would, I think, be guided to a central sore point in the German complaints of being unloved, namely, the angry warmth with which they repudiate the so-called war-guilt lie of the Treaty of Versailles. I do not propose to embark on the complex historical study of the causes of the last war, but it seems to me likely that anxieties aroused among Germans by the immediate post-war years—I refer to the hunger, currency inflation, political uncertainty, and so on—found considerable food for reactions to guilt in the memories of the blustering and aggressive behaviour of German rulers during the twenty years preceding the war.

This phenomenon of wholesale methods of suggestion naturally leads one to what has perhaps always been the central problem of mass psychology, namely, the inner meaning of the relationship between the leaders and the led. Those specially interested in this subject may be referred to Freud's *Group Psychology and the Analysis of the Ego* in which he makes some very important contributions to our knowledge of it. One of the points he makes is that it is impossible for stability to be brought about in a group unless something common to the ego ideals of all members of the group can be incorporated in a suitable leader. This leader then represents the qualities that the various individuals have been striving after, and so he will be looked up to and admired. Since Freud's book was published more knowledge has been gained about the relationships of this ego ideal which throws an even more important light on the function of the leader in this respect. The ego ideal, that is, the group of conceptions of which the ego most highly approves and towards the realization of which it strives, is only one aspect of an important institution in the mind which nowadays is called the super-ego. The super-ego is charged not only with the maintenance of high ideals and standards, but also with the duty of punishing and crushing anything that offends against them. Moreover, it is only on the conscious level that it exercises these functions, which are akin to what we are familiar with in our judiciary. In deeper layers of the mind its standards, far from being idealistic, are based essentially on whatever it believes will protect against anxiety, standards which are often extremely irrational as judged by our conscious knowledge. Its checking and punishing activities, furthermore, are in these deeper levels often carried out with an attitude of insensate brutality, of which the self-inflicted sufferings of our neurotics are only one manifestation.

The upshot of these considerations is that there is a close connection between leading or governing and cruelty. It would be more accurate to say that the connections lie so close to each other in the unconscious mind that there is always a risk of apparently paternal benevolence in a ruler deteriorating, either temporarily or permanently, into inhumanity and ruthlessness. One could cite any number of liberal rulers whom this fate has befallen; the Czar Alexander I of Russia is one of the first examples that occurs to one's mind. Were it not for this unfortunate propensity more people would hail government by a benevolent autocracy than in fact do. Experience has shown that only very exceptional men can be trusted to continue in their benevolence when given supreme power. Various political means have, therefore, been devised to exercise check on the possession of supreme power. These checks are not always so potent as is popularly believed, and it is likely that a democracy exercises less influence on those in the key positions of state than is sometimes thought. This is most evident, and perhaps necessarily so, in times of emergency. We experienced a striking example of it during the recent war crisis. When it came to the point of crucial action, it was found that the decision depended on the will of one man alone who, for all we know, may not have communicated his inmost thoughts and intentions even to his own Cabinet, let alone to the democracy he was representing. Politically speaking, this introduces an unknown element and an uncertainty into our social life which is very disconcerting. We have found various rough-and-ready means for selecting our leaders by appraising their political capacity in the narrow sense of the word, and we apply to them certain minimum standards of intelligence and respectability. It has occurred to hardly anyone, however, to demand more than this, to ask for any reassurance that the inner psychological stability of, for instance, our Prime Minister, or Foreign Secretary, should be one of a satisfactory order. I could easily give you examples of the way in which unresolved personal conflicts in the individual's unconscious may cause his judgement and conduct to deviate alarmingly from the rational in times of crisis, and I am persuaded that, in a sane society, a leader would be required to pass certain elementary psycho-analytic tests, if not to have been properly analysed himself.

From the descriptions I have just given of the rôle of the leader, it follows that he has to represent various more or less abstract ideas, to stand for a particular policy or cause. Sometimes, when these ideas are sufficiently definite and coherently grouped, the personality of the actual leader becomes of less importance. We may, in this respect, contrast the wave of nationalism that has passed over Europe in the last hundred years with the earlier forms of nationalistic uprisings where the personality of the leader was all important. We cannot fail, for instance, to associate the resurgence of Scottish nationalism with the names of William Wallace and Robert Bruce, but personally I cannot at the moment recollect who it was that made Belgium into a nation a hundred years ago. I am venturing on sociological ground here, but it is hard not to connect the recent wave of nationalism, to which most of you would, I am sure, ascribe many of our present woes, with the manifest decline in religious beliefs that has taken place in the same period. The fate of the Roman Catholic Church of late, for instance, has been most striking. With the exception of the Irish Free State and certain parts of America, it may be said to have lost most of the political influence and power it had a hundred or even fifty years ago. It is being reduced to the status of an Italian National Church and, even there, only this week, we have been astounded to observe how an appeal, written by the Pope himself to Mussolini imploring him to stay his hand and not violate the Catholic doctrine on the important subject of marriage, was not only ignored in action, but actually not even answered. It would be tempting to speculate on the reason for this remarkable state of affairs, and I can make the following psychological comment on it. The history of both the individual and of mankind at large shows a curious oscillation between, on the one hand, a revolt against external authority and the desire to establish personal freedom of conscience and responsibility and, on the other hand, a shrinking from responsibility and a desire for someone else to take over the burden of one's conscience and to issue dictates accordingly which the individual then gladly obeys. The wave of emancipation to which we give the names of Renaissance and Reformation was followed by a couple of centuries—until the French Revolution—of increased conservatism and even servitude. The second wave of emancipation associated with scientific progress and the industrial era has now been followed by a vehement clamour for authority which has proved highly perturbing to those brought up in the liberal traditions of the last century. Whatever may have been the sociological causes of these emancipatory movements, it is fairly evident that they overshot the mark and imposed on the people a strain of individual responsibility greater than they could bear.

Whenever this happens, and the people clamour for an authoritative government to guide and support them, the inner weakness and flinching from responsibility which this betokens set into action certain primitive mental mechanisms of which I will mention one here. It is the belief in omnipotence, akin to the belief in the absolute of which I spoke earlier in another connection. The people then demand that the authoritative rulers they have clamoured for should possess this quality. The belief in human omnipotence is an extremely troublesome thing, both individually and socially. It arises, as I just hinted, in a very primitive region of the mind, at the earliest infantile level, one we call the psychotic region because of its resemblance to the manifestations of the insane. It is the part of the mind that is most obviously divorced from reality. Even in our own so-called democratic country we are familiar with the constant cry, 'Why doesn't the government do something about it?', and a great deal of social discontent and resentment is the result of disappointment at finding this infantile belief unfulfilled. At times people cling to the belief in the face of all evidence to the contrary by means of imputing evil designs to their rulers—the train of thought being: 'We know they are omnipotent and so if they do not do this desired thing it can only be because they are wicked'. It was a similar train of thought that led to the invention of the devil and, incidentally, it could have been predicted that once the belief in the devil waned, that in God must also in time weaken because of the difficulty of making him carry the weight of both good and evil. In more dictatorial countries than ours the demand for omnipotence in rulers is so strong that the latter have to make constant efforts to meet it. This is the psychological reason why the position of dictators is so notoriously delicate, and why they are so sensitive to any loss in prestige, that the temptation to retrieve it by a violent *coup* may be overwhelming. It is extremely difficult for a dictator to act this part for long without being captured by the belief itself and thus becoming megalomaniac. Even Napoleon lost, at the end, his usually close touch with reality. We often see great dictators express this attitude by mystical beliefs in their destiny or mission, divine or otherwise; they are apt to be religiously God-inspired or to usurp the station of God himself. Cynical criticism makes them out to transcend even this, as in the story of the angelic messenger anxiously searching for a first-class psychiatrist to treat an illness that had befallen the Almighty who, the messenger said, was suffering from megalomania and believed that he was Hitler.

I spoke earlier of the connection between the belief in omnipotence and the mechanism of projection. Now this mechanism has, in the infantile psychotic layer of the mind, a close connection with a tendency which in psychiatry we term paranoid. A prominent manifestation of it is what are known as delusions of persecution, the belief that the whole world is against one and is plotting to compass one's ruin. We have seen, of late, tragic examples of this in Germany, and particularly in Russia. I have not heard, however, of any Foreign Office consulting psychiatric experts on the safest ways of coping with this dangerous complaint.

I will finish what I have to say with some words on a cognate subject, on an attitude of mind which emanates from the same early layer of mental development. When faced with a frustration or thwarting, the wise man measures the strength of his thwarted desire with the strength of the opposition to it, and then takes the most appropriate steps, which may be of the most varied kind, for overcoming the opposition. When he knows that the frustration is not to be overcome he 'tholes' it, to use a good Scottish word. This mode of response, however, is the product of a complex mental development. It is not at all a primitive and, so to speak, natural reaction. The latter is seen rather in the convulsive fits of the thwarted infant, in the tantrums of nursery years, in the loss of temper which is gradually educated out of the schoolboy and in the attacks of furor which occasionally seize even adults. The important point about the primitive reaction is that it is an indication of weakness or even helplessness rather than of strength. Now side by side with this instinctive response goes a mental attitude which, in later stages, we may term a belief. It is the belief that force is the strong man's response to frustration, one of the most fateful beliefs entertained by mankind. I am not, of course, saying that a strong man would never use force, but I do say, as a psychologist, that the tendency to resort to force, and especially violence, as the *first* response instead of the last, is a sign of inner weakness, of lack of self-confidence, and not at all of strength. Violence, *i.e.* uncontrolled force, may undoubtedly produce consequences, but they are seldom either effective or lasting ones. Talleyrand once justly said: 'You can do anything with bayonets except sit on them'. On the other hand, it is equally true that to be blind to a real danger from the fear of having to use force is not the sign of a balanced mentality. I will leave it to the discussion to bring out the implications of this in current affairs.

XVIII

EVOLUTION AND REVOLUTION[1]

From the previous lectures in this course you have heard in considerable detail something of the more important respects in which psycho-analysis has contributed to our knowledge of social-psychological problems. From this final lecture, which is intended to some extent as a summary of the others, you may well wish to gather some hints of a practical nature about what it is desirable to do in the way of dealing with these problems. Science, however, has a tantalizing way of refusing to answer questions of this sort, rightly regarding them as outside its sphere when cast in such a form, and confining itself to stating—whenever it can—what measures have to be adopted to achieve such and such an effect, granted that someone desires to achieve that particular effect. Psychological science goes even further on this annoying path and, turning on the questions themselves, converts them into an object of study for its own purposes. Instead of answering the question, it proceeds to take an interest in the reasons for asking it and the motives behind the wish to answer it.

Least of all can I gratify the wishes of those who may look for any psycho-analytical philosophy of life or *Weltanschauung*. There can, in the nature of things, be no such conception, any more than there can be a botanical or a chemical philosophy of life. All we can offer is a set of facts, of conclusions and considerations, which it is advan-

[1] Lecture delivered at the Institute of Psycho-Analysis, May 23, 1939. Published in the *International Journal of Psycho-Analysis*, vol. xxii.

tageous to bear in mind when reflecting on certain problems. Nevertheless I would not underestimate the value of what we have to offer. The prevailing muddle, to use a mild expression, into which the social relations of mankind have obviously landed, both intra-nationally and inter-nationally, is more than anything else due to ignorance of just those unconscious forces on the nature of which psycho-analysis is throwing so much light. To control and manipulate those forces, as we can do with so many other natural agencies, may prove to be difficult enough, but it is evidently altogether impossible so long as we do not even know of their existence. Psycho-analysis has already done very much more than reveal their existence. It has been able to tell us a great deal about their nature, and even about the conditions on which the control and modification of them depends.

The word 'Evolution' has many connotations, among which the biological one is perhaps the most prominent. Here we are, of course, concerned with it in a sociological context, but we shall find that it is harder to separate the biological and sociological contexts than might be thought. It will be more convenient to begin with the other concept in the title, that of 'Revolution'. Most people, especially nowadays, are apt to be confident about what is meant by a revolution in society, and what are the characteristics of such a change. I do not myself find it so easy to apprehend the essential ones, and will invite you to follow my efforts to do so. This will necessitate a slight incursion into history before we can consider the psycho-analytical implications of our theme.

I suppose that the criteria which would most readily come to the mind in distinguishing a revolutionary from an evolutionary social change are the *speed* with which it was brought about, the *scale and importance* of the change, and the *violence* of the means used to effect it. Now let us see how these criteria really apply to the facts. In the first place, we have to distinguish between political, social, and material revolutions. Such a distinction has this much artificial in it, that it is hard to get one without the others following in its train. Perhaps the political revolution is the one that comes nearest to existing in a relatively pure form. When it does, however, we often do not call it a revolution; it somehow does not seem important enough. We do not think of the replacement of the Lancastrian by the Yorkist dynasty, bloody enough as it was, as a true revolution; it was so much of a replacement of one thing by another very similar in kind. The French in 1848 had a revolution whereby they replaced a monarchy by a republic, but we do not speak of the subsequent *coup d'état* by which Louis Napoleon replaced the republic by an Empire as a revolution, although the change had a certain amount of importance. Is it that in both these cases the agent of the change was not massive enough? Must a revolution be effected by a large number, perhaps the majority, of the population? This is seldom, if ever, so; revolutions are usually engineered by an active minority and not even desired by the majority, though means may later be taken to secure the acquiescence of the latter. We describe the recurrent *coups d'état* of South American republics as revolutions, when the number of people concerned, or interested, is often very small. Perhaps the best recent example in Europe of a political revolution was the *coup d'état* by which Mussolini not only seized administrative power but radically changed the form of government, though the change appears to have been approved by only a minority. The Nazi revolution in Germany differed in having a certain show of legality in its early stages, so that at least a thin thread of continuity persisted in the change. Both these political revolutions have been accompanied by considerable social changes and by some amount of material ones, the changes being much greater in Germany than in Italy. If we turn to our own country we can perceive a feature which will prove of some theoretical interest. What we call the Glorious Revolution of 1688, in which Parliament ignored the established laws of succession, was, strictly speaking, not so much a sudden revolution as one of the two or three peaks in a lengthy process whereby the Commons successfully asserted their supremacy over the Crown. This process, if we date its culmination by the Septennial Act in the reign of George I, extended over three-quarters of a century and has indeed gone on operating, in ever-diminishing measure, to the present day. Similarly, the great French Revolution of 1789 itself was not extinguished when Napoleon seized power. It was followed by three smaller ones which in the course of a century achieved its aims of breaking the power of both the Monarchy and the Nobility. What the British call the American Revolution, termed by Americans the War of Independence, was again essentially a political revolution, but, trenchant as the event was, it may be also regarded as an episode in the long endeavour to emancipate America from European influence—a process which some Americans complain is still not completed and which undoubtedly never will be until the stream of influences flows in the reverse direction, as it is visibly on the point of doing.

These last reflections suggest that some revolutions at least are only modifications of evolution and we may put the instructive question: is this true of all revolutions and, if not, what is the difference between those of which it is true and those of which it is not?

Let us turn now to revolutions of a different order,

namely material revolutions. I will mention two of them. The great Industrial Revolution in England was most active from the middle of the eighteenth to the middle of the nineteenth century, although its operations extended a century before and a century after this period. Though essentially of a technical nature, it brought with it vast social and considerable political changes. One has only to think of the displacement of the landed gentry by the new plutocracy, the extension of the suffrage, and so on. In our own days we have seen a somewhat similar revolution initiated by Benz's discovery of the internal combustion engine. This has led to an ever-increasing tempo in daily life, to a greater informality in dress and social manners, to an extensive urbanizing of the country and, above all, to the loosening or destruction of local topographical bonds through the greater ease of communications. Now it will be noted that these material revolutions do not satisfy very well the criteria from which we started. They were not accomplished swiftly nor were they brought about by means of violence. They were not, it is true, entirely dissociated from violence. In the former revolution many lives were lost in industrial rioting against the new machinery, while the complacency with which we regard the horrific annual slaughter on our roads betokens an attitude towards violence which psychologically is not altogether remote from a willingness to inflict it. Furthermore, at least in the industrial revolution, a ruthlessness was manifested which, in its callous disregard for human suffering and in its replacement of beauty by ugliness, could only have proceeded from a group of instinctual activities similar to that which in other circumstances results in open violence. Possibly it is the dim perception of this feature that makes us unhesitatingly apply the term revolution to a process which at first sight would appear to differ greatly from the other changes we class as revolutionary.

The French Revolution of 1789 and the Russian Revolution of 1917 are perhaps the best examples of social revolutions. Naturally they brought with them both political and material changes as well, but essentially they aimed at changing the social relationships subsisting between different classes in the community, the French one by attacking the social privileges of certain classes, the Russian one by attacking what is called the exploiting powers of certain classes. Of the three classes of revolution the social one undoubtedly evokes the most bitterness and hatred, a fact which leads us directly to consideration of the essential nature of revolution.

I would here put forward the thesis that revolutionary changes are, with a single exception, evoked by the identical forces that bring about evolutionary ones. We have seen that the element of time is not decisive: revolutionary changes may take centuries to produce their effect, while evolutionary ones need not necessarily demand a notably long period for their action. The vastness of the scale may be similar in both, even if this feature is sometimes more visibly striking with the revolutionary changes. The element of violence is not always prominent in revolutionary changes nor always absent from evolutionary ones. At most the degree of tension preceding the change may vary somewhat in the two cases.

Yet the exception I hinted at is of profound significance. What really marks off revolutionary changes in the strict sense from evolutionary ones is the feature of *destructiveness*. The practical test of its presence is whether the former and now displaced conditions are permitted to survive and co-exist with the new ones, or at least are transformed in such a fashion that their essential elements persist even if in a new guise.[1] When the avowed object of the change is the annihilation of something that went before, and the consignment of it to complete oblivion, then we can truly speak of a revolution. The attitude of Bolshevism to Christianity is perhaps the most striking modern example of this, and the intensity of it may be measured by the relentless way in which the truths of history are sacrificed in its interest.

By far the most pungent writing on the subject of revolution, at least so far as I know, is Bernard Shaw's *The Revolutionist's Handbook*. From its Preface I will quote the following passages that connect with my next theme:

> Any person under the age of thirty, who, having any knowledge of the existing social order, is not a revolutionist, is an inferior.
>
> All who achieve real distinction in life begin as revolutionists.
>
> The most distinguished persons become more revolutionary as they grow older, though they are commonly supposed to become more conservative owing to their loss of faith in conventional methods of reform.
>
> And yet Revolutions have never lightened the burden of tyranny: they have only shifted it to another shoulder.

The last sentence brings us back, almost cynically so, to the *astronomical* meaning of the word 'revolution', which there relates to the way in which a celestial body, with eternal recurrence, traverses a curved path to regain its original position. Is it really possible, as Bernard Shaw's historical studies lead him to insist, that—apart from the element of destruction—revolutions merely re-establish on another plane similar conditions to what had gone before?

We come at last to the psycho-analytical contributions that can be made to this subject. Bernard Shaw was

[1] I owe this formulation to my son, Mervyn Jones.

EVOLUTION AND REVOLUTION

doubtless right in saying that anyone under the age of thirty who is sensitive to life must be a revolutionary; it is the natural path to manhood. But what does that mean in the language of the unconscious? Surely no more and no less than the impulse of youth to displace the old, or, more specifically, the Oedipus wish to kill the father. This audience must already be so familiar with that theme, and all the previous lectures in the course have dealt so fully with it, that I do not intend to develop it here except to add one consideration of interest. It is often charged against revolutionaries that they crave for change for the sake of change rather than from a true desire for the new, and this charge is commonly enough borne out in the pathetic, and indeed tragic, feature of revolutions that the leaders, after their success, tend to reproduce just the attributes of their predecessors against which they had most vehemently inveighed: again we may quote a simple example of this from Russia, where the Cheka, later the Ogpu, exactly reproduced the notorious 'Third Section' or Ochrana of the later Czarist regime, the descendant of the Oprichnina of Ivan the Terrible. We know that the attitude of the boy to his father is usually an ambivalent one, composed, on the one hand, of admiration with the desire to emulate him and, on the other hand, of hostility with the desire to replace him. The influence of the paternal figure may be so great that the boy, instead of developing something new and individual wherewith to express his own personality, often aims at simply displacing the father with the object of reigning in his stead in the same fashion as his father did and with his same attributes.

We know that a revolution is no time for timid leaders, and we are familiar with the tendency of power to pass into the hands of extremists, of those who have no compunction in taking matters to the uttermost point—that of murder of the Father figure. We are also familiar with the tendency to subsequent reactions and successful counter-revolutions which—as with the Restoration of 1660—are often joyfully greeted by the populace. Both these features are intelligible in the light of the Oedipus complex. Those in a state of misgiving attempt half-measures which are swept away by the more full-blooded rebels. Then comes the later wave of remorse that favours the counter-revolution unless the previous regime, as in Russia, had become completely despicable.

The most interesting question, however, and by far the most important one sociologically, is why it is that some revolutionaries are content with seizing power and changing social or political conditions, while others are possessed with a fury of destructiveness that cannot contemplate any continued existence of the things displaced. Whence this bitter hatred and intolerance, the effects of which are always regretted by later generations who realize what they have lost for ever? We find the same contrast in our patients. With some the Oedipus complex follows a straightforward path of development which enables the individual to oppose, resist, fight, and even dispossess his various rivals in life with a relatively easy conscience: it is of the essence of life that every generation strives to measure itself with, and where possible surpass, the preceding one. With others the matter is more grim. For them life is not a game, or even a battle, but a very deadly affair in which everything is at stake—something that is more than life itself. They take very literally the old saying: all is fair in love and war. And they are prone to descend to the most malicious and underhand ways of gratifying their hate, gloating over the discomfiture or destruction of their opponent, and trampling with fury on his remains or possessions. To what can we ascribe this remarkable difference in the two cases?

You will probably know that at present much of psycho-analytic research is concentrated on the difficult problem of the aggressive or destructive impulses, and that investigation is being eagerly carried out into their nature and their relationships. It is a study that is very far from being completed, and there is a considerable divergence of opinion among analysts over several of the issues. You will know, for example, that Freud's suggestion of an innate self-destructive tendency, which he calls the 'death instinct', has not found very wide acceptance among analysts. This is not the place for me to enter into a discussion of these vexed problems, which are certainly not solved at present. But I should like to offer two contributions which I think most analysts would find their experience confirms.

The maliciousness, hatred, and often cowardice that so characterize the destructive type of revolutionary indicate, as indeed we find in our actual clinical practice, that such a person has not less sense of guiltiness, but more, than the more moderate variety. Something, therefore, must have happened internally to allow him to pursue his murderous aim with the callousness, ruthlessness, and apparent freedom from guiltiness that are the attributes of the typical destructive revolutionary. The Jacobin has been able to do something about his sense of guilt which the Girondin could not. It is not a simple matter of repression. In my experience, what has happened is that the sense of guilt in such people has been disposed of, or successfully kept at bay, by their developing in a specially high degree the paranoid mechanism of projection. They have persuaded themselves that their opponents are so unspeakably evil that they deserve no better fate than torture and death, and that, to inflict this, so far from being a guilty act, is a laudable one. They feel as noble as St. George did when crushing the dragon. In their state of exalted conviction they find it easy, in certain circumstances, to infuse a following with both dread of the wicked enemy and loathing for him, and at the same time to inspire them with confidence that if they follow their noble leader the good cause must triumph. We reach thus the conclusion that a successful revolutionary must be more than a little mad and I leave it to you to judge whether experience does not bear this out.

The mechanism of projection is of course in itself quite normal, and there are stages of infantile development where it plays such a prominent and unmistakable part as to suggest the use of the term 'paranoid stage of development'. We are constantly learning more about the factors that stimulate it, the interrelation between it and states of depression, etc., but these are technical questions that I cannot pursue here. It is extremely probable that the strength of this mechanism, and the extent of the use made of it, vary also with the inborn constitution. Please do not think, however, that I am recommending this type of constitution as a recipe for the manufacture of revolutionary leaders. On the contrary, the large majority of people of this type, if they do not develop actual insanity, become querulous, resentful, suspicious, and unhappy creatures who are useless to themselves or their fellows. It is only in highly special circumstances, both personal and social, that one of them finds an opportunity to achieve notoriety.

My second point is perhaps best introduced by means of an illustrative example. In the second millennium before Christ there lived an Egyptian King, Amenophis IV (later rechristened Akhenaten), who deserves to be recognized as the first revolutionary of whom we have much knowledge. On succeeding to the throne he overthrew the local prevailing religion, with its Theban God Amun, and for the first time in history instituted an universal monotheism. The story has gained in historical interest since Freud (1939) in his recent book on Moses has made it highly probable that here is to be found the genesis of both the Jewish religion and, indirectly, the outstanding characteristics of the Jewish people. The revolution was of a peculiarly destructive kind. Towns associated with the previous God Amun were deserted or destroyed, the word itself was obliterated from the name of the Pharaoh and his father, and immense energy was expended in erasing it from all inscriptions throughout the land. Twenty-seven years ago Abraham (1912) wrote an essay on Amenophis's revolutionary deed, which he explained in the light of the Oedipus complex as a revolt against his father. This explanation is doubtless correct, but it has been amplified in an important respect through later knowledge. Mr. Strachey (1939), in a recent paper, has pointed out that Amenophis, according to recent Egyptological discoveries, was almost certainly extremely feminine in disposition, so that he probably possessed what is called a negative Oedipus complex in addition to the familiar positive one. This Mr. Strachey correlates with the pronounced ambivalence of the Pharaoh towards the divine Father substitutes, the annihilating hatred towards Amun and the adoration of the universal and omnipotent Aten.

Now I would venture a wide generalization from this example. It has long been known, particularly from Freud's (1911) Schreber analysis, that paranoia is especially closely related to homosexuality, and I am inclined to think, also on the basis of my own analytic work, that there is a specific connection between the deadly and destructive kind of hate and the action of a paranoid defence against sex inversion, or—more strictly—against the incorporated 'bad objects' resulting from this inversion. If this proves to be true, then we shall have acquired some valuable knowledge about the psychology of revolutions and shall have a basis to work on when we begin to inquire into the practical possibilities of increasing the good and diminishing the harm pertaining to this recurrent social phenomenon.

I will now pass to the less stormy, but no less difficult, problem of social Evolution. This is, in the first place, bound up with the question of social progress. In the second half of the last century few would have doubted the reality and solidity of not only social progress but also human progress. The difference between the assumedly bestial cave man, on the one hand, with his savage propensities and his almost certainly un-dainty behaviour at the dinner table, and the refined Victorian gentleman, on the other hand, was so very striking that it was hard not to regard them as essentially different beings and to preen oneself on the enormous change that had come about in our species in the past 10,000 years. To-day our perspective is in many ways different. We know now that in all probability there were high civilizations 10,000 or perhaps more years ago, and that the species *homo* may well be a million years old. More critically objective standards have been applied to the nature of different culture levels. And, last but not least, we have seen in our own generation famous civilizations deteriorate to a level that would have been completely unbelievable forty or fifty years ago, to a level that has only occasionally been reached in the history of mankind. All this must make us very sceptical about identifying social with human progress, for it is certain that great social changes can be brought about without in any way altering man's essential nature.

When speaking of revolutionary changes, I called attention to the destructive elements that so often accompany them and said nothing about the creative, altruistic, and idealistic elements that are at least as important. It is generally found more convenient to treat of these in connection with the process of evolution, but I want to guard against simply identifying the destructive elements with revolutionary changes and creative ones with evolutionary ones. Both may be operative in either kind of change, which is why I do not make the usual sharp distinction between the two kinds. I consider the positive motives are fundamentally similar with both, although I do think that the circumstances accompanying revolution tend specially to favour the action of destructive forces, and that, when that is so, the amount of destruction is usually grosser and more irreparable than it is in evolutionary changes. At all events, let us now inquire into the nature of the idealistic and creative forces, those which are often called the forces of progress.

Psycho-analysis has contributed a great deal to our knowledge of these forces, and previous lecturers in this course, particularly Dr. Rickman, have already expounded much of it. We are far from the days when analysts were prone to cite the blessed word 'sublimation' as the *deus ex machina* in all social and idealistic impulses. Things have proved to be very much more complicated than they seemed in the early days of psycho-analysis.

The outstanding discovery of psycho-analysis in this context has been that many—and some analysts would be inclined to say all—of the original discoveries and betterments and improvements of all kinds that previously were attributed to the action of purely creative impulses are rather to be regarded as by-products resulting from the action of certain defensive mental mechanisms. The endeavour to escape from unconscious guilt and anxiety leads to infinitely varied mental activities, some of which produce what may socially be called 'improvements'. To the idealism and self-esteem of mankind it is a chastening reflection that so much of what he is most proud of is merely an accidental result of the flight from fear and pain, that a bad conscience should prove to be one of the prime motors in even our loftiest strivings. Still, if it is true, we must make the best of it and learn modesty in the process. I would warn, however, against premature generalizing in this matter. While it appears to be true that the genesis of idealistic and altruistic strivings is much more complex than used to be thought, and that in this genesis what may be called negative, reactive or defensive agents undoubtedly play an important part, that does not at all exclude the operation of more purely positive, creative agents—broadly speaking, those emanating from the love instinct—which indeed may well be factors in guiding the former set into less egotistic directions. The discovery of the importance of hate, for example, does not necessarily diminish the importance of love: it may even enhance it. In our investigations we have perforce to concentrate for a time on one or another aspect of these problems, but in presenting our results we should do our best to retain a sense of balance and proportion.

The evidence at present available goes to show that both evolutionary and revolutionary movements affecting a community are extensions of mental processes that are essentially individual in origin. By this I mean that individuals, in attempting to deal with their personal (and therefore family) conflicts, make use of the idea of society in general as a region where their conflicting impulses may be depicted, expressed, or worked out. I shall say something more presently about this process, which might be called the socialization of personal impulses.

What now can be said about the motives that impel an individual to effect changes in his surroundings? When does his dissatisfaction with them wax so great that he is led to act? Psycho-analysis demonstrates a very close correlation between this outer dissatisfaction and the inner dissatisfaction with the self. It is truly astonishing how someone possessing inner self-content can placidly endure surroundings that most people would consider urgently call for radical alteration. The internal agency that registers self-dissatisfaction Freud terms the super-ego, and the quantity of self-dissatisfaction can otherwise be expressed as the degree of tension between the super-ego and the ego. At this level the conflicts have been extensively moralized, so that we may equally well speak of the degree of reprobation with which the super-ego regards the ego for failing to reach its ideal standard. But behind this unconscious sense of guilt lies the still deeper problem of anxiety. The criticism on the part of the super-ego is ultimately, therefore, a defensive mechanism designed to prevent the generation of anxiety in the ego, or—put in more ideational language—to protect the self from the supposed dangers arising from id impulses. In the last resort, therefore, we may say that inner content is equivalent to a sense of security.

The ideas of danger are visualized by the unconscious ego as concrete evil objects, derived from distorted pictures of either persons or bodily parts of persons, principally the parents. The dangerous objects are alternately imagined to be within the self—or rather the actual body of the self—or in the outer world. There are two fundamental ways of countering them, apart from other defence-mechanisms to be found on a higher level. Either one attacks them in the hope of sadistically destroying them or one seeks for safe, 'good' loving objects which shall neutralize their evil power. In the Middle Ages one either prayed to God to be protected from the machinations of witches or else one burned the supposed witch. A third method, and the one most extensively used of all, is to allow the evil powers to operate in phantasy, checking their action in reality with the aid of various devices, and then to counter their bad effects by reparative or restitutive processes that are intended either to undo these effects or to make them good by compensating for them.

According as one or other of these three mechanisms predominate with a given individual so will a particular type of personality result. We are familiar with the way in which in religion love of 'good', leading to piety and charity, alternates with hatred of 'evil', leading to denunciation and intolerance. Micah, Jesus, and St. Francis contrast here with Savonarola, Calvin, and John Knox. It cannot be denied that the latter make the more vivid and lively personalities, but it is probable that the teaching of the former has the more lasting effect. What is true of religion here is true of life in general.

The first type, where the desire to love and be loved predominates, is found *in excelsis* in the *saint*. The saint, as distinct from the ascetic, does not cope with the evil of the world; he averts his gaze with a sigh. Nietzsche said once: 'Where one can no longer love, there one should pass by'. At the other extreme we have the personality where the internal turmoil is so vehement that it can be dealt with only by provoking and thus reproducing a corresponding violent turmoil in the outer world. Such a person makes the typical social agitator or, on another level, the nihilistic *revolutionary*. Between these extremes there is the dissatisfied meliorist, whose restitutive impulses acting in a piecemeal fashion make him into a *social reformer*.

The reason why these distressed personalities become people with a pronounced attitude towards the universe, or, more strictly, towards society, is that the fundamental mechanisms of introjection and projection permit of extensive displacements. In the place of the parents who are alternately loved and injured, or towards whom complex processes of restitution are set in motion, there appears the concept of society as a whole with all its rich 'good' and 'bad' components. The impulses of love and hate, of reparation and restitution, together with the sense of guilt and the ever-present anxiety, undergo a tremendous socialization. The person is convinced that what he is thinking or feeling began with the idea of society and solely refers to it. He is quite unaware that only a part of it really relates to society and that the greater part was generated in a more personal field, that of his attitude towards himself (his body and its impulses) and his parents, a field which has now been replaced by the social one.

I pointed out years ago that there would appear to be an optimum point, where there is neither too much nor too little repression, in relation to which the maximum amount of sublimation occurs. One may venture a similar statement on the conflict between the search for 'good' and the destruction of 'evil', between the forces which Freud has personified under the names of Eros and Thanatos. The former would seem to have more lasting qualities, the latter more dramatic ones.

The further question is, in what circumstances do these socialized motives of individuals coalesce to produce mass effects? Previous lecturers have to some extent considered such phenomena as mass infection, mob manifestations, and so on, and Dr. Bibring has dealt at length with the important problem of leadership. I will only say in regard to this, that the hope and sense of omnipotence which leaders offer, naturally make their greatest appeal when the opposite attitudes are widely prevalent, namely depression (with perhaps despair) and the sense of inferiority or unlovedness. We know, from the psychology of individuals, that the presence of these attitudes indicates a deep-seated sense of guilt which is being inadequately met by other measures. The source of this guilt is sometimes a sociological problem, but we have to remember the latent sense of guilt in all human beings which is apt to be stirred by any great misfortune or privation. The Hebrew custom of meeting misfortune by having recourse to sackcloth and ashes was a frank recognition of this, but more often the sense of guilt is denied and replaced by projective accusations against others in an attempt to ward off unhappiness and feelings of inferiority. In short, the preliminary condition necessary to the emergence of a forceful leader is suffering. Whereas, however, the saint responds with a 'Come unto me all ye that labour and are heavy laden, and I will give you rest', the leader of revolt cries, 'Follow me, and I will give you revenge on those who caused your misfortunes'. In the latter case Evolution becomes Revolution.

I come, finally, to the most important topic of all, to the difficult questions of whether any biological evolution is taking place in the sphere of the mind and of what constitutes permanent progress. Here the distinction between the effects of tradition on the one hand, and of true evolutionary changes on the other, can be extensively paralleled by the distinction between material and spiritual progress respectively; for it is material progress that is handed on by tradition, while innate spiritual changes would have to be biological.

It is evident that most of what we prize as civilization and culture, whether in the sphere of knowledge or in that of social institutions such as law and religion, has been laboriously acquired by individuals, made the common property of their fellows, and then passed on to successive generations, each of which has to acquire it afresh. To take an example: if a human community had to begin again in some isolated continent, aeons would have to pass before it would once more develop a knowledge of insulin therapy or of wireless technique. It is only the ignorant who suppose that a garage mechanic, because he can use the telephone and manipulate an internal combustion engine, is intrinsically superior to, or has a better brain than, an Athenian gentleman of the fifth century B.C. who had none of the requisite knowledge at his disposal. And in the course of millennia knowledge and social institutions grow to a high level and are again and again utterly destroyed. The sole agency that can preserve them from such a fate is a continuous tradition; if this is badly interrupted, most or all is lost, and mankind has once more to resume its painful efforts. Calamities of nature such as those leading to famine, may thus interrupt the continuity, but much more potent are the human activities of War and Revolution. Most, and possibly all, that distinguishes us from primitive man, what we treasure most highly and preciously, is safeguarded by one thing only—*continuity of tradition*. This is a consideration often lost sight of, but always at a heavy cost.

Turning now to the matter of progress in the realm of the spirit, we must confess that we find ourselves in a region of obscure speculation with hardly any light of knowledge to guide us. Almost the sole ray is Freud's theory, to which I adhere, concerning the development from the pre-totemistic level of the primal horde. It seems to me probable that the chain of links: parricide—talion fear—guilt—remorse—homosexual, fraternal bonds, does provide a chronological series leading from primitive man to complex social life. But it is hard to get further than this. Freud's opinion that these traumatic events leave inherited traces that accumulate is quite incompatible with modern biological theory and, to me at least, would seem inherently improbable. It is not hard to suppose an alternative: that the social utility of these processes has in itself enough selection value to have effected some biological change. But if such change has come about at all in the past half-million years it must still be a very slight one, as is evidenced by the readiness with which regression so often takes place.

Yet any permanent and innate change in the spiritual nature of man can, so far as we can see, be brought about only by a process of selective breeding. The feeble and chaotic attempts hitherto made in this direction, for instance by our nobility, have produced too indefinite and inconstant results to permit of any useful conclusions being drawn from them. The science of heredity cannot get to work on the problem until something is known of the mental elements with which we have to do, the genes of the mind. And in my opinion it is only psycho-analysis that will enable us ever to isolate and define these. Freud has provided us with an invaluable tool for research. When enough knowledge has been accumulated by such research there will arise some day a genius who will place the necessary conclusions at the disposal of practical geneticians. And then, perhaps, a ruler may appear who shall put their advice into operation. He would be the first wholly beneficent Revolutionary, and it may well be that he would confirm Bernard Shaw's interesting prediction that 'superiority in the unconscious self will be the true characteristic of the Superman'.

REFERENCES

ABRAHAM, K. (1912). (*Trans.* 1935.) 'Amenhotep IV (Ikhnaton)', *Psychoanal. Quart.*, vol. iv, p. 537.
FREUD, S. (1911). (Trans. 1925.) 'Psycho-Analytic Notes upon an Autobiographical Account of a Case of Paranoia', *Collected Papers*, vol. iii, p. 387.
— (1939). (*Trans.* 1939.) *Moses and Monotheism.*
STRACHEY, J. (1939). 'Preliminary Notes upon the Problem of Akhenaten', *International Journal of Psycho-Analysis*, vol. xx, p. 33.

XIX

THE PSYCHOLOGY OF QUISLINGISM[1]

I WILL begin what I have to say with the following propositions. The two decisive factors on which the outcome of the present war apparently depends are aircraft production and civilian moral. We need not therefore emphasize any further the importance of the latter subject, with which we are here concerned. It is, it is true, a wider field than that of Quislingism, but this constitutes not merely a special aspect of the whole: it is a chief and most important part of the whole. Furthermore, while we do not know what Hitler had in mind when he used the words 'secret weapon', there is no doubt that Quislingism and its many variants are Hitler's most valuable secret weapon, the one to which he mainly owes his spectacular successes both in his own and other countries. Although there is no reason to suppose that he has any conscious knowledge of the deep workings of his weapon, he has undoubtedly an intuitive grasp of the way in which certain aspects of human nature can be exploited to his advantage. His victims are singularly unaware of the process by which they are affected, so that it remains a *secret* even more to them than to those who engineer it. The form the phenomena in question have taken is a relatively new and startling one, a fact which in itself must engage the attention of any serious psychologist. The challenge to psychoanalysts is even more direct, inasmuch as the very secrecy

[1] Read before the British Psycho-Analytical Society, June 12, 1940. Published in the *International Journal of Psycho-Analysis*, vol. xxii.

and mystery with which the phenomena are invested indicate the operation of some deep agencies in the Unconscious, *i.e.* in the sphere of our special work. We have, therefore, strong motives, both practical and scientific, for trying to understand as much as possible about this important problem.

My next proposition is that the key to the understanding of Quislingism and the other phenomena connected with it is that they are all based on a peculiar inability to face, or even to recognize, an enemy. By an enemy I mean someone whose interests and endeavours run diametrically counter to one's own, so that one has no other emotional relationship to him than an attitude of sheer opposition. It is not common for a situation of this degree of purity to arise in life, but it is of the utmost importance both for mental integrity and for the practical issue that an individual should be able to recognize and to face such a situation when it does arise. We are concerned here with the problem of how it is that many people fail to do so, especially at a critical juncture.

Let me turn now to some purely descriptive aspects of the matter. The problem of pure Quislingism, curious as it is, would not be so difficult were it not complicated by an extensive aura of attendant phenomena, the connection of which with Quislingism has been generally overlooked. Leaving on one side for the moment the fully developed Quislings, I would call your attention to the following types which, I maintain, represent stages in that development. All of them indicate either denial or else approval of the aggressiveness of the enemy, but the important point is that there is a curious connection between these two attitudes of denying and approving. At one end of the scale we have a person, perhaps a slum dweller, who says he would be no worse off under the Nazis and that it makes no difference to him who governs the country. Then we have the escapist who used to be sure that there would be no war, though still more sure that there need be no war, and maintained that it could be avoided either by talking matters over reasonably with the opponent or by the subjects on both sides refusing to fight; what this person refused to believe was that the opponent was determined to force a fight. A next step is shown by the man who admitted the presence of a certain amount of aggressiveness in the Nazi regime, but thought that this degree was so small that it could be allayed by giving it some vent, *i.e.* by the policy of appeasement. Such a man was particularly sensitive to the possibility of increasing the aggressivity by provocation. We come, then, to the man who admitted aggressiveness but held that it was mainly justified and in no way savage or irrational. He would assert that the English would have behaved in just the same way as the Germans if they had been debarred the full use of their own country, as the Germans were in the Rhineland, or forbidden to unite with their compatriots such as the Austrians and Sudeten-Germans. This moral justification can pass over into actual admiration, such as that of the man who says, 'We could do with a bit of Hitler here' or is impressed by the efficiency and positive achievements of the Nazi regime. Even so, the transition from this type to the fully fledged Quisling is not an easy one, and particular factors have to operate before it can be brought about.

There would appear to be two main classes of people who tend to be seduced into the more manifest Quisling direction: the dissatisfied and the insecure. Both of these elements may, of course, be present together. The experience of Austria in particular shows that the Nazi infiltration took place largely among the dissatisfied and ambitious, often junior, members of firms, banks, or

THE PSYCHOLOGY OF QUISLINGISM

government departments. I can recall instances myself of men who had been previously dismissed for incapacity or dishonesty and who made out that they had been unfairly treated; the motive of revenge is here evident. The element of disgruntled ambition may also be active among scions of the well-to-do classes. In the upper classes a special mechanism is sometimes at work, actuated by the fear that the privileged position of the person's class may be destroyed by what he would probably call Bolshevist tendencies. He deals with his fear of this by allying himself with the forces of destruction in the hope of emerging as a leader in the new regime. Such a person has often been afflicted with a sense of guilt about his privileged position, which for personal reasons he feels he does not deserve, and hopes to win back his self-esteem by allying himself with the forces that condemn such privileges; his bad conscience has made him side with that condemnation. In all those types there is present a dissatisfaction with, or hostility to, the present rulers of the country.

Coming now to the psycho-analytical problem concerned, I may assume that every analyst has had ample evidence of the identification of the enemy in question with certain aspects of the formidable Father imago. The torture dreams about Hitler, and the still more revealing ones of friendly intimacy with him, are apt to occur in contexts that render this interpretation inevitable. Furthermore, it becomes plain that the attitude towards the external persons is profoundly affected by the attitude of the ego towards his own internal objects, there being a constant tendency to identify the two. There is both introjection of, for instance, Nazi leaders and also projection of id impulses on to them. The cardinal attribute of what I have called the formidable Father imago is his irresistibility. There are two main reactions to it, which are apparently opposed in kind. One consists in denying the person's serious aggressivity behind the irresistibility, *i.e.* in the denial of danger and therefore in the repression of fear. The second consists in admiration of the irresistibility, often, though not always, accompanied by the tendency to identify oneself with the irresistible person. Incidentally this provides a very nice problem for those in authority: if they decry the invincibility of the enemy they play into the hands of those who complacently deny his dangerousness, whereas if they emphasize his power so as to arouse the nation they run the risk of stimulating the morbid reaction to the idea of irresistibility with which we are here specially concerned. Fortunately the question can be properly answered by paying heed to the matter of tempo.

From my own psycho-analytical data I have come to the conclusion that the fundamental process in these two apparently dissimilar reactions is really the same. It may be described as an attempt, often by devious and desperate devices, to convert the imago of the evil Father into that of a good one.

Now this attempt would surely in itself seem to be in a quite healthy direction, but everything depends on the way in which it is carried out. If it consists in strengthening the confidence in the internal good objects, with a corresponding diminution of anxiety about the dangers of the internal bad objects, then it is possible to effect a satisfactory identification between oneself and the friendly aspects of the Father imago. The Quisling direction, however, is quite other than this. A profound self-deception takes place. A belief is established in the power, in the inevitable success, and therefore in a sense in the goodness, of the internal evil objects and impulses, and this belief is then applied to the external enemy himself.

The important step in this process is indicated by the word 'therefore'. Why should inevitable success be necessarily equated with goodness? It sounds like the old doctrine that might makes right.

Subtle mechanisms may be at work here, some of which I shall presently indicate, but the fundamental reason underlying them would appear to be the identification of sadism with sexual potency.

Our starting-point in any constructive analysis must surely be the fear of the dangerous Father or of one's own dangerous impulses towards him. If one is unable to face this situation, then there remain only two alternatives: to submit to him, or to ally oneself with the dangerous forces through the mechanisms of acceptance and identification. These alternatives are not so mutually exclusive as they might appear; often they are both operative in the same person. On the whole, the former is more characteristic of the passive homosexual type, the latter of the active one. Both are *exquisitely homosexual solutions*, there being always some complex emotional relationship with the enemy in place of an attitude of *aloof opposition*. The fear is both sexualized and moralized. Passivity and masochism play an obvious part in the former process, and I may quote an example of how this may be interrelated with the guilt factors that underlie the moralization. One patient maintained that Hitler's very insistence, and the enormous energy he has devoted to achieving his aim, in itself put him in the right. It turned out that insistent 'wanting' of that degree could only mean 'wanting back', so that Hitler had a right to demand the return of what had been taken from him, all this being of course rationalized in terms of Germany's reactions to the Treaty of Versailles. The analytical point is that *primary* aggressive wanting was so repressed as to be inconceivable, though its existence was, after all, implied in the idea of the Father demanding back the penis of which he had been robbed. That this cannot be an isolated reaction is shown by the inactivity of the Allies for so many years under the illusion that Germany's conduct was a more or less proportionate response to the aggressivity of the Allies immediately after the first war and therefore need not be supposed to betoken any innate aggressivity of her own. Such is the revenge of a bad conscience; it tends to paralyse the power of resistance.

This type, in which the submission depends upon a secret hostility that cannot be accepted, is both more passive and more sexual than the next one we have to consider. Here we see the faint beginnings of a positive admiration. I am speaking of the type in which the idea of aggressivity is denied and the hope entertained that it should be possible to appease the enemy by making suitable concessions. The admiration may be somewhat masochistic and accompanied by the hope of obtaining a kind of protective security through coming to terms with the enemy. Politically this may go with a fear of 'Bolshevism', *i.e.* of a chaotic mob, which may afford grounds for identification with the powerful dictator. Perhaps this was the characteristic attitude in Denmark and Norway and it may be likened to that of the younger brother. The most complete forms of identification, however, occur where the homosexual trends are of a more active kind. With such persons tyrannical tendencies are already present which render an identification easy. One imagines this to be so with the well-known Fascist leaders in the various countries. It is probable, however, that when the alliance is complete even the most active of these types is forced to regress to the deeper level of passive homosexuality. Mussolini will probably yet follow the path of Seyss-Inquart, Henlein, and Major Quisling himself.

THE PSYCHOLOGY OF QUISLINGISM

All we have said so far, though it may go some way to explaining the ambiguous attitude of various types towards the foreign dictator, does not account for the more heinous deed of betraying one's own country and shooting one's own countrymen. It is plain that here there must always have been present some divided attitude towards the latter. I have not had the occasion of analysing a fully-fledged traitor, though I have had two patients who hoped Germany would win the war, but with several patients there has been present enough of the tendency to make me surmise that the secret of it lies in some unsatisfactory attitude towards the Mother. Treachery, by allying oneself with the conquering enemy, would seem to be an attempt sadistically to overcome the incest taboo by raping the Mother instead of loving her. Perhaps this is why it is generally regarded as the most outrageous and unnatural of crimes, since it combines disloyalty to both parents.

In conclusion, I would suggest that the people who are most subject to the wiles of Nazi propaganda are those who have neither securely established their own manhood and independence of the Father nor have been able to combine the instincts of sexuality and love in their attitude towards the Mother or other women. This is the psychological position of the homosexual.

Postscript.—Ciano's diary and much other subsequently published material have amply justified this prediction.

XX

THE PSYCHOLOGY OF THE JEWISH QUESTION[1]

I

By the Jewish Question is presumably meant the problem of what measures are feasible to render possible a more satisfactory life, and perhaps status, for Jews. It turns, more than anything else, on a study of the nature of racial prejudices in general, and of anti-Semitism in particular, matters on which remarkably little exact knowledge exists. A social anthropologist, such as I happen to be, will in the course of decades—if he is specially interested in questions of racial and national differences—assimilate from various sources a great number of impressions which ultimately broaden into opinions; but he should remember that the individual methods thus employed render the opinions reached peculiarly liable to revision on the appearance of fresh or more precise data. I shall, furthermore, confine my observations here to a few psychological aspects of the problem, being more qualified to deal with those than with the political or economic ones.

An outstanding feature that can be predicted about any racial prejudice (the word 'racial' must be begged for the moment) is that it always contains important elements of an irrational kind. The classical current example is, of course, Hitler's attribution of all manners of misfortune, with the possible exception of unseasonable weather, to the all-powerful machinations of the Jews.

[1] Contribution to a symposium entitled *Gentile and Jew*, edited by C. Newman, 1945.

This assertion may be a truism, but two less obvious corollaries follow from it. One is that to a psychologist the word 'irrational' betokens 'of unconscious origin', *i.e.* emanating from deep regions of the mind of which we are totally unaware. The consequence of this is that most people who debate such matters are really talking of things the nature and origin of which is quite unknown to them. The second corollary is perhaps the less surprising. When one says that a given mental attitude is irrational, it does not at all follow that therefore the person displaying it can be easily argued or reasoned out of it. On the contrary, it is just such attitudes that are most refractory to reasonable considerations, even when the person may be persuaded to yield temporary lip service to them. They proceed from regions of the mind where the emotional logic of phantasy, a logic which though coherent in itself is very distant from what we commonly understand by the terms, holds an almost unchallenged sway. Yet such is the faith in our own particular prejudices, which we commonly mistake for reason, that we are constantly deceived in our expectation of converting other people to what we maintain is obvious. An internationalist and a nationalist, for instance, are always surprised at the obtuseness of the other.

The first of these corollaries will probably have carried little weight from the mere statement of it. Let me, therefore, illustrate it from the present context. Analytical studies of individuals who manifest pronounced racial prejudices have revealed the curious part played in it by the simple matter of pigmentation. The fact itself is familiar enough. Indeed, it will be hard to find an example of racial prejudice against a people who were less pigmented: the Red Indians, it is true, called the invading Europeans 'Pale Faces', but it would be hypercritical to designate as prejudice their antagonism to people bent on exterminating them. Now the association between 'dark' and 'evil' is also familiar enough, as is that between blond and pure (*'non Angli sed Angeli'*, as Pope Gregory said). But what analytic studies have revealed is that this dark evil is, in the unconscious mind, related to the contents of the bowel, to material believed to have been obtained by angrily greedy impulses and invested with various intense emotions such as guiltiness, disgust, and fear. It is easy to observe how readily this association leaks through into consciousness. Every anti-Semite, for example, speaks of 'dirty Jew', ignoring their millennia-old pioneering in the field of personal hygiene as well as the fact that their cleanliness in respect of food is still a model to the rest of the world. What is of practical importance here is not the mere association with bowel content as such, but the fact that strong emotions are equated with a material substance —a phenomenon alien to the life of consciousness—and that this substance can be either incorporated or expelled. To have close contact with a dark foreigner, still more to marry one, thus comes to mean to admit some poisonous material into the system—the familiar Nazi delusion of blood contamination. On the other hand, any evil impulses the existence of which is not admitted by consciousness, can be dealt with by expelling them through what psychologists call 'projection' on to dark foreigners, and particularly such as reside in one's midst and form, in fact, part of the national entity. This is surely the explanation of the enthusiastic relief with which the troubled German mind received Hitler's evangel that all their sufferings during and after the first world war were due not to anything wrong with 'pure Germans' but to the poisonous element in their midst—German Jews. It perhaps also explains why Mediterranean peoples are less afraid of being swamped by intermarriage with dark foreigners than are more northern ones who have more blondness to lose.

Another characteristic feature of racial prejudice, none the less important for being familiar, is its quantitative aspect. Whatever the source of the idea of 'badness' in the foreigner—and there are many such—it should seem that every population has the capacity of assimilating a definite quantity of it without experiencing any sense of being harmed. This capacity varies with many factors, which is simply a way of saying that there is more prejudice against some foreigners than others and in some circumstances than in others. But it is none the less limited and definite for all that, so attempts to force an artificial increase in it is apt to be resisted very tenaciously. Let a negro, for instance, settle in an English village. If well conducted he will probably be regarded as a curiosity and treated with friendliness. But let a dozen settle there, and still more let them persist in their own alien customs, habits, speech, etc. The reaction on the part of the natives can then be predicted with certainty. It is ultimately based on fear, or a sense of danger to their standards, traditions, beliefs, customs—to the ideals that constitute that sense of personality and self-respect. Everything seems at stake, and the danger must be curbed or, better still, driven away. This simple numerical factor is only one of many. Nor does it always work out directly; it sometimes happens that an increase in the number of foreigners actually diminishes the prejudice, probably through the natives discovering that they are not as bad as they thought, *i.e.* that the danger to themselves is not as great as they feared. This is obviously more likely if the foreigners wish to adapt themselves to the native life or if they bring material advantages with them; the skilled Huguenots in England are an example of both.

II

This is not a treatise on racial prejudice in general, and I must hasten to the main theme. I will do so by raising the question whether anti-Semitism is merely a typical example of such prejudice in an acute form or whether it has distinctive features of its own. It would appear to have two such.

With the exception of the Gypsies, the Jews are the only emigrating people who, having no national home, nevertheless refuse to acquire one by assimilating themselves to the people among whom they dwell, and claim the privilege of residing in any country they choose while remaining in certain essentials apart from the other inhabitants. It may be objected that that state of affairs is largely out of Jewish control—it is obviously far more complex than here presented—but for the moment I am concerned with the volitional element in it that undoubtedly exists and which is the one that excites prejudice. What I am suggesting, in other words, is that the factors in Jews themselves resisting assimilation are as important from the point of view of prejudice as the numerous extrinsic ones impeding that process. What has become of the Goths, Vandals, Huns, and Continental Celts in the past fifteen hundred years? Except for the rapidly diminishing group of Bretons they have all vanished as such and lead a transformed existence as Spaniards, Italians, Frenchmen, and so on; the same fate has befallen the Ancient Romans. Nothing of the sort has happened with the Jews.

The baneful effects on the relations between Jews and Gentiles of this aloofness or separation, from whichever side it proceeds (and it obviously, in fact, proceeds from both), are only too painfully manifest, and need not be detailed here. In essence they consist in a latent mistrust on the part of Gentiles that, in any important situation needing co-operative action, Jews may subordinate to their own interests those of the community among whom they dwell. In every community there are, it is true, social and anti-social units, but these are seldom organized in a group and are still more seldom at all likely to join cognate groups—in possibly hostile countries.

This is an occasion for remarking on a feature of prejudice that has always to be taken into account in any context; namely, that it follows a tendency of the unconscious mind to generalize wildly wherever any strong emotion is felt. Thus what is felt to be typical of any nation is by no means what is of frequent occurrence in it. It is grossly unfair, but it is quite useless for Jews to protest that only a small minority of them would participate in a black market, for instance, so long as such conduct is for various reasons felt to be typical.

There is much reason for thinking that the primary explanation for the non-assimilation of the Jews lay in the peculiarly exclusive and arrogant nature of their religious beliefs, including that of possessing a specially favoured and more intimate relationship with the Celestial Powers than other people, except perhaps the Japanese. Among the more emancipated Jews of the past century this factor appears to have been replaced by an equivalent in the form of a curious 'superiority complex' in respect of brain power; one not very amply sustained by their achievements in the fields of art, music, science, or philosophy.

Superiority of endowment or culture need not lead to racial prejudice. In favourable conditions, *e.g.* with the Romans in Gaul or elsewhere, it may be accepted and even in time proudly incorporated in the native tradition. Naturally its existence has first to be admitted, and, whatever Jews may think to the contrary, this has, on the whole, not been so. The only exception has been in the moral and ethical sphere—I refer to the teachings of the Old Testament. So far, however, has this been from redounding to the credit of the Jews, that for three reasons, it has in fact had very much the opposite result. Moral teachers are often feared and sometimes respected, as the Old Testament itself amply illustrates, but they are seldom loved or even liked. To be liked they have to combine the unpleasant effect of their teaching on the conscience with the mollifying influence of an endearing personality; no Gentile would maintain that this has been a prominent feature of Jews. Then the moral doctrines in question were not presented as a generous gift to mankind—the 'chosen' theory excluded that—but was taken from the Jews in very special circumstances, for the main part by the Protestant rebels against Roman Catholicism. Finally, and by far the most important, there was what to Christians seemed like the unreasonable contumaciousness of the Jews in refusing to pursue their own Messianic doctrine which had, apart from them, become the essence of the religion universally recognized by the white races in every continent. This more than forfeited any advantage the Jews might have gained from their moral primacy.

III

The second distinctive feature of the historical causes of anti-Semitism is closely related to the first one. It is that, for more than two thousand years, Jews have been disliked and have suffered from persecution. We have mentioned one of the early reasons for this, namely, in the religious history of the Jews, but, once established, it seems to have resulted in a vicious circle peculiarly difficult to resolve. Psychologists, particularly medical ones, are far from being as enthusiastic as many theologians seem to be concerning the beneficial influence of suffering on character, even when it comes from objective misfortune such as physical accidents, and when it is the result of being disliked they would, I think, be unanimously sceptical about its beneficent workings. It might be pointed out that nevertheless with the Jews, beneficial effects of suffering are to be found in the form of noble resignation and endurance, profound wisdom about life, etc., but even so there is a heavy balance on the debit side which it is perhaps not necessary to particularize. Again, a biologist might question my equating the ascertainable effects of suffering on an individual with the alleged ones on a race, to which the answer is that the mental characteristics in question would seem to be at least as typical of Jews in the mass as are their physical ones, so that it is irrelevant to the present argument whether they are derived from direct inheritance or from recurrent individual experience under the influence of environmental tradition.

One feature resulting from persecution may be singled out to illustrate both the complexity of the theme and the depths to which its resulting impressions may reverberate in the minds of the environment. From the Old Testament accounts it would appear that the ancient Hebrews were a pretty savage *Herrenvolk* in their part of the Near East, invasion and utter destruction of their neighbours being as ruthless and as marked by self-approval as anything we have known in later times. It is perhaps not fanciful to suppose that the destruction of Jerusalem, after their spirited and desperate defence of it against an invincible foe, was followed not only by the changes incident on the loss of their country, but also by a revolutionary change in the mentality of the Jewish people. It is as if they said to themselves, once and for all: 'We have tried to achieve our ends by physical means, and we perceive they do not meet with success; from now on we will eschew violence and seek whatever other methods are open to us'. However that may be, it is surely beyond doubt that pugnacity is not among the prominent characteristics of the Jews. Criminological statistics, as well as numerous Jewish jokes on the topic, confirm the impression of their aversion to physical violence.

The primitive mind, as we see with infants, readily resorts to violence as the most obvious way of countering frustration, while a civilized mind holds it in reserve to be used if need be; it would seem to be characteristic of the Jews that it be kept to the very last resort. This may well be the hall-mark of a higher type of civilization which we shall all one day reach, but whether that is so or no, it is not, unfortunately for the Jews, so regarded at present. On the contrary, it is despised as a sign of unmanliness. Take the case of a German-Jewish refugee who has become a naturalized British subject before the outbreak of war. One might expect to find him burning with zeal to do all he can to oppose the persecutors of his race and thus to save those of them still left in the horrors of the Continent. Instead he may be found discussing with his friends, as if it were the most natural thing in the world, his chances of evading the military service that has become one of his new civic responsibilities. The actual frequency of such cases is not important; what matters is whether they strike the Gentile as being characteristic; if so, then generalization will follow readily enough.

To illustrate the psychological complexity of such questions I will add that the topic just mentioned can often be shown to become associated in the unconscious mind with two physical features of the Jews. One is circumcision. The Biblical story about this being introduced to mark off the Jewish nation has at last become true; the quite recent surgical craze for the practice among well-to-do Gentiles has done little to alter this. Actually the story itself must have been a later priestly interpolation, because at the time of Moses it could not have fulfilled that function; it was familiar knowledge that the practice was general among the Egyptians, from whom the Jews had recently escaped, as well as elsewhere in Africa. It must almost certainly have originated in the castration threats so characteristic of initiation ceremonies at puberty, being subsequently transferred (like baptism) to the period of infancy. The repercussion the idea may have in the Gentile mind is well featured in Browning's poem 'Cleon'. The second physical feature alluded to is the Hittite nose, so suggestive of deformity, which the Jews unfortunately picked up in their wanderings, and which, by an unlucky chance, is associated with a dominant gene.

The link connecting these topics is indicated by the term 'castration fear', which is universally present in the unconscious mind. Characteristics, whether mental or physical, that tend to stir this, lead inevitably to a sense of aversion.

No one, however, even in the unconscious, regards the Jew as a passive creature. The aggressive impulses attaching to the male will, if their direct outlets are blocked, find indirect ones. When a Gentile complains that Jews are pushful, assertive, and given to getting their way by sharp practices or even underhand methods, what he is really trying to express is that they are persons whose manliness has been impaired and who have thus been driven to adopt what he feels to be effeminate (not feminine) methods of dealing with his fellow-men.

How irrational all this is (as I indicated at the outset) and how unfair! And yet how human! What a vicious circle! One side complains that first he is persecuted and then that he is reproached for the deleterious effects this has on his character. The other side remarks that people who do things to make themselves disliked should not then complain that they are unpopular.

IV

It will now be asked what practical bearing have psychological considerations such as these on the urgent problem of the future of the Jews.

The main conclusions we are led to, which, if true, should be constantly borne in mind in discussing any solution, are two: first, that the roots of anti-Semitism go very deep, and that it is illusory to suppose they can be eradicated by superficial methods such as appeal by propaganda; secondly, that the causes of anti-Semitism are not due solely to Gentile depravity, but reside in a vicious circle contributed to by both sides and therefore alterable only by mutual concessions and modifications of attitude.

So far as I know, only three possibilities for the future have been suggested, and I will discuss them briefly in turn.

National Separation

The Zionist movement, which has gained a constantly increasing impetus in the past forty years and will presumably receive a further increase when the war is over, has been actuated by fairly obvious motives: powerful reasons of sentiment, the need for a refuge from persecution, and so on. Much of the support by Jews who do not intend to migrate to Palestine themselves derives from a motive of especial interest to us here, namely, the perception that much of the opposition to Jews proceeds, as was indicated above, from their being strangers in the land. This has been confounded with the fact of homelessness, and it is believed that, were this remedied, Jews would gain both in self-respect and in the esteem of their neighbours. It is a final attempt to assert their national individuality.

It would be unseemly for a Gentile to comment on the religious and sentimental reasons impelling towards Zionism; that is a matter that concerns Jews alone. But a political psychologist may be permitted to express doubt concerning the accuracy of the calculation of the effect on the relationship with other peoples. There are two grounds for this. To begin with, the movement asserts more forcibly than ever that Jews are a distinct and separate people, or race, and that they intend to remain so and to retain any national characteristics they may possess, a right accorded to all other nations. That in itself is a just claim, but it is one which we have seen to be the basic cause of anti-Semitism, and so can only exacerbate it. The argument passes by the crucial fact that the relative tolerance accorded by one nation to another depends on the main mass of the nationals residing in their own country, so that the small overflow visiting, or even settling, in another country does not surpass what may be called the digestive capacity of that other, a capacity we have seen always to have definite limits.

The claim to be a separate nation with a country of one's own and yet to have 95 per cent of one's nationals residing in other people's countries is one that has never been accorded freely and probably never will be. It savours too much of what many Gentiles feel to be the arrogant pretension to uniqueness inherent in the Jewish religion and philosophy. The question frequently to be heard among the lower classes, 'Why don't you go to Palestine?' is likely to be reiterated with insistence. And, finally, the precise coincidence of the rise in Zionism with the extraordinary increase in anti-Semitism in all countries may not be altogether fortuitous.

Persistence

By this I mean the continuation of the past relationship between Jews and Gentiles in the vague hope that it may somehow improve without any fundamental change being brought about, and that if it does not it must be borne with the tough endurance and resignation that most Jews have acquired. This would seem to be the attitude of most Jews in Western countries, particularly of those who have taken little interest in Zionism. It betokens inertia, and perhaps resignation tempered with pessimism.

It is a solution—or rather non-solution—that no active or progressive mind should accept, and yet, current factors being what they are, all the available evidence suggests that it is the main one likely to be adopted, being only in some degree modified by the Zionist addition.

Such a prospect is very unsatisfactory, for even though gross persecution can be ruled out in Western countries as being repugnant both to civilized behaviour and common sense alike, nevertheless it leaves the Jew subject to endless unpleasantnesses which inevitably have deleterious consequences—not least in the important field of psychoneurosis.

Assimilation

All the experience of history goes to show that no group of people retains its separate identity indefinitely, so that if Jews are subject to the same social and historical laws as other people, and are not really unique, it follows inevitably that sooner or later assimilation will prove to be the definite solution of our problem.

Immediate protest will probably be raised against this conclusion. What, it will be said, after preserving our identity for over two thousand years in the face of the most formidable odds, for a longer period than any other nation in the world, with the possible exception of the Chinese, we are to lose it in the end? Well, two thousand years is a good run; few other nations, even the Romans, have had more than one thousand. But resistance to the laws of nature can only delay their operation; it can never avert it. And obdurate resistance to change, as one sees politically, commonly has the effect of the change coming about in disadvantageous ways instead of advantageous ones.

A more superficial objection, doubtless derived from the same emotional source, asserts that this particular change has already been tried and has failed. In few countries have Jews imbibed the surrounding culture more than in Germany and Hungary, and look at the result. They are more violently repudiated there, perhaps, than ever before; Hitler has called attention to many a man's Jewish descent which he himself had almost forgotten. These impatient critics, however, would appear to have made little historical study of the process of assimilation. It is ludicrous to imagine that it could be accomplished in a single century by individual attempts, often enough clumsy or half-hearted, on the part of a minority of the community. Let us contemplate the record of our own island. It took four hundred years to fuse the small number of Normans with the rest of the population—indeed, it is only after nine hundred years, in the last half century, that 'Norman blood' has ceased to have social significance—and it took more than a thousand years to turn the Cornish into Englishmen; fusion with the Welsh and Scotch is evidently going to take a good deal longer.

The assimilative capacity of the body politic bears many resemblances to that of the body itself. Here a foreign body may be one of three kinds. Food itself is, to begin with, a foreign body, but if it is of a suitably nourishing order its constituents are absorbed and preserved, though its original form is lost. Then it may be inert like an old rifle bullet. Finally, it may be an irritant, in which case the surrounding tissues react violently and make every effort either to isolate or to expel the offending body (ghetto or diaspora).

Resistance to the decrees of Nature brings friction and discomfort, or even misery, in its train. Acceptance of them ensures the easy working whereby the best qualities can be preserved.

Influences operate in both Jew and Gentile to oppose that approximation between them in which lies the only hope of a harmonious relationship. Of the former, something has already been said. With the Gentile one observes the cautious conservation, born of xenophobia, which is parallel to the attitude to foreign words. The English, for example, borrow words from all over the world, but they impose a probation period of testing, marked by the use of inverted commas or a semi-foreign pronunciation, before the word is finally accepted and is felt now to be English. Gentiles are harsh on what they often feel to be premature, ostentatious, or awkward attempts of some Jews to exchange their nationality, and miss the tact and patience, the easy gradualness, so necessary for the overcoming of xenophobic resistance; then we have the cruel *Punch* caricatures of the rich Jews' supposed antics on the grouse moor or in a deer forest. If, however, the aim of approximation were consistently pursued on both sides, a great deal could be done to soften the transitional period. I repeat 'on both sides', for it is incorrect to regard anti-Semitism as a spontaneous, unprovoked disease; to change the metaphor, it represents a vicious circle which can be broken only by mutual endeavour. It is for both Jew and Gentile to search their hearts.

I do not propose to say anything on the former score; it is for Jews to speak to Jews. But as to Gentiles, I would express the opinion that more satisfactory methods could be found than the one most used nowadays. To try by preaching to make all Gentiles feel ashamed and guilty for the ill-treatment of Jews certainly provokes corresponding emotional reactions, for there is such a large floating body of guilt in every human heart that it is easy to stir it, but they are reactions that are apt to be temporary and to be succeeded by resentment against the occasion for them. To raise the general standard of decent behaviour in general is less spectacular, but in the long run more effective. The best propaganda is to explain to Gentiles the real truth of the matter, namely, that anti-Semitism, like any other racial prejudice, is a sign of weakness, not strength, proceeding as it does from irrational fears that bring with them the risk of paranoid delusions, of which the *Elders of Zion* was a flagrant example. Tolerance betokens self-confidence and sanity; intolerance betokens fear and insanity. Against such weaknesses ridicule is the most formidable weapon. It is the cowering Hitler and Streicher that should be caricatured, not the cruel ones; these can only be deplored, and, wherever necessary, removed.

Postscript.—The historical tenacity of the Jewish people made it easy to predict that they would unhesitatingly decide for the nationalist solution mentioned above.

Whether they are right in believing that this will diminish anti-Semitism remains to be seen; it will certainly provide new problems for the bulk living outside the national state. In any event it is desirable that it should be supplemented by all other possible methods of combating the scandal of anti-Semitism.

XXI
PSYCHOPATHOLOGY AND INTERNATIONAL TENSION[1]

A SPECIAL interest attaches to tension between powerful nations in that the culmination of it may be catastrophic and world-wide, but psychologically the causes and motivation of such events cannot be fundamentally different from those of minor conflicts, *e.g.* between two Red Indian tribes or between a majority and a minority in a given area (Ireland!). We shall be well advised, therefore, to consider a broad view of the problem, and this has the further advantage of freeing us from a particular topical tension where it is hard to avoid the bias of emotional prejudice.

A full discussion of the topic in general could profitably take place only among a group of those fully informed on various aspects of it, including the biological nature and development of human instincts, the psychology of the derivatives of those instincts, the economic history of man, and the history of national policies and ambitions. Here, however, we are restricted to one aspect of the whole: namely, the contributions that a knowledge of psychopathology can make to our understanding of it.

The first observation that may be made, dating from the time of Le Bon, sixty years ago, is of a purely descriptive nature. It concerns the remarkable contagiousness of certain emotions, often with corresponding behaviour, when a group of people are closely linked together—either with physical propinquity, as in a crowd, mob, or

[1] Contribution to a symposium published by the University of Cincinnati, 1949.

meeting, or with any other bond of common interest and means of swift communication. When these conditions are present, the display of an emotional attitude on the part of one or more assertive members of the group may often arouse in an extraordinary degree similar ones throughout the group. Fear, anger, hatred, enthusiastic acclamation, may in this way, given certain conditions, spread with terrific speed and ever-increasing intensity. The important thing is that other mental attitudes of a more critical nature, which otherwise would check or guide the emotion, are far more easily suspended in a group than in an individual. Hence the notorious fickleness and irrationality of mobs.

The difficult problem at once arises of estimating the relative importance of the instigator of the emotion, one who commonly becomes a leader, and the spontaneous activity of the crowd. At one extreme of the scale, where the external situation speaks for itself, he may be quite insignificant; when a theatre is burning, it does not matter who starts the panic by shouting 'Fire'. At the other extreme a powerful personality may infuse a group with emotion that beforehand would have astonished its individual members. It is most noteworthy how extraordinarily rare it is for a nation to refuse to follow its leaders into war. The Government has to be totally discredited and the army itself faced with overwhelming defeat, as with the Russians in 1917, before insubordination and mutiny occur. This weighty fact must signify either that the commands of leaders are of decisive importance or that they divine the will of the people beforehand with peculiar accuracy. The latter thesis is the harder to maintain. When one thinks of the dynastic wars of the Middle Ages, or the probable outcome of the American Civil War had not the great figure of Lincoln insisted on the relentless pursuit of it despite the apathy and opposition of so many of his people, one must suppose that there is more power behind the leader's voice than is to be explained on purely rational grounds, that there is some deep irrational tendency to support and obey him (or the government, which may be regarded as one Big Man) irrespective of whether individual members would agree with his policy if they were in a position to estimate it coolly. Even the Communists, who might be supposed to be furthest away from class distinctions and the worship of individuals however prominent, have deified Lenin and Stalin to a height perhaps unequalled in history—one which most Roman Emperors would have envied.

Subsequent ages, with the opportunity for more detached appraisal, have seldom been able to share entirely the contemporaneous attitude towards these leaders, despite the sporadic appearance of such hero-worshippers as Carlyle. It would therefore seem that the supra-rational or magical powers they often display must have some personal origin. The group who responds has to feel that he is 'our leader' or 'my leader'. It was Freud who made this addition to Le Bon's original description, and it was also he who divined the source of the leader's magical powers. This remark takes us at once to the heart of modern psychopathology, and it cannot be expounded without first making clear the essential contributions that this branch of science has made to our knowledge of human nature.

They may be summed up in two words; the 'unconscious' and the 'infantile', two concepts which are closely related. We mostly live our lives without extreme manifestations of passion. When these occur, in the form of devoted adoration, deadly hostility, bloodthirsty cruelty, and so on, they are apt to be alarming and often dangerous;

control and criticism are swept aside. Now, according to psychopathology, all these manifestations are revivals of corresponding, but inexpressible, passionate attitudes experienced in infancy. Freud discovered that the mind of the infant contained—perhaps inborn—asocial wishes whose nature would be described by such words as 'savage' or at least 'uncivilized'. Sexual and murderous impulses, of the utmost significance to the individual, are examples of what had not previously been recognized as part of infantile life. The infant has to effect extensive changes in its mind, taming, renouncing, controlling, etc., before it consents, so to speak, to become a child —at about the age of three or four—and many have great difficulties in doing so and only imperfectly achieve this desirable transformation. The child, from then till puberty, plays at life, tries not to take its passionate irruptions as seriously as formerly, and more or less patiently passes through a period of physical and intellectual growth, until at puberty the emotional life once more comes into its own.

Among the truly unconscious attitudes of infancy, an extremely important one is that towards an image, highly charged emotionally, of a powerful Father. This is independent of the actual male parent, often an ineffective enough figure in reality, and, indeed, even of his existence (*e.g.* with orphans). A rich complex of emotions clusters around this image: adoration, hatred, dread, and so on. And the interplay of them is fateful for the social (and religious) reactions of later life. An easily intelligible component in this complex is the wish to be protected from danger and the belief that the great Person has absolute power to protect one. Oddly enough, this goes hand in hand with the opposite attitude of protecting Him, presumably because of his being vital to one's own safety or existence. This is often illustrated in warfare, where men will fight with the utmost desperation to protect a leader or king, whose life or standard is in jeopardy.

Akin to this theme, but much more connected with the maternal parent, is the alternation in infancy between the extremes of helplessness and omnipotence. The latter attitude normally gets toned down by experience into self-confidence, which in its turn diminishes the dread of helplessness. Nevertheless, it is astonishing to find how much of these extreme attitudes may persist in the unconscious mind of adults, and how seldom is a perfect balance struck even in consciousness. A great obstacle to the attainment of this desirable goal is the fact that other agencies than the original one enter into the situation. If strong inferiority feelings develop (which, incidentally, always originate in sentiments of moral unworthiness, *i.e.* guilt), the individual may react to them by reverting in the direction of one of these two early attitudes. On the one hand, he may feel unequal to coping with the guilty aggressive impulses that lie behind the inferiority feelings, and so come to depend on some strong being who is supposed to protect him from himself. Or, on the other hand, he may defiantly proclaim himself above any guilt feelings and turn into a bully. Both of these results have profound political effects when, as was mentioned above, they assume a mass form, *i.e.* become part of the reaction of a group. The Germans after the first world war gave an excellent illustration of what is meant. The majority reacted to the 'Guilt Clause' of the Treaty of Versailles (and all that went with this) with feelings of inferiority and displayed a lack of self-confidence, and consequently of capacity, in conducting their own affairs, *i.e.* governing themselves in a democratic fashion. A minority, on the contrary, were defiantly aggressive, and the strength and confidence this simulated made such an appeal to the majority that for the most part they followed them in a pathetically docile manner, evidently hoping they could regain their self-respect or more by leaning on this great Führer and the small group around him.

One sees this same alternation in many forms. The history of mankind could well be depicted as a struggle between the desire for freedom, self-confidence, and self-dependence, on the one hand, and the craving for protection and help from stronger beings on the other. Perhaps there are even cyclical periods in history where one or other of these opposing tendencies gain the upper hand. The nineteenth century, for instance, was characterized by, among other things, a widespread desire for freedom and self-government. This was manifested not only by the emancipation of many countries (Italy, Hungary, etc.) from foreign rule, but also inside a country by the increasing revolt against the previous ruling oligarchies or monarchies, by universal suffrage, emancipation of women, and many more cognate movements. The cry for freedom was a favourite theme for the poets, who passionately declaimed it as the highest good, and the dramatic cry of Patrick Henry, 'Give me liberty or give me death', was echoed and acted on over and over again. The twentieth century, on the other hand, has seen the rise in one country after another of powerful dictatorships whose tyranny has seldom been equalled in history, and more significant than the forcible suppression of individual liberty has been the extensively successful denigration of the very concept of freedom, which so far from being the highest virtue is now widely regarded as an out-moded superstition if not actually an anti-social vice, and is to be replaced by the nobler one of docile 'loyalty' to the current regime or 'cause'.

The psychopathologist, being accustomed to view genetically all adult manifestations as derivations of early tendencies, believing to the full that 'the child is father to the man', would connect the epoch-making happenings just mentioned with the infantile conflict between dependent helplessness and omnipotent phantasies.

These examples, presented in a highly condensed fashion, may serve as a bridge between the purely descriptive observation with which we started and the more dynamic considerations that modern psychopathology can contribute to the general problem. The outstanding one is that *any emotional attitude disproportionate to the actual situation is derived from associative stimulation of a corresponding one in infantile life still persisting in the unconscious mind.* With this formula as a basis, one is in a position to investigate more profitably innumerable historical and diplomatic problems where argument often takes the place of illumination.

We meet at once, however, the formidable difficulty of determining what emotional attitude is disproportionate. One may count with almost certainty on the person concerned being unable (or unwilling) to co-operate in answering the question. On the contrary, he maintains inflexibly that his emotional attitude is a normal, natural, and inevitable response to the situation that has evoked it and is precisely proportionate to its objective significance. This has some truth in it; the reaction may be proportionate to the significance the situation has *for him*, but this still leaves open the difficult matter of ascertaining why it has. Few more important tasks lie before psychology than to provide objective criteria for answering these two questions. The daily experience of psychopathologists with individuals, by now very extensive, has already begun to contribute material for the formulation of such criteria.

In the first place, we may assert that the disproportion in question is much commoner and more extensive than not only the individual concerned but also the general run of people think. The world is very lenient towards manifestations of the unconscious; or perhaps it would be nearer the truth to say that it enters into a general conspiracy to overlook such manifestations. One of the many characteristic signs of their presence is inability on the part of the person concerned to discuss the matter, an outburst of anger often taking the place of a free discussion. There are many such indications which psychopathologists have learned to recognize; it is an important part of their daily technique, often very complicated, and, to study them, reference must be made to the appropriate text-books. What is important here is that in certain circumstances particular situations can acquire an increasing emotional significance because of their becoming more and more closely associated with unconscious ideas that they symbolize, until a point is reached where they function as a vital 'test case' where everything of value is felt to be at stake. What is then happening in the unconscious is that some literally intolerable idea is being stimulated, at first slightly and from afar and then more and more poignantly until some violent defence mechanism has to be brought into play to prevent—what? Chaos, collapse, extinction? What lies behind this notion of an intolerable idea? Evidently something dominated by acute and unbearable 'anxiety', as dread and panic are technically designated in psychopathology. Certainly one cannot exaggerate the central part that 'anxiety' plays in the unconscious; it is the key to most problems there.

This picture of man as fundamentally a fearful animal is very alien to our usual view of him. The reason for this is that only a very small proportion of the unconscious anxiety, even in the universal psychoneuroses where it is most often manifest, is allowed to come through to consciousness as such. The greater part is prevented through the action of various defence mechanisms, which vary in form and intensity from one individual to another. So important is this matter of protection against anxiety that the greater part of a person's character is made up by the various defences he has learnt to employ in the course of his early development. When one or another of them is so exaggerated as to form a striking characteristic of his personality, it may afford a broad hint of the amount of underlying anxiety and, furthermore, of its particular type.

The contribution made by the unconscious to a person's response to various current situations relates not only to its content, *i.e.* the type of attitude concerned, but also to various psychological mechanisms characteristic of the unconscious. There are a good many such, and I will select one or two of them to illustrate what is meant. In the unconscious there is no discrimination, there are no nuances, and attitudes akin to judgement are often of the 'all or nothing' type. This often affects consciousness in the way of over-ready generalizations, which play a prominent part in international relationships. Nothing is commoner than remarks like, 'I hate the French', 'All Americans are arrogant', 'All Italians are thieves', and the like, where reasonable discrimination is completely absent. It is evident that these national prejudices must, in their nature, be extreme generalizations from very limited data, since few if any people possess a really extensive knowledge of the national group that is being condemned and, moreover, some of the strongest examples of such prejudice may be found among people who have had no experience whatever of the nationals in question. An experimental proof of the truth of this statement was afforded recently by a study in the United States correlating various types of prejudice. The investigators slipped in names of three or four non-existent nations among those about whom inquiry was being made, and a certain number of the subjects expressed in their replies a considerable measure of animosity towards those unfortunate ghosts!

Another familiar, and even more important, example of the unconscious mechanisms that often influence conscious attitudes is that called by psychiatrists 'projection'. By it is meant the ascribing to a person or persons in the environment ideas, intentions, and emotional attitudes that strictly belong to the subject himself, but which have been repudiated—usually unconsciously. He then not only believes intellectually that the other person displays the attitude in question, but feels it in a direct way and responds to it emotionally, often very strongly. It is seen in its grossest forms in various insanities, *e.g.* when a patient believes so firmly that someone has evil intentions on his life that he protects himself by forestalling him and carrying out a prophylactic murder. This very example must remind one of the so-called 'preventive wars' and opens up the question of the original source of the aggressive intentions.

What is, in some respects, the opposite to this mechanism is the more obscure one called 'introjection'. Here the observed attitude of another person (or nation) is incorporated within oneself and often becomes a permanent part of the personality. Much of what is regarded as the child's 'imitation' of the parents is of this nature. In the unconscious phantasy, however, the process goes further, and the other person is actually imagined, *and felt*, to be inside one. Naturally much then depends on whether the incorporated person is regarded as friendly, kindly, and helpful, or, on the contrary, unkind, harmful, and evil. Curiously enough, there are motives impelling towards the introjection of both kinds, so that both 'good' and 'bad' objects, as they are called, live side by side within and may act on each other. Fear lest one's precious objects (together with one's own capacity for love) may be destroyed by the evil influences is common and leads to complex defensive reactions. In international relations similar processes are at work, and similar variations may be observed. A good example was the attitude of the English (and presumably also the Americans) towards Russians at different periods in the last ten or twelve years. Before the war the prevailing attitude was of aloofness, doubt, and suspicion. During the war they were welcomed with open arms and incorporated as 'one of us', 'one of the Allies', and so on. After the war resurgent doubt deepened into first suspicion and then fear that after all they might turn out to be hostile, and that the United Nations had incorporated a 'bad object' into their midst.

* * * * *

After this brief but necessary introduction on the psychology of the individual as seen through the eyes of a psychopathologist who has to investigate the deeper layers of the mind, we have to turn to our theme proper—the bearing such knowledge may have on the sources and nature of international tensions. It is natural that we should think first of modern conditions, of nations with their popular opinions pervading them, of responsible governments negotiating with other governments, and so on, but we should do well to keep in mind a broader historical perspective. For essentially what we are concerned with is the problem of latent hostility between groups, small or large, particularly, of course, when this reaches a dangerous degree of tension, and history is only too replete with instances of this phenomenon in all forms of social organization. When the Mongol hordes swept westward into Europe, that was certainly not because of any unfortunate conflict between their leaders and the leaders of other countries which after much argument had to be settled by force: naked force was the first indication those unfortunate countries had of any 'Mongol problem'. Nor were the Jews the first or the last exponents of genocide when three thousand years ago they set out to exterminate the Amalakites, Canaanites, or whoever else stood in the way of their intentions, irrespective of any 'diplomatic incident' or disagreement between governments. We have, in short, to do with not merely any such recent matters as the mischief of armament makers, the iniquities of 'secret diplomacy', or the evils inherent in the 'capitalistic system', but with a far older, deeper, and more general tendency of human groups to generate hostility among themselves. That men can so readily hate and destroy members of their own species is a prerogative that they share with no other vertebrate animal, though it is displayed by many of the insects. With those insects also man has shared the propensity to devour his fellow-creatures, and although he has now for the most part (if by no means altogether, as the last war illustrated) learned to refrain from this logical culmination of killing, it is disconcerting to know that cannibalistic impulses are a regular constituent of the infantile mind and remain one of the common features of the adult unconscious.

All this signifies that there is in mankind a permanent capacity for hostility, aggression, and cruelty towards their fellow-creatures; whether this capacity, mostly dormant, is best described as a propensity, a trend, or an innate instinct is a difficult problem about which there is much discussion.

Such statements as those just made are so unpalatable and so hard to accept that one is not surprised at the various attempts that have been made to discount or deny them. Some anthropologists, for instance, have insisted that primitive man is a peaceable creature, living in harmony with his fellows and his environment until artificially stimulated. No doubt it is possible to find isolated communities living in favoured circumstances where this description appears to hold good, but it is certainly far easier to find primitive ones where it does not; hence the term 'savages'. It is also possible to find civilized nations who are exceptionally peace-loving—Scandinavia is at present a notable example—but all these observations simply present us with an important problem: how comes it that the latent hostility psychopathologists know from their studies of the unconscious to be *always present* sometimes lies long dormant in an individual or a community and at other times becomes only too manifest?

Let us consider a few historical examples. A thousand years ago Danes were, to the coastal inhabitants of the British Isles whether Celts or Saxons, people who looted, raped, and murdered without the slightest provocation from their unhappy victims, and their incursions culminated in their seizing the throne of England. About the same time their Norse neighbours became the terror of Europe as far as ships could sail—from France to Sicily and Cyprus. Their seizure of the throne of England in 1066 proved more lasting. To Russians with any historical memory, Swedes signified the conquerors of most of their country—and the word 'conquest' is generally a euphemism for many things—whose activities there continued into the seventeenth and eighteenth centuries. In the fifteenth century the Swiss pikemen were the most dreaded warriors in Europe, as Italy in particular knew to her cost. Yet in the whole world there are no more pacific peoples to-day than the four just mentioned, nor peoples whose neighbours may feel safer from any aggressive tendencies.

These are very striking examples of a complete reversal of behaviour. Other cases of change are not so unambiguous. What the English did to the native inhabitants of America, Australia, and Tasmania who objected to their land being seized stands on record, and only in New Zealand did they establish an amicable relationship. Their treatment of the natives of Ireland and India is a more controversial question, but the fact remains that they have peaceably withdrawn from both countries, and there is every sign of their days of aggressive expansion being finally past. The conduct of the Spanish in Central and South America is only too notorious, but perhaps it may be said that their aggressive tendencies were not glutted thereby, as with the other nations we have considered, but continue internally against their own people. The Greeks managed to combine their internal dissensions with external expansion from the seventh to the fourth century B.C., and have never been able to dispense with the former type of hostility. The Germans have lived fairly peaceably for centuries, except when disturbed from without, and even without many internal conflicts (between state and state), but their recent history appears to betoken a reversion to the characteristics ascribed to them by the Romans. Similarly the Jews, according to their chronicles, must have been among the most ruthless peoples of antiquity, but for two thousand years they have been noted for their abhorrence of any kind of violence; it is possible we may now be witnessing a resuscitation of qualities long dormant.

Most striking of all instances of unprovoked aggression is the story of the Mongol incursion, and a study of the career of Genghis Khan is indispensable to anyone concerned with the investigation of aggressive impulses. But history is replete with examples in every area of the world, so we need not continue in our relation of them.

We have therefore the picture of periodic surges of aggression on the part of one community after another, whether a nation or not, surges which then, equally mysteriously, die down and apparently disappear. There we have the naked form of aggression, but actually they constitute only one type of situation where hostility culminating in war occurs. There are the more complex cases where suspicion, rivalry, and hatred between two nations proceeds until an outbreak comes about. Here it is not a case of an overwhelming aggressiveness against which nothing can prevail except, in fortunate cases, a successful military defence, as when the Huns were checked at Châlons or the Goths at Tours.

It is at this point that we acutely feel the need of co-operation with good historians, trained in both economics and psychology, who might be able to unravel both the underlying and the inciting causes of a series of wars, and in that way to afford some sort of classification from which further investigations could proceed. Two broad kinds have just been singled out, which for the present may be termed 'aggressive wars' and 'quarrel wars' respectively, but plainly this is a very rough grouping between two types that cannot be sharply divided and which needs very much refined modification. Nevertheless we may start with it, if only for the practical reason that the treatment of them must differ: the technique of stopping the rush of a mad bull is quite other than that of settling a dispute.

A noteworthy feature of the second group of wars is that so many of them would seem to have been easily avoidable if only a modicum of good-will and tolerance had been allowed to operate. Examples of this are the British-American war of 1812, the Crimean War, the Franco-Prussian War, and even the first World War (the second surely belongs to the other group). It is probably true of the American Civil War, and certainly of the English one. The more fortunate outcome was often prevented by suspicion, *i.e.* the imputing of exaggeratedly bad motives to the other party, with the fears that always underlie that. There is no more delicate task for the diplomatist than to measure the exact degree of danger in an apparently aggressive neighbour; he could do so much more accurately were he able first to allow for the probable projections from his side. There are, of course, always real issues of a complicated kind, but it is suggested that these are seldom of so acute a nature as to preclude a working compromise. When, however, any compromise is felt to be a surrender which the other party will regard as a weakness and of which he will proceed to take further advantage, the case is difficult, and it may need a considerable measure of good-will and self-confidence (based on easy conscience) to succeed.

If we ask in what circumstances a government will decide to use force rather than other means, we come to an extremely complicated problem, since at first sight the motives appear to be so manifold that one might well despair of reducing them to their fundamentals. Most governments, though not all, are prepared to fight if the alternative is slavery or domination, *i.e.* to fight for their freedom and independence. It is perhaps the clearest case.

INTERNATIONAL TENSION

But beyond this there are many situations where the importance of the issue is judged very subjectively, where it is estimated quite differently by the parties immediately concerned and by others at a distance in either space or time. Few foreigners, for instance, could understand why Great Britain should have thought it necessary to fight the Boer War, and the number of British that thought it necessary has diminished with the passage of time, although the large majority thought so at the time. Then we have the question-begging phrase 'vital interests', which covers a vast scale of varying degrees of importance from the rare instances where it might be appropriately used (*e.g.* when the supply of food is imperilled) down to those where only some minor economic interest is concerned. This leads on to the equally ambiguous term 'prestige', one that usually applies to strong Powers who insist on weak ones paying them due respect, *i.e.* admitting that they have reason to fear them. Not long ago, if Albania had blown up two British destroyers, Great Britain would certainly have landed troops to demand forcibly that she be accorded due apology and reparation, a course now forbidden by the thought both of Russia and of the United Nations; the insult, *i.e.* the lack of deference to her strength, would have been felt to be intolerable.

The comments a psychopathologist has to make on these complex matters are as follows. In the first place, when a nation strongly feels a certain interest to be 'vital', when it is plain to other people not concerned that the phrase is very exaggerated, the exaggeration represents an addition of emotion derived from unconscious sources. It is psychologically the same sort of surplus that the neurotic exhibits when he dreads suffocation if he enters a closed place. The interest that is felt to be vital, although not actually so in itself, has come to *symbolize* one of the few unconscious ideas than the unconscious truly regards as vital. Death or castration, for instance, represent attacks on what the unconscious regards as vital interests, and so extensive are the latent fears in mankind that there is an exaggerated sensitiveness to any stimulus that may, however indirectly, stir them. The conclusion is that many violent decisions which produce an appearance of aggressive assertiveness are much more defensive in their origin than might be thought; more will be said presently about the important theme of 'aggressive defence'. The conclusion just enunciated needs to be confirmed by analyses of specific instances of 'vital interests', 'prestige', and so on, but it is highly probable that these concepts would be shown to be unconsciously associated with more fundamental ones characteristic of the unconscious.

Here we have been considering cases where the attitude of the government is representative of that of the people, but there is an extensive class of case where its attitude is more concerned with its own interests, separate from and often opposed to those of the people. When this is so, the leader may be concerned with his own interest only—those behind being either commanded to follow or, as with William the Conqueror's invasion of England or Napoleon's invasion of Italy, induced to do so by promises of loot—or again, and this is a much more sinister situation, he may be concerned with the mutual hostility between himself and his nation and decide to deal with them by deflecting both in the direction of external aggression, proceeding to pick a quarrel with some neighbour. There is indeed a social theory according to which foreign wars are characteristically of the latter nature, being designed to divert the tension between different classes in the community, a theory connected with the common suspicion that wars are deliberately brought about by rulers, 'capitalists', and 'the old men' to further their own interests only, but it can be sustained only through considerable distortion of both historical events and human motives. Rulers are seldom so Machiavellian, and Oxenstjerna's famous remark to his son Annescis, 'quantilla prudentia mundus regatur!' ('Do you not know with how little wisdom the world is governed!') is much nearer the truth.

Although psychopathologists can never forget the permanent aggressive impulses deep in man's nature, they would probably agree with the prevailing sociological opinion that in an organized community the impulses of individuals can for the most part be kept within tolerable bounds. There are many outlets available for indirect and relatively harmless expressions of them in the way of rivalry, ambition, sport, competition, the surmounting of difficult tasks, and the achieving of emulous aims (exploration, scientific discovery, and so on). The sporadic exceptions in the form of criminality could be brought within much narrower bounds than at present by an adequate social psychiatric service and advances in police efficiency. The danger of serious outbreaks of hostility, therefore, is confined to mass combinations: internal revolution and international tension, two manifestations which, as were pointed out above, are by no means always disconnected. It is for the sociologist and historian to study the various situations in which these eventualities occur, but the psychopathologist would maintain that, in the nature of things, the agents bringing them about must ultimately be of the same order as those that evoke an outbreak of hostility (murder, etc.) in the individual and that they must operate through similar mechanisms.

Psychopathology can show that an uncontrollable outburst of aggression in the individual is always due to frustration or fear (or, of course, both). With the infant of a month old anger is evoked by unavoidable, and what may be called 'normal' frustration, *e.g.* the fact that the nipple is not available at every moment. Later, when the child has acquired some capacity for tolerating frustration, it needs a larger amount, one that mostly may be called undue or excessive frustration, though the measure of this varies greatly with different individuals. The part played by fear is both less evident and more important. We are familiar with the observations that a cornered rat may in its desperation turn savage and that the ferocity of a tiger increases with its sense of danger, but these are reactions of aggression to manifest fear. What we are here concerned with are similar reactions of man to invisible fear, to the unconscious anxiety of which he is not aware but which is the mainspring of various other emotional attitudes.

Although the instinct of fear appears to be universal throughout the animal kingdom, even among the most powerful animals, with man it has certain unique features. Like other animals, he can be afraid of dangerous aggression spontaneously emerging from the outside, but he can also be afraid of external aggression conceived by his conscience as retaliation or punishment for his own aggressive impulses and, moreover, he often projects these on to the outer world and responds with fear to what may in that case be a largely imaginary danger—the typical paranoid reaction. Much more important than all these, however, are the purely *internal* sources of anxiety. It would seem that the primitive mind, *i.e.* of the infant and of the adult unconscious, regularly reacts with anxiety to its own aggressive impulses, and this reaction has many fateful consequences. It is important to remember that, although some of this anxiety may leak through, especially with neurotics, and although much of it may betray itself through various indirect effects, it is essentially unconscious, so that there is always far more anxiety present in any individual than is externally manifest to either himself or others. Many elaborate defences are developed to cope with it. An unfortunate one is a defiant increase of external aggressiveness, as anyone who listened to one of Hitler's characteristic tirades will recognize. In the political sphere it is indifferent whether the aggressive impulses of rulers leading to unconscious anxiety are primarily directed against foreign natives or against their own people or, as in Hitler's case, against both. But when they lead to great anxiety the aggression is often further increased; aggression is then both the cause and the effect of the anxiety.

Another equivocal defence against unconscious anxiety is an increased harshness of the super-ego, that warning agency of which the conscious manifestation is the sense of conscience. Unconscious guilt plays a most important part in political life. Its presence, for instance, is a typical precondition for the projection that so disturbs any hope for the reasonable discussion of sundering issues. A specially interesting problem in this connection is the case where the pangs of guilt are so intolerably painful that secondary defences have to be erected against it, or some mysterious transformation of it has to be effected. The colonizers who exterminated native races seem usually to have been successful in that respect, and one would greatly like to know whether William the Conqueror or Genghis Khan ever experienced any such pangs. Henry V persuaded himself so thoroughly that he was the rightful King of France that when he invaded Normandy he was preposterously outraged at the 'treasonable' behaviour of the French in opposing their lawful sovereign; on the other hand, Shakespeare, with his usual insight, saw deeper and credited him with many painful qualms on the night before Agincourt.

It is possible to summarize in one sentence the gist of this brief essay: What the psychopathologist has to contribute to the understanding of international tension is to point out the significance of aggression, guilt, and, above all, anxiety in the unconscious mind, with the effects of these on behaviour.

XXII

THE DEATH OF HAMLET'S FATHER[1]

WHEN a poet takes an old theme from which to create a work of art, it is always interesting, and often instructive, to note the respects in which he changes elements in the story. Much of what we glean of Shakespeare's personality is derived from such studies, the direct biographical details being so sparse. The difference in the accounts given in *Hamlet* of the way the King had died from that given in the original story is so striking that it would seem worth while to look closer at the matter.

The most obvious difference is that in the Saxo-Belleforest saga the murder is a public one, with Shakespeare a secret one. We do not know, however, who made this change, since an English play called *Hamlet*, thought to be written by Kyd, was extant some twelve years before Shakespeare wrote his; and he doubtless used it as well as the Belleforest version. That play no longer exists except in a much later and much distorted German version, but a Ghost probably appeared in it, and one can hardly imagine any other function for him than to disclose a secret murder. There is reason to suppose that Shakespeare may himself have had a hand in the Kyd play, but at all events he made the best possible use of the alteration.

In the old saga, Claudius (there called Feng) draws his sword on his brother the King (Horvendil)[2] at a banquet and slays him 'with many wounds'. He explains to the

[1] Published in the *International Journal of Psycho-Analysis*, 1948.
[2] It was Shakespeare who changed this name to Hamlet, thus emphasizing the identification of son and father.

assembled nobles that he has done this to protect his sister-in-law (Geruth) from ill-treatment and imminent peril of her life at the hands of her husband—a pretext evidently, a reflection of the infant's sadistic conception of coitus. Incidentally, in the Saxo saga (though not with Belleforest), there had here been no previous adultery with the Queen, so that Feng is the sole villain, and Amleth, unlike Hamlet, unhesitatingly kills him and reigns in his stead as soon as he can overcome the external obstacles. In *Hamlet*, as is well known, the plot is intensified by the previous incestuous adultery of the Queen, which convulses Hamlet at least as much as his father's murder and results in an animus against women that complicates his previously simple task.

In the *Hamlet* play, on the other hand, Claudius disclaims all responsibility for his brother's death and spreads a somewhat improbable story of his having been stung to death by a serpent while sleeping in an orchard. How he knew this we are not told, nor why the adder possessed this quite unwonted deadliness. There is much to be said about that 'orchard', but we may assume that it symbolizes the woman in whose arms the king was murdered. The Ghost's version was quite different. According to him, Claudius had found him asleep and poured a juice of hebana into his ears, a still more improbable story from a medical point of view; he further tells us that the poison rapidly spread through his system resulting in 'all his smooth body being barked about most lazar-like with vile and loathsome crust'. Presumably its swift action prevented him from informing anyone of what had befallen him.

The source of this mysterious poison has been traced as follows.[1] Shakespeare seems to have taken the name, inci-

[1] See Hy. Bradley, *Modern Language Review* (1920), vol. xv, p. 85.

THE DEATH OF HAMLET'S FATHER

dentally misspelling it, from the juice of 'hebon', mentioned in a play of Marlowe's, who himself had added an initial letter to the 'ebon' (ebony) of which the walls of the God of Sleep were composed (Ovid). Shakespeare apparently went on to confound this narcotic with henbane (hyoscyamus), which at that time was believed to cause mortification and turn the body black.[1] Two interesting beliefs about henbane are mentioned by Pliny: (1) that it is a remedy for earache, and (2) when poured into the ear it causes mental disorder.

The coarse Northern butchery is thus replaced by a surreptitious Italianate form of murder, a fact that has led to many inquiries, which do not concern us here, concerning Italian influence on Shakespeare. The identical method is employed in the Play Scene, where a nephew murders his uncle, who was resting after coitus, by dropping poison into his ear and immediately afterwards espouses the widow *à la* Richard III. Hamlet says he got the Gonzago story from an Italian play, but no such play has yet been traced. There had, however, been two instances of murder in an unhappy Gonzaga family. In 1538 a famous Duke of Urbino, who was married to a Gonzaga, died under somewhat suspicious circumstances. Poison was suspected, and his barber was believed to have poured a lotion into his ears on a number of occasions. So the story goes: whether poison thus administered is lethal to anyone with intact tympani is a matter we must leave to the toxicologists. At all events the Duke's son got the unfortunate barber torn in pieces by pincers and then quartered. In the course of this proceeding the barber asserted he had been put on to commit the foul deed by a Luigi [2]

---

[1] W. Thistlton-Dyer, *Shakespeare's England*, vol. i, p. 509.

[2] From whom Shakespeare perhaps got the name Lucianus for the murderer in the Play Scene.

Gonzaga, a relative of the Duke by marriage. For political and legal reasons, however, he was never brought to trial.[1] Furthermore, in 1592 the Marchese Rudolf von Castiglione got eight bravoes to murder his *uncle*, the Marchese Alfonso Gonzaga, a relative of the Duke of Mantua. Rudolf had wished to marry his uncle's daughter and had been refused; he himself was murdered eight months later.

The names used make it evident that Shakespeare was familiar with the story of the earlier Gonzaga murder, as he possibly was with the later one too. The 'poison in the ear' story must have appealed to him, since he not only used it in the Gonzago Play Scene—where it would be appropriate—but also in the account of Hamlet's father's death.

If we translate them into the language of symbolism the Ghost's story is not so dissimilar from that of Claudius. To the unconscious, 'poison' signifies any bodily fluid charged with evil intent, while the serpent has played a well-known rôle ever since the Garden of Eden. The murderous assault had therefore both aggressive and erotic components, and we note that it was Shakespeare who introduced the latter. Furthermore, that the ear is an unconscious equivalent for anus is a matter for which I have adduced ample evidence elsewhere.[2] So we must call Claudius' attack on his brother both a murderous aggression and a homosexual assault.

Why did Shakespeare give this curious turn to a plain story of envious ambition? The theme of homosexuality itself does not surprise us in Shakespeare. In a more or less veiled form a pronounced femininity and a readiness

---

[1] See G. Bullough, 'The Murder of Gonzago', *Modern Language Review* (1935), vol. xxx, p. 433.

[2] *Essays in Applied Psycho-Analysis* (1923), pp. 341-6.

to interchange the sexes are prominent characteristics of his plays, and doubtless of his personality also. I have argued[1] that Shakespeare wrote *Hamlet* as a partly successful abreaction of the intolerable emotions aroused by the painful situation he depicts in his Sonnets, his betrayal by both his beloved young noble and his mistress. In life he apparently smothered his resentment and became reconciled to both betrayers. Artistically his response was privately to write the Sonnets (in the later publication of which he had no hand) and publicly to compose *Hamlet* not long afterwards—a play gory enough to satisfy all varieties of revenge.

The episode raises again the vexed question of the relation between active and passive homosexuality. Non-analysts who write on this topic are apt to maintain that they represent two different inborn types, but this assertion gives one an unsatisfied feeling of improbability, and analytic investigation confirms these doubts by demonstrating numerous points of contact between the two attitudes. Certainly Claudius's assault was active enough; sexually it signified turning the victim into a female, *i.e.* castrating him. Hamlet himself, as Freud[2] pointed out long ago, was unconsciously identified with Claudius, which was the reason why he was unable to denounce and kill him. So the younger brother attacking the older is simply a replica of the son-father conflict, and the complicated poisoning story really represents the idea of the son castrating his father. But we must not forget that it is done in an erotic fashion. Now Hamlet's conscious attitude towards his father was a feminine one, as shown by his exaggerated adoration and his adjuring Gertrude to love such a perfect hero instead of his brother.

[1] Ernest Jones, *Hamlet and Oedipus*, 1949.
[2] *Die Traumdeutung* (1900), p. 183.

In Freud's opinion homosexuality takes its origin in narcissism,[1] so that it is always a mirror-love; Hamlet's father would therefore be his own ideal of himself. That is why, in such cases, as with Hamlet, suicide is so close to murder.

My analytical experience, simplified for the present purpose, impels me to the following reconstruction of homosexual development. Together with the narcissism, a feminine attitude towards the father presents itself as an attempted solution of the intolerable murderous and castrating impulses aroused by jealousy. These may persist, but when the fear of the self-castration implied gains the upper hand, *i.e.* when the masculine impulse is strong, the original aggression reasserts itself—but this time under the erotic guise of active homosexuality.

According to Freud, Hamlet was inhibited by his repressed hatred of his father. We have to add to this the homosexual aspect of his attitude, so that Love and Hate, as so often, both play their part.

[1] Freud, *Collected Papers*, vol. ii, p. 241.

INDEX

Abraham, 20, 54, 265
Absolute terms, 244, 250
Adaptation, 144
Aggressive impulses, 211, 280, 305, 308, 309, 314, 315, 319, 320
Akhenaten, 264
Amphimixis, 159
Amun, 265
Anderssen, 166, 175, 181
Andrea del Sarto, 22 *et seq.*
Anti-Semitism, 290 *et seq.*
Anxiety, 210, 214, 225, 242, 243, 247, 268 *et seq.*, 280, 320
Aristocracy, 233
Artistic sensitiveness, 194
Aten, 265
Atteridge, 39
Autocracy, 247
Auto-erotism, 152

Bacon, 68
Baring-Gould, 104
Barrie, Sir James, 104
'Bellezze di Firenze', 24
Berlin decree, 40
Bibring, E., 272
Binet, 120
Biology, 135, 157
Birth phantasies, 9, 11, 12
Bisexuality, 155
Böcklin, 106
Bottari, 24
Bradley, Henry, 324
Bramwell, Milne, 179

Browning, 24, 26, 37, 38, 191
Brun, 159, 162, 163
Bryan, Douglas, 188
Bullough, G., 326

Cambacérès, 43, 47
Carlyle, 303
Champagny, de, 46
Chess, Chapter XIII
Christianity, 238
Ciano, 283
Civilization, Chapter XVII, 273
Claudius, 323, 324, 327
Clinical psychology, 113
Collins, Michael, 111
Conflict, 197
Conscience, 212
Conversion hysteria, 213
Coprophemia, 91

Darwin, 135, 157
Dead souls, 13
Death, 9, 105, 108
Death instinct, 147, 148, 162, 263
Defences, 242, 309
Delusions of jealousy, 52
persecution, 52
Depression, 272
De Valera, 110
Devil, 251
Doheny, M., 100

Edge, F. M., 171, 172, 178, 184

Ego-dystonic, 142
  ideal, 147, 247, 271
  syntonicity, 141
Ehrenberg, 148
Einstein, 231
Ellis, Havelock, 34
Empress, 10
Environment, 209
Eros, 148
Erotic cathexis, 195
Erotogenic zones, 159, 160
Ethnology, 150
Evolution, Chapter XVIII

Falkbeer, 171
Father imago, 280
Fechner, 147
Ferenczi, 89, 91, 159, 162, 163
Flügel, J. C., 54
Force, 216, 252
Frazer, Sir James, 89, 90
Freedom, 306, 316
Freret, 109
Freud and biology, 135, 139, 157, 161-2
  on aggression, 85, 86
  on bisexuality, 155, 328
  on coprophilia and birth, 4
  on death, 13, 14, 263
  on emotional paralysis, 18
  on genetic outlook, 118 *et seq.*, 274
  on leadership, 246, 303
  on masochism, 9
  on Moses, 265
  on sexuality, 82
  on the meaning of neurosis, 125, 207
  on the pleasure principle, 20

Freud on the significance of words, 89, 90
  on the super-ego, 269
  on the unconscious, 58, 92, 137, 143 *et seq.*, 198
Furtmüller, 13

Gallon, 92
Genius, 194
Giulio Romano, 24
Glover, Edward, 76, 195, 225
Gonzaga, 325, 326
Gonzago, 325, 326
Government, 217
Gross, 89
Guilt, 242, 243, 246, 263, 268 *et seq.*, 279, 305, 321
Guinness, 23, 24, 25, 30, 31

Haeckel, 161
Hamlet, 13, 243, 323 *et seq.*
Han-sing, 171
Hanusch, 12
Harp, 108
Harrwitz, 172, 184
Heine, 10
Helplessness, 305
Henbane, 325
Heredity, 160, 274
Hitler, 251, 276, 278, 279, 284, 286, 297, 321
Hock, 12
Holt, 119
Holy Grail, 108
Homosexuality, 155, 265, 274, 326-8
Horst, 12
Hortense, 49
Huss, John, 171

INDEX

Hutchinson, 110
Huxley, 157
Hypochondriac, 42
Hysterical conversion, 159

Id, 201
Id impulses, 269
Impotency, 221
Inbreeding, 158
Incest, 150, 155, 158
Infantile sexuality, 82
Infantile theory, 11
Inferiority complex, 128, 129, 215, 227, 272, 305
Insatiability, 10
Introjection, 244, 271, 310
Ireland, 95 *et seq.*
Irresistibility, 280

James, William, 73, 170
Janet, Pierre, 120
Jews, Chapter XX
Jones, Mervyn, 260
Josephine, 48
Jubainville, 107
Jung, 21, 146

Kant, 13
Keating, Geoffrey, 101
Killiher, 110
King Francis, 29, 30
Klein, Melanie, 204
Kleist, Heinrich von, 9-14
Krauss, 12
Kyd, 323

Lamarck, 161
Layard, Sir Henry, 23, 31
Leaders, 247, 248, 264, 272, 279, 302, 303, 305

Le Bon, 122, 301, 303
Lebrun, 47
Lenin, 303, 318
Libido, 146, 160
Loewenthal, 165, 180
Louis Bonaparte, 39
Love conditions, 12
Lucrezia del Fede, 27

Macdonnell, 178
McDougall, W., 88, 121
Malinowski, 223
Mansar, 171
Marlowe, 325
Marriage, 218 *et seq.*
Masson, 39
Matrilineal society, 223
Maurian, 186, 195
Mead, 186
Medical psychology, 113
Megalomania, 251
Mendel, 133
Mental deficiency, 205
Mental heredity, Chapter XI
Mental hygiene, Chapter XIV
Michelangelo, 22
Misogyny, 49
Monarchy, Chapter XVI
Mongredien, 182
Monotheism, 265
Morphy, Paul, 165 *et seq.*
Moses, 265
Murray, 170, 175
Mussolini, 249, 256, 282
Mythology, 161

Napoleon, 39, 251
Napoleon the Third, 47, 50
Narcissism, 146, 152, 328

Necrophilic tendencies, 11
Niagara Falls, 16
Nietzsche, 67, 84, 270
Nutt, Alfred, 107

Ochlocracy, 233
O'Donnell, Hugh, 100
Oedipus complex, 69, 98, 108, 156, 220, 223, 224, 228, 262, 265
Oligarchy, 233
Omnipotence, 250, 272, 305
Ontogeny, 161
Oxenstjerna, 319

Paranoid syndrome, 52, 252, 263-6, 320
Parnell, Charles Stewart, 109
Parricidal impulses, 195, 274
Pathopsychology, 114
Paulsen, 172, 179, 181
Pearse, P., 100
Phylogeny, 161
Plasticity, 159
Pleasure-pain principle, 143, 144, 147, 162
Pliny, 325
Plutocracy, 233
Primal horde, 274
Prince, Morton, 113, 120
Projection, 263, 264, 271, 310, 321
Psychoneurosis, 199, 208
Psychopathology, 114, 148
Punishment, 211, 221

Queen, 10
Quislingism, Chapter XIX

Rank, Otto, 20, 104, 106
Raphael, 22, 37
Reality principle, 144
Regression, 159, 274
Religion, 217
Reparation, 271
Repetition compulsion, 145, 147, 162
Repressed homosexuality, 52
impulses, 79, 80, 137, 151, 160, 199, 200, 211, 263, 271
Restitution, 271
Reti, 175
Reumont, 25, 30, 36
Revolution, Chapter XVIII
Rickman, John, 267
Rocquain, 39
Romanization, 97
Rousseau, 165

Sadger, 9, 10, 12, 13, 14, 19
Saint-Amant, 180, 181, 192
Scalzi frescoes, 24, 30
Schreber, 265
Scott, Leader, 23, 33, 38
Scott, St. J. G., 171
Scott, Sir Walter, 44
Searl, 160, 188
Self-dissatisfaction, 269
Sepp, 12
Sergeant, P. W., 184, 189, 196
Sex inversion, 266
Sexuology, 148
Shaw, Bernard, 260, 275
Sistrum, 108
Slang, 93
Socialization, 269, 271

INDEX

Social psychology, 62,
    Chapter IX, 206
Sociology, 240
Sophocles, 235
Specht, Wilh., 114
Spencer, Herbert, 228
Stability law, 147
Stalin, 303
Staunton, 172, 180, 182, 183, 191, 193
Steinitz, 179
Stekel, 9, 20
Strachey, J., 265
Strindberg, 33
Sublimation, 77, 143, 170, 195, 267, 271
Suggestion, 244-6
Super-ego, 142, 202, 203, 212-214, 217, 247, 269 *et seq.*, 321
Symphilia, 164

Talleyrand, 253
Temple of Aesculapius, 19
Tennyson, 107
Thanatos, 147, 271
Thiers, 230
Thistlton-Dyer, W., 325
Timocracy, 233

Trotter, Wilfred, 63, 123
Truth, 13
Tylor, 89

Ulster, 112
Unconscious, 79, 92, 120, 130, 137, 141, 142, 151, 198, 201, 210, 228, 248, 255, 261, 277, 285, 303, 308, 318

Valetudinarianism, 42
Van der Linde, 170
Varchi, 24
Vasari, 24, 25, 26, 28, 29, 33, 34
Violence, 253

Wales, 128
War, 55, 224
Wasmann, 164
Wheeler, 164
Wish-fulfilment, 80
Witches, 270
Wordsworth, 103, 105
Wundt, 122

Yeats, W. B., 102

Zenge, Wilhelmine von, 12

333